A CLUTCH OF REDS AND DIAMONDS
A Twentieth Century Odyssey

By Albert Jolis

EAST EUROPEAN MONOGRAPHS, BOULDER
DISTRIBUTED BY COLUMBIA UNIVERSITY PRESS, NEW YORK

1996

EAST EUROPEAN MONOGRAPHS, NO. CDLXVII

For Mona, who made all the difference

CONTENTS

COMMENT

Albert Jolis' autobiography is by far the most interesting I have seen for many years. It covers the almost incredible range of his activities in the thick of the political struggle the world over, and it is written in a notably sympathetic and readable style. A great book!

Robert Conquest,
author of *The Great Terror, The Harvest of Sorrow, Kolyma – the Arctic Death Camps, The Last Empire*

*

This book is certainly much more than a personal memoir. Considering that Bert Jolis became an active participant in almost every major event of the twentieth century, we are entitled to question his claim to have been just an „ordinary witness." For if that were true, why did we not have more people like him – more such „ordinary witnesses?" I have no doubt that the whole story of our turbulent century would have been quite different, if his sense of history and his moral commitment had been shared by more of his contemporaries.

Vladimir Bukovsky,
author of *To Build a Castle – My Life as a Dissenter* (Andre Deutsch, London, 1978)

and *To Choose Freedom* (Hoover Institution Press, 1987), former Soviet dissident, who was forcibly expelled from the Soviet Union in 1976, after suffering 12 years in Soviet labor camps and psychiatric prison hospitals, and was the first to draw international attention to the Soviet practice of using mind-altering drugs as an instrument of political repression.

*

I have read with great interest the autobiography of Albert Jolis since it concerns two subjects on which I have written books, Diamonds and Espionage. I found the manuscript fascinating. It tells the story of a man who has lived through some of the most interesting events of this century and presents them through a unique perspective. I also thing it is an important book of human rights. I strongly recommend its publication.

Edward J. Epstein,
author of *Legend – The Secret Life of Lee Harvey Oswald,* and *Deception – The War between the CIA and the KGB*

Albert Jolis – 1972

AUTHOR'S NOTE

For the longest time I resisted this undertaking; but friends kept telling me "Do it. Do it."

And I would reply: "But why? I am not famous; I have never been elected to public office; I have not commanded victorious armies in battle; I have not figured as the accused in a famous murder trial, (not yet at least.) I am not a public figure; I am a private figure. What is more, I have never been too comfortable talking about myself. I have an instinctive reluctance to discuss my private life in public. I have no reason to write an autobiography. There is nothing special about me.

"That is just the point," answers my son Alan. "You are special because you're not special. Your story is interesting because you lived through the ideological battles of the twentieth century, not as a major player, but as a private citizen, sucked into the conflict because it was not in your nature to stay on the sidelines."

"But that can be said of millions of us," I reply. "The life of every one of us has been affected, one way or another, by those tidal flows."

"Exactly," interjects my daughter-in-law, Cilla. "That is exactly what we mean. Why don't we call you a 'Twentieth Century Everyman'?"

So here I go, in my 85th year, setting it down as best as I can remember, and promising to try my hardest to keep it honest.

My story spans most of this turbulent and bloody century; the century plagued by the twin-evils of Nazism and Communism. As a young man in England, I was caught up in the ideological ferment that followed the end of World War I, and the pull of ideology never left me. There is nothing original about this. Many of my friends and contemporaries have travelled the same road, and their lives have been similarly touched, The literature of our times is rich with such experiences. But each person travels alone. Each must choose his own path, make his own choices, follow his own counsel.

Let me say at the outset, this is not another story of "one who broke with Communism." I never broke with Communism because I never embraced it. On the contrary, I fought against it throughout my adult life. What then is this "pull of ideology?"

As a teenager in the 1920's, the emotional impact of listening to the ghastly horrors of World War I trench warfare on the Somme caused me to become a pacifist. I believed in Ghandian non-violent resistance. I became attracted to the British Labour Party, and for a while was a Fabian Socialist. I was never a Marxist, but I met British Communists who tried earnestly to lure me into the Party. I refused. Marxists were men of violence and I was a pacifist. But I accepted that they were "on our side" against the rising menace of Fascism and the threat of Hitler. And having accepted that, it was but a small step to condoning, or at least shutting my eyes to their methods. For a while, I became without knowing it, one of Lenin's "useful idiots." But it was short-lived. The Spanish Civil War caused my pacifism to evaporate, and what I learned about Communist behaviour in that conflict, convinced me that Communism and Nazism were twin-evils of equal malevolence. At this point, the "pull of ideology" was no longer emotional, it was intellectual as well.

Throughout these years I have had to ask myself: If Communism and Nazism were the overriding evils that bedevilled our century, a fact which at last, few would dispute, why was it that the West adopted such a lopsided manner of dealing with them? For the truth is the West obstinately refused to equate the ideology of Marxist-Leninism with that of Hitler's National Socialism. If crimes against humanity committed for political ends are to be measured by body count, then Communism bears a far greater burden of guilt than Nazism; infinitely greater when Mao Tse Tung's and Pol Pot's victims are included.

Under Nazism you were sent to the gas-ovens because of **who you were.** Under Communism you were sent to starve in the Gulag, tortured and shot because of **what you thought.** Twin evils under the skin to be sure.

Why then the double standard? Nazism was recognized as evil, and rightly, crushed. Communism on the other hand, with a few exceptions, was at first ignored by the West, then tolerated, explained, apologized for, and in certain cases even supported. And when it's aggressive intentions could no longer be evaded, the West never really fought back with conviction. The West invented a figleaf called Containment, an exercise in self-deluding hypocrisy, whose object was to halt further Soviet expansion. What it did was to confirm Soviet enslavement of East and Central Europe while the West shed a few crocodile tears, and all the while making half-hearted efforts to deter Soviet strategic and political expansion in the rest of the world. And where Communist armed aggression forced us to take up arms. Did we fight to win? No. We accepted a less-than-honorable truce in Korea and a humiliating defeat in Vietnam; not a military defeat, a political defeat.

We are told it was the danger of nuclear war that made the difference. This undoubtedly influenced some, during the Cold War, but it is not the whole reason. The double standard has deeper roots, and they take us back to the very beginning. Democratic socialists have never been able to rid themselves of the feeling that Marxist-Leninists were wayward brothers, dedicated to the same ultimate goals, but unfortunately using unacceptable methods. This was my own case as a young man. Jeane Kirkpatrick, former United States Ambassador to the United Nations in the Reagan administration, expressed it precisely in her illuminating work, "Dictatorships and Double Standards."

She wrote:

Socialism of the Soviet/Chinese/Cuban variety is an ideology rooted in a version of the same values that sparked the Enlightenment and the democratic revolutions of the 18th century; because it is modern and not traditional; because it postulates goals that appeal to Christian as well as secular values (brotherhood of man, elimination of power as a mode of human relations,) it is highly congenial to many Americans at the symbolic level. Marxists speak the language of a hopeful future while traditional autocrats speak the language of an unattractive past Because left-wing revolutionaries invoke the symbols and values of democracy, emphasizing egalitarianism rather than hierachy and privilege – liberty rather than order, activity rather than passivity – they are again and again accepted as partisans in the cause of freedom and democracy.

Nowhere is the affinity of liberalism, Christianity, and Marxist socialism more apparent than among liberals who are "duped" time after time into supporting "liberators" who turn out to be totalitarians.

In Western Europe, approximately fifty percent of the voting public has traditionally voted socialist, and in the United States a goodly proportion of our population thinks and votes along similar lines, though it does not call itself socialist. For these people, the evils of Communism, even when recognized in the abstract, never inspired the same horror and revulsion as those of the Nazis because they were committed in pursuit of ultimately desirable ends, the Socialist Utopia.But in all fairness, I must add that the Left was not alone; the Right also shared in the failure, albeit to a lesser though critical degree. Top leadership, even when conservative and instinctively anti-Communist, was all too often ignorant of Communist methods. Minds were focused on conventional warfare and military hardware instead of where the real threat lay. They did not understand that in perfecting the techniques of Active Measures, Disinformation, and political subversion, the Soviets had at their disposal a weapons system which was permanently deployed and in constant use, against which we had no defence. On the one occasion when America almost rose to the challenge, a well-intentioned but clumsy Senator Joseph McCarthy handed the enemy a priceless victory by sheer overreach – a victory the Communists exploited so successfully, we never quite recovered.

In looking back through my life in this "totalitarian century," I was always aware of my good fortune. I was not one of it's victims. I was born into the lap of luxury and could have ignored it all. But I was filled with the romantic illusions of youth – a belief in the perfectibility of man, in a world free of poverty, war and hunger. Not to take a position in those days was in itself a statement, and one I was not willing to make. I could not sit on the sidelines. My political thoughts began to develop along lines best expounded by George Orwell, except that I did not possess his genius. Later, I had the good fortune to meet him, and I count it as one of the high points of my life that George Orwell became one of my friends.

A personal conviction that the defeat of Communism was just as important as the defeat of Nazism, if we wished to preserve Western Civilization, has been a guiding tenet for all of my adult years. And because of this, many of my contemporaries, and yes, even friends, considered me an oddball, irrationally obsessed with the subject. I was a "kook", an extremist. It caused me to lose friends. The prevailing philosophy in Washington, DC was to seek peaceful coexistence with the Soviet Union, which to me tasted like (and indeed was) nothing but defeatism. Because of my strong views, I lost access to influential government officials. It shaped the course of my life.

But while I was frustrated that so few shared my views, I cannot say I was alone. Embattled, yes, but not alone. In addition to George Orwell, I was lucky to have been able to counts among my circle of friends such staunch anti-Communists as Eugene Lyons, Sol Levitas, Editor of the *New Leader*, John Dos Passos, Sydney Hook, Bert (*Three who Made a Revolution*) and Ella Wolfe and Manes Sperber, author of *A Tear in the Ocean.* And there were others whose names I no longer recall, but who shared the same sense of commitment. Arthur Koestler, I only knew slightly, but having previously read **Darkness at Noon** he was totally familiar at first meeting. And of course, outside my immediate circle there were many, known to me only by name, who made milestone contributions to the process of disenchantment. I read their works and followed their careers. They became vicarious friends. One of my great regrets is never having met Whittaker Chambers.

We were a minority, and always it seemed, on the losing end, believing but not wanting to admit, that the cause was hopeless. My good friend, Frank Barnett, who joined with me in helping Soviet prisoners-of-war and displaced persons avoid forced repatriation to the Soviet Unions at the end of World War II, and who later founded the National Strategy Information Center, used to distribute a calling card on which was inscribed "The League to Save Carthage."

I knew that all these friends shared with me the view expressed by Edmond Rostand that "Only the hopeless causes are worth fighting for."

In the end, the impossible happened. The enemy gave up.

I do not agree with the commonly held notion that we won the Cold War. It is my contention that we never seriously fought the Cold War; that is to say, we never fought to win. We fought for a stand-off, while the enemy fought to win. To me, this was a sure formula for defeat; defeat by the salami method. And we were retreating, step by step, in one Third-World country after another; resisting every Communist advance with half-measures, paralyzed by Leftist protest in the Media, in Academia, and in the Congress. In the end though, extraordinary and unexpected as it may seem, the tables were turned and we won by default, because the enemy collapsed from exhaustion.

And here, William J. Casey, my old OSS friend of forty years standing, deserves eternal recognition and gratitude from freedom lovers the world over. For his voice rang loudest and clearest among those advising President Ronald Reagan. As a result, the enemy's collapse was hastened by the deployment of Pershing missiles in Europe, by the Strategic Defense Initiative, and by Ronald Reagan's denunciation of the "Evil Empire."

Most of these friends have now passed on. Even Bill Casey was not permitted to see the end.

God has granted me a long life, and I have been privileged to play a small role in this adventure. I was tempted to say I lived to see the dragon slain; but in truth I did not. I lived to see the dragon commit suicide. What an extraordinary outcome. But is the dragon truly dead, or is it going to rise up Phoenix-like from the ashes? As the century winds down, disturbing portents abound. The totalitarians still hold sway in China, Cuba and North Korea. The Khmer Rouge threaten a come-back in Cambodia; and Communist apparatchiks under new labels cling relentlessly to power in much of East and Central Europe and in all of the countries of the old Soviet Union.

In writing this account I have thought repeatedly of my grandchildren, seven at last count, Oliver, Timothy, Lucy, Janie, Annie, Jake and Jeremy. You, dear children, will learn the history of the twentieth century from the perspective of the twenty-first. What will you learn? Will the revisionists have turned everything upside-down? Already we are hearing that the Cold Warriors prolonged the Cold War; that the United States was even responsible for the Cold War. I want to tell you it is not so. I was there.

Or will you be told that the Soviet Union was gradually evolving into something more akin to Western democracy, while we in the West were becoming more like them? It was a fashionable idea among Soviet apologists at one time, and went by the name of the Convergence Theory. Those who preached it, and you yourselves will no doubt meet similar types in Academia, insist that it was we – Cold War fanatics and warmongers – who stopped it from happening, by frightening the Soviets.

Children, don't you believe it. I have listened to those who lived for forty-five years under Communism in Eastern Europe, and to those who survived the Gulag and the psychiatric prisons. I tried to help them. They never experienced any "convergence." There are those who tell us there was never a Holocaust – never any gas-ovens. They are the re-writers of history, a totalitarian speciality. The Nazis learned fast. But the system was invented and perfected by Marxist-Leninists and their fellow-travellers, who practiced it since Day 1.

There will of course, come a time when the ideological wars of my century will seem to future generations as unreal and remote as those between the Guelphs and the Ghibelines in medieval Italy, or the Wars of the Roses in medieval England. In the meantime, children don't let yourselves be fooled.My story is not a political treatise, it is a personal account of a journey that began before World War 1 in England – a journey that took me as a young man to the United States, and then to France and tropical Africa, and then back again to the United States. Family life, my business life in the diamond industry, and the thread of ideology are all intertwined in a continuous weave. It is the story of one citizen's personal Hot and Cold War. All persons and events described herein are real.

April 1996

PROLOGUE

Visitors to Geneva, Switzerland are familiar with the fountain on the lake which sends a jet of water high into the air just east of the Rhone Bridge. A visitor, happening to walk out of the Hotel des Bergues, at the foot of the Rue du Rhone, would see the fountain on the left, and straight ahead across the bridge, he would see a row of elegant medium-size office buildings, and if he looked up he would see high up on one of the facades in large letters, the name HARRY WINSTON. This is the Geneva office of New York's famous Fifth Avenue jeweller.

On September 20, 1977, having looked for him in New York, and having been told where to find him, I made a special trip, and now sat before the legendary man in his Geneva office.

As the purveyor of world-class diamonds to the stars of Hollywood, Arab princes, Wall Street tycoons and jet-set millionaires, and as the man who constantly appeared in the gossip columns in connection with such activities, it was no surprise that when Dolly sang "Diamonds are a girl's best friend," it was Harry Winston's name that always sprang to mind. He occupied a unique position in the diamond industry, at the opposite extremity from mine. I had no contact with the public or the world of glamor. I was exclusively engaged in securing a supply of rough diamonds from the source, and in marketing them to industrial end-users and the diamond polishing trade.

But we shared a common attribute. Both of us were dependent upon the De Beers organization as our main source of rough diamonds. Both of us chafed at the constraints and limitations imposed on us by the De Beers monopoly. Both of us had in the past sought to develop independent sources of diamonds, his firm in Angola and mine in Central Africa. Both of us had incurred the wrath of De Beers for our efforts.

I had a special interest in making the trip to Geneva to see Harry Winston. It had to do with a small country situated on the west coast of Africa between Sierra Leone, Senegal and the Ivory Coast. The country was Guinea.

Diamonds had been discovered in Guinea during the nineteen thirties, when the territory still formed part of colonial French West Africa. These diamond deposits had been exploited by a British company, Consolidated African Selection Trust (CAST), and marketed through De Beers. When, during World War II, the colonial governor of French West Africa a threw his support to the Vichy government of Marshal Pétain, CAST had been obliged to withdraw.

In 1958, under the leadership of Communist-leaning President Sekou Touré, Guinea walked out of "l'Union Francaise," (France's post-colonial commonwealth) and opted for what it preferred to call "true independence". President Charles de Gaulle was furious and cut Guinea off from all further French support. Sekou Touré was prepared. As he had planned to do all along, he turned to the Soviet Union.

The Soviets, delighted to oblige, took Guinea under their wing with assurances of undying and unlimited fraternal socialist support. True to their word, the Soviets delivered. The support arrived, high on rhetoric, low on substance. Soviet engineers attempted to run the old CAST diamond mines, (now nationalized), but were signally unsuccessful. Nor were they successful elsewhere. Guinea's economy foundered; it's standard of living sank lower and lower, while that of it's neighbors, especially the Ivory Coast, flourished.

It took time before the idea finally sank in. But in the end, Sekou Touré had to admit that what his country needed was an infusion of private investment from the hated capitalist West. He put as good a face on it as he was capable of and let it be known that he was now prepared to grant mining and exploration rights for diamonds, and would welcome bids from the private sector.

I proposed to Harry Winston that his firm and mine form a joint-venture to explore for diamonds in Guinea. His response was instantaneous. Without pausing to consider it, he exclaimed: "Sure, why not? I think its a great idea. But you'll have to work out the details with my son Ron."

All this is but a prelude to the day, on March 3, 1978, when, accompanied by Ronald Winston and our respective negotiating teams, I arrived in Conakry, capital of Guinea, on a Sabena flight out of Brussels. On my team were Francois Lampietti, chief geologist and Peter Wragg, my lawyer, who had had previous experience in Guinea. Accompanying Ronald Winston were Nick Axelrod, his chief diamond specialist and a young woman aide whose name I don't recall.

The road from the airport, "L'Autoroute Fidel Castro," with weeds sprouting through the cracked and pitted concrete, was lined with peeling billboards proclaiming "Victory for Socialism" and "Long Live Che Guevara."

Conakry itself was dilapidated and depressing. Crumbling walls, garbage-strewn pot-holed unpaved streets. Hardly anything new had been built since colonial times; with one exception, a one-story rambling hotel, just built by an Italian contractor in response to Sekou Touré's plea for private investment. This is where we checked in.

Our negotiation got off to a good start under the chairmanship of the President's brother, Ismael Touré, Minister of National Economy.

On the second day, he opened the session by inviting us to accompany him up country to the town of his birth, to attend a local celebration, "Le Bal de la Monnaie." He explained that this would give us an opportunity to get first-hand knowledge of local conditions. Of course, this was not the reason at all. His real reason, as we discovered later, was to stage a self-promoting public-relations event in his own political fiefdom by parading us as evidence of his brother's success at attracting foreign investment.

Next day, we all piled into a three-car convoy of old-model Peugeots and Renaults, and set off on the four-hour journey, with the

Minister in the lead car (later model, of course,) and we following behind in his dust.

"Le Bal de la Monnaie" was staged in an open-air enclosure. All the local leading personalities were there, with their ladies, many wearing extraordinary headdresses. At the head table on a raised dais, Winston and I sat on either side of the Minister, who presided, while the other members of our party sat alongside among sundry dignitaries.

Non-stop music was provided by the local Afro-Carribean combo.

At the end of the meal, Minister Touré stood up to deliver a speech, in which he introduced us, explaining we were there in direct response to his bother's invitation.

He went on to describe the extraordinary benefits that would accrue to the local community as a result of the infusion of money we would bring to our mining project. Then, after a routine eulogy to "our great leader-father of our country, President Sekou Touré," he sat down. It was now my turn. As I began to rise, the Minister stopped me with a restraining hand. "Pas encore", he whispered. "Not yet."

Then I saw why. The welcome was not yet over. A group of entertainers marched in and took their position at the back of the assembly. About twenty African teenagers, boys and girls, wearing red berets, white shirts, and red scarves.

As the leader tapped his baton, twenty clenched fists were thrust into the air, and with Marxist fervor they began to sing:

"A bas le Capitalism, vive le Socialism!" "Down with Capitalism, up with Socialism!" "A bas l'imperialism, vive le proletariat," "Down with imperialism, up with the proletariat!" "Down with the exploiters of the masses!" The chant went on for several verses, all carrying similar messages.

Could this be sophisticated african humor, I wondered, as I turned inquiringly to the Minister? He gave no clue. He was watching the performance with sympathetic interest. Nothing seemed to be bothering him. My companions had difficulty to concealing their horror. Then it dawned on me that this was not supposed to be humorous at all. This was straight. Good lord, was it possible somebody got the signals crossed and nobody noticed the difference? But of course, there was no difference. This was all according to regulation; the official song-and-dance routine, brought on stage for every public event. And until the Central Committee, or "our beloved leader" ruled otherwise, it would remain unchanged.

We had, in other words, entered the world of transition. Portent of things to come. Eighteen years later we are still in it, and it is not over.

At the end of the performance, I finally got up to respond, but the words I had mentally prepared earlier, obviously no longer fitted. So I ad-libbed:

"Dear Friends", I began, "Let me address my words to the charming group that has just entertained us. It is impossible for me to express to you how touched I am by the warmth of your welcome. I have no hesitation in saying that in the entire history of economic development, I doubt that any foreign investor has ever been received with more spontaneous encouragement. On behalf of my colleagues and for myself, I wish to express our gratitude and appreciation."

I sat down. Everyone applauded. Minister Ismael Touré smiled at me and nodded. If he sensed any irony in my words, he did not show it. In fact, the whole episode went off in an atmosphere of utter normalcy, as though nothing untoward had happened. I whispered to my colleagues: "Play it their way." Only once back in the comparative safety of our hotel rooms did we dare give vent to laughter.

The negotiation resumed next day. In due course an agreement was signed and the project was launched. The slip-up was never mentioned. Slip-up? Who mentioned slip-up? There was no slip-up.

Worried about the post-Communist investment climate? Stay flexible and think fast. Better yet, don't think.

"Curiousier and curiouser," cried Alice.

Of course, Lewis Carroll had it right. The more absurd the circumstance the more important is it that it be treated with the utmost solemn gravity. Many times I encountered such moments along my journey. They were moments to be treasured, and I remember what fun it was to keep a straight face when confronted by absurdity, and simply dart down that rabbit-hole again with Alice.

CHAPTER ONE

THERE'S NO WAY TO AVOID A BEGINNING

I like to think of myself essentially as a Transatlantic man. Nothing special about that. Most Americans are Transatlantic. In my case though, you might say there's an extra element. I am a pure blooded Jewish-Dutch-British-French-American – a genetic cocktail. Born in 1912 in London, England of Dutch parents, I spent my first 24 years as an Englishman, before coming to the United States in 1936. As an American citizen, I served in the United States Army in World War II. Then in the post-war years my business called for me to live in France. This I did for some twenty years, enabling me to pass almost unnoticed as a Frenchman. Multiculturism is much in vogue these days, whatever that term is intended to convey, and being suspicious of it's ideological overtones, I prefer not to feel multicultural. What I do feel is being completely at home in all of the above environments. But before all and above all, I feel American. And that, if you will, is more than just a U.S. passport. Some have called it an idea, one of the greatest, and I agree. But there is more to it. Other than those two honored gentlemen of the 18th Century, Tom Paine and the Marquis de Lafayette, how many Englishmen or Frenchmen can ever consider themselves to be Transatlantic? Only an American can enjoy that special feeling.

The cocktail gets more mixed in the case of my four sons, whose mother was half Spanish, and as of this writing, again more mixed in the case of two of my seven grandchildren, who are half Swedish.

The known generational ladder of the Jolis family does not go back much earlier than the 1830s, though one thing is clear. We are Sephardic Jews whose ancestors fled to Holland from Spain and

Portugal during the Inquisition. Outside of our family, there are few Jolises. I once discovered a watchmaker named Jolis in Grenoble, France. Then, around 1950, I came across an item in the Paris daily, *Le Monde,* reporting that a certain Albert Jolis had been arraigned before a judge in Versailles, accused of murdering his mother. It was not me.

Neither the travel agent named Jolis whom I discovered living in Burke, Virginia, nor the half-page list of Jolises listed in the Barcelona telephone directory are relatives. There are names similar to Jolis, for instance, Jolles and Joly. These are also not relatives, nor is the avant-garde writer, Eugene Jolas, for whom I was once mistaken.

It is in Holland that we began, and the family's destiny has been inextricably linked with diamonds.

In the 16th Century, trade with India, which had been opened by the early Portuguese explorers, flowed into Europe through the Hanseatic League, an association of North European cities which controlled most of the trade and commerce at the time. It's merchants and bankers became rich on trade with the East. Rough diamonds were brought to Amsterdam, a League member, from the Golconda mines in India, near Hyderabad, and Sepahardic Jews from Spain and Portugal polished them into brilliant gems for the adornment of Europe's nobility and royalty.

Until the mid-19th Century, when they were discovered in Brazil, and later in South Africa, the only source of diamonds had been India. But this remained a relatively small industry until 1867, when diamonds were discovered in Kimberly, South Africa. Then the whole world of diamonds changed. An extraordinary "diamond rush" took place, involving adventurers, fortune-hunters, grub-stakers, and con-artists. It produced such legendary characters as Barney Barnato and Cecil Rhodes. This event, coupled with the discovery of gold on the Rand, led to the Boer War, "Oom" Paul Kruger, and the whole subsequent history of South Africa. But that is another story.

The diamond-cutting industry in Amsterdam expanded dramatically.

At the turn of the century, my grandfather, Bram Jolis, lived with his family in Amsterdam, in one of those beautiful 17th Century houses with stepped-up gables that line the canals; in his case, the most fashionable canal, the Kaisersgraacht. Bram Jolis was a prosperous and respected master diamond cutter; his factory was a model in the industry; his business was flourishing. In 1902, his eldest son Jacob (known throughout his life as Jac) was 16 years old. Bram Jolis decided that the boy had had enough education and the time had come for him to learn the trade – the art of diamond-cutting. So Jac was ordered to appear the next day in the factory and report to the head foreman, where he would be enrolled as a new apprentice. An apprentice sits at the bench opposite the master-cutter and learns the skills, step by step, for months on end, maybe a year or more, until his teacher pronounces him proficient.

At the end of the first week, the foreman came respectfully to Bram Jolis and most deferentially announced there was a small problem. The problem was this, he explained: the employees were attempting to form a trade-union (The entire industry had no union in those days.) The workers' demands were twofold: a limit of eight working hours per day, and a limit to the number of new apprentices to be admitted year by year. "The real problem is" added the foreman, "our apprentice quota for this year is filled, and the men don't think it is right for an exception to be made for Jac."

Bram Jolis exploded. "You mean to say," he thundered, "I cannot teach my own son my own trade in my own factory! Never on your life! Over my dead body! The boy will go back to the bench tomorrow, and I don't want to hear any more about it." The foreman retreated, abashed and uncomfortable.

At the end of the second week the foreman returned, this time leading a delegation. Once again they most respectfully explained that the apprenticeship of Jac Jolis was not acceptable, and would Bram Jolis kindly withdraw his son from the plant. And once again, Bram Jolis, in the most polite and measured Dutch, told them he would see them in hell first.

At the end of the third week, no more delegations; the men went on strike. The plant was shut down tight. Bram Jolis was not a man to be trifled with, and his dander was up. He called a meeting of the employers' association, the Diamond Manufacturers' Council. "What is the world coming to" he inveighed, "if a man cannot teach his own son his own trade in his own factory?" His fellow-employers, duly sympathetic, and realizing they would be the next targets, expressed their solidarity. They declared an industry-wide lockout. Overnight, the entire diamond-cutting industry in Amsterdam was shut down and thousands of men were thrown on the streets. There was no strike pay, no unemployment benefits, no social safety-net in those days.

The lockout lasted for nine months. It is considered by some to have been one of the landmark disputes in the history of labor relations. It has also been reported, though I am unable to verify this, that Samuel Gompers, founder of the American Federation of Labor and himself a Dutchman, was involved in the conflict.

As the strike/lockout dragged on and the weeks ran into months, tempers frayed and nerves cracked. Young Jac Jolis would come home time and again, beaten up and bloody, after being attacked in the street by sons of the unemployed diamond workers. For them, the matter was simple; young Jac Jolis was the reason they had no food on the table. The day came when my grandmother, a patient but determined woman could stand it no longer. She rounded on her husband one day when young Jac entered the house in a particularly gory condition. "I have had enough!" she stormed at Bram Jolis, "You are too proud and obstinate to realize you are destroying your family. Are you prepared to wait until your son is killed before you come to your senses."

Bram was shaken. His wife had never spoken to him thus. He decided the time had come to send his son Jac out of town. He called him into his study. "All right, my boy," he said, "we're going to send you away. I have business friends in Paris and in London, and in either place you will continue learning our trade. You have a choice; which will it be, Paris or London? Think carefully before you answer. Jac did not need to think. "Paris," he said without a moment's hesitation. He had heard from friends that the girls were "easier" there, but this he kept to himself. "Good," said Bram, "then we'll send you to London.

Next day Bram telegraphed his friends at the Premier Diamond Mining Company in London, from whom he bough this rough diamonds, to ask whether he could send them Jac until the trouble blew over. "Sure," they said. Bram Jolis was a valued customer. So, Jac was duly packed off to London, whence he never returned. The Premier Diamond Mining Company eventually became absorbed into the De Beers Diamond Syndicate.

The strike/lockout was at long last settled, but it was too late for Bram Jolis. He was ruined. The union was recognized. The industry had in the interim, moved south to Antwerp where the union eventually but much later, cought up with it. Antwerp became the main diamond center, which it remains today, and Amsterdam never fully recovered.

Jac Jolis returned a few years later, but not to Amsterdam, this time to Antwerp, and with only one purpose, to pick his bride. She was Rosette Couzyn, with whom he had been carrying on a distant and surely platonic flirtation for some time. Very pretty, taller than Jac, speaking fluent French, she was also Jewish. Her father, Emmanual Couzyn ran a small jewellery shop on the Rue Carnot, where she and her sister Clara served behind the counter helping customers make their choice from trays of rings and baubles. Jac had happened to drop in one day and cought Rosette's eye. The Couzyn family were also Dutch, but had moved to Belgium. It did not make much difference in those days, since the two countries had only been separated in 1830. Rosette's mother was the daughter of the Zondervan family, about whom little is known except what is probably an apocryphal story of the name's origin. It seems that when soldiers were being drafted into Louis Napoleon's army (Bonaparte's brother, remember?), the conscripts were lined up and had to call out their names. "Van Gelder!" "Van Houten!" "Van Damme!" "Van Berg! and so on. When it came to our man, he hesitated and mumbled. He had no "Van" in front of his name. So the recruiting sergeant wrote down "zonder Van." The word "zonder" in Dutch means "without" So Zondervan stuck.

Jac took his bride back to London, where in due course I saw the light of day, in a modest house on the edge of the city, 22 Dukes Avenue, Chiswick, to be exact. It was April 27, 1912. By a strange quirk, the vicissitudes of the trade-union movement caused me to be born an Englishman. Some thirty years later, organized labor was once again to affect the course of my life.

CHAPTER TWO

WORLD WAR I

What is remembered? How much is imagined, suggested, or thought to be remembered? Some childhood events are recounted to us over the years, and they enter our "memory". We think we had the real experience. A few vivid images nonetheless are truly real.

By 1915, we had moved from Chiswick and were now living in Bayswater, the district west of Marble Arch in central London. It was a top floor apartment in what was known as Prince Edward Mansions. There was the daily walk in Kensington Gardens accompanied sometimes by a nanny, sometimes by my mother. The routine was always the same. One-year old brother Bernard in the "pram", me walking alongside holding on. Every day we walked past the Peter Pan statue. There was Peter standing with one arm raised, his face lifted to the sky, and the rabbits running around his feet. There were always wounded soldiers in sight. Clad in pale-blue flannel pyjama suits, they hobbled on crutches or were wheeled in invalid chairs. And then there was always the balloon seller standing at the Bayswater Gate.

Why do I especially remember the wounded soldiers in their blue pyjamas? Because of Alfred. He was a wounded soldier in a blue pyjama suit. But he was more than that. He was the boyfriend of our cook, Ada, and he used to come around and sit in our kitchen and have tea. He didn't look all that badly wounded, though it was said he'd been gassed. I was four years old and was allowed to sit in the kitchen and have tea with Alfred. What impressed me most about Alfred was his amazing shiny black hair. Tea consisted of bread and butter and jam, and sometimes also cookies. On one occasion I took a slice of bread which had been generously buttered for me and smeared it all over my head. To the horrified protests of the grown-ups – "What on earth are you doing? " they gasped, I replied: "I want to look like Alfred."

The best fun of all was the occasional air-raid. This is World War I, mind you, not World War II. It went like this. There were no sirens. The air-raid alert was given by boy-scouts riding through the streets on bicycles blowing a whistle and shouting: "Take cover! Take cover!" It was always at night, which made it more exciting. We would scramble out of bed, and head for the cellar where all the other residents of the apartment building were gathered. There we would sit while all the grown-ups discussed the raid, and listened to the occasional boom in the distance. Candies were always handed out, and we didn't mind how long it went on. In the end the boy-scouts on their bikes would ride through the streets again, blowing whistles and shouting "All clear! All clear!" and we'd regretfully return upstairs to bed.

I once saw the Zeppelin; it was a daylight raid – a huge silver cigar that filled the sky. It nearly blacked out the daylight.

My mother played the piano, and when she played "Roses of Picardy" I stood by the piano and cried. Eighty years later I can still hum "Roses of Picardy" perfectly, but it no longer makes me cry.

The grownups were always talking about "this terrible war." It was never clear to me what it all meant, but I figured somehow it had to do with those wounded soldiers in the park in their pale-blue flannel pyjama suits.

On one occasion I rode with my mother in a "Hansom" cab from Knightsbridge to Hyde Park Corner. I can still hear the horse's clop clop, and the the coachman's voice urging it along from above our heads.

I was six years old when the war ended and remember watching from my father's office near Holborn Circus, as a huge military victory parade wound its way through London's streets.

CHAPTER THREE

GROWING UP IN ENGLAND

In 1919, we moved again, this time to Wimbledon where they play tennis. We lived in a large Edwardian house in a secluded lane, about half a mile from the All-England Tennis Club. Every summer when the matches were on, my brother Bernard and I would smuggle ourselves through the back entrance and watch the play gratis. It was much more relaxed than the highpowered show-biz industry it is today. No professionals, all amateurs. The public never let themselves go beyond polite clapping. The men all wore long white flannels. The French dominated everything. We saw Borotora in his Basque beret, Lacoste in his buttoned up shirt, Brugnon in buttoned-down long sleeves and cap. We once saw Suzanne Lenglen throw her racquet to the ground and storm off the Center Court in an emotional outburst. The public was shocked; it was a front-page story. We saw Big Bill Tilden. The English were nowhere, except for a second stringer called Fred Perry.

Wasn't it Bernard Shaw who said "England and America are two nations separated by a common language."? Nowhere is this truer than in the field of education. In England a prep school is a private, *primary* level, educational establishment, either day school or boarding, for boys aged 7 to 12 or 13. In the United States a prep school is a private *secondary* educational establishment (high school level), usually fairly snobbish, roughly comparable to an English public school, which of course, is not public but private and, oh yes, snobbish. In America a public school is what it says it is, free tuition and taxpayer supported. In England this is called a grammar school.

At least that is the way it was in those days. Now, I'm told all is different.

I attended primary school (prep school in England) at Kings College School from 1922 to 1925 and bicycled there from home every day along Wimbledon Common, 2 miles there, 2 miles back, rain or shine, with a homework-packed satchel on my back.

Time went by very slowly; it always does for kids, except when the summers came around. Then there were summer holidays on the beaches in France and Belgium, Blankenberghe, Le Zoute, Cabourg, Dinard, La Baule. I learned a smattering of French. My parents spoke English to me and Dutch to each other.

In due course the time arrived when it became necessary to decide which public school (prep school in the USA) I would go to. My parents decided I should attend Westminster School, one of the most prestigious of the public schools, second only to Eton and Harrow. Located in the heart of London, it stood in an ancient pile, nestled up against Westminster Abbey. The students wore top hats and black suits and were easily recognizable on the streets of London. I took the entrance exam and passed. We waited and waited. No communication came from Westminster School. One day the headmaster of my prep school, Mr. Woodley, called on my parents to inform them that to his deep regret I would not be admitted to Westminster. When pressed for an explanation, since after all, I had passed the entrance examination, he confessed in much embarrassment that he had been informed it was because we were Jewish.

For me this was a bombshell. I had no idea I was Jewish. My parents were non-observant and never discussed religion. I was not even sure what it meant. At school we had morning prayers before class, and I recited the Lord's prayer along with the others and thought nothing of it. To be refused admittance after passing the entrance test was unthinkable. Was I unclean or something?

Having been shielded and protected from the real world so far, I now received my first baptism of fire. I was beginning to grow up.

My parents were likewise shaken. Recognizing the need for some corrective action, they decided it would probably be a good thing if I were Bar Mitzvahed. Besides, my maternal grandfather was unhappy that I was receiving no religious education. So, in preparation for this event I was packed off three nights a week to sit for a couple of hours with a Rabbi to learn about being a Jew. He didn't teach me anything; nothing of the Torah, of the meaning of Judaism, of the history of the Jews. I learned to recite a few prayers by rote – "Baruch Ato Adonay" – to read a few words in Hebraic script, and remembered to open the book backwards. It was an unpleasant experience. The Rabbi smelled, had food stains on his clothes and food scraps in his beard. I found it hard to accept that he was a man of God.

A few years later, at a Church of England Christian school, in Divinity class, I learned about the Jews in the books of the Old Testament. Mandatory, wonderful reading; I loved it – found it utterly fascinating.

The Bar Mitzvah came. I stood in the Synagogue, nervous in my best suit and my yarmulke, and said my piece. What remains in my memory is the singing of the cantor, a surprise, and astonishingly beautiful to my ears. Then the party, the presents, the family, and finally it was over. Whew!

So, I am now a Jew. What does it mean? Do I feel different? Yes and no. Inside my skin I'm exactly the same. Outside, I'm not so sure. People look at me differently, or do they? At least I feel they do. It would be some thirty years before I got an insight into these questions, when I had the good fortune to meet Will Herberg, and enjoyed the exciting experience of reading his *Judaism and Modern Man*. (Farrar, Strauss & Young, 1951.)

Meanwhile my religious education took another tack. The disappointment of Westminster was forgotten. I entered Bradfield College, not as prestigious to be sure, but an honorable public school nonetheless, in the hallowed tradition of Rugby's "Tom Brown's Schooldays." Bradfield was "Church of England." If there were any Jewish students besides myself, I never met them. For that matter, there were no Catholics either. We attended chapel every morning; twice on Sundays – dressed in the mandatory mortar-board cap and gown. All students, in rotation, were required to read the lesson in Chapel for three consecutive days at a time. I was no exception.

Standing before the huge bible on the brass lectern, I intoned before the congregation – in the manner I'd heard others do it before me – "Here beginneth the first verse of the fourth chapter of the Gospel according to Saint Matthew." – or whatever the text was. It terminated with "Here endeth the lesson." – and then I returned to my seat in the pews.

The only thing I enjoyed about chapel was the singing of hymns. I bellowed: "Onward Christian Soldiers, marching as to war." – with gusto, along with four hundred other young voices, equally exuberant. We lifted the chapel roof. The preacher's sermon's on the other hand, I found boring and unreal.

When the time came for my class to be "confirmed", it was perfectly natural that I would be included. So, in due course I participated in the confirmation rites, and was duly recorded as a member of the Church of England.

I was now a Jew and a Protestant and have remained a religious hybrid ever since. A Judeo-Christian if there ever was one. The trouble is, I never was particularly religious. In truth, not religious at all. But neither was I a true non-believer. I felt the pull, but never took the "leap of faith."

The quandary is described by Will Herberg thus:

"Every man has his faith whether he recognizes it or not, whether he avows it or not; the beliefs which a man really holds, it is well to remember, are not necessarily those he affirms with his mouth but those that are operative in his life. The real decision is thus not between faith and no-faith, but between faith in some false absolute, in some man-made idol – the construction of our heart or mind – and faith in the true Absolute, in the transcendent God. This is the decision, and it is a decision that wrenches man's whole being. For it means a decision once and for all to abandon all efforts to find a center of existence within one's self, a decision to commit oneself to God without qualification or reservation. It is not easy for us to abandon confidence in self, in ourselves, in our ideas and enterprises; it comes only after a desperate inner struggle in which the victory is never final. That is why the decision of faith is not merely an intellectual judgment but a total personal commitment reaching down to the foundations of existence."

I resisted that decision, and consequently never made it, but at the same time I never failed to respect those who were able to do so.

At age 14 or 15, such considerations hardly occur, if at all. Life is lived from day to day, competing for a niche in the stratified social order of the student world; competing in sports, competing in class, staying ahead and building friendships. Cosmic curiosity was a rare flash.

*

Some fifty miles west of London, half hidden in the hollows of Berkshire's rolling green farmland lies Bradfield College, a nineteenth century establishment dedicated to the education of the sons of English gentlemen.

Approached along narrow winding hedgerowed lanes, it suddenly appears around a bend at the corner of a little travelled cross-roads. A red brick half-timbered Tudor covered gatehouse ushers the visitor into the outer courtyard. Beyond, a three-sided quadrangle with the fourth side open to a vista of endless playing fields, is formed by the Great Hall, the Dining Hall and the Chapel. High windows all around; stained glass by Burne-Jones. In the center of the "quad" stands an out-of-character grey stone monument – the World War I memorial, engraved with the names of the alumni who fell.

Bradfield operated, as all public schools did, on the prefect principle. That is to say, a kind of student police force, recruited from members of the senior class, wielded authority, kept order, and on occasion administered corporal punishment. Prefects were sometimes feared, never to be trifled with, and always respected. Since prefects, after all, were only students themselves and hardly mature reasoned adults, abuse of authority was not uncommon. If the system appeared to the victims as sometimes unjust, there was always the satisfaction of knowing that some day, with luck, one might become a prefect oneself. In my senior year, I too became a prefect.

Life was spartan. Compulsory cold showers every morning summer and winter for everyone without exception, except if on sick leave. The prefects were there with wet towels to flick the bare bottoms of reluctant stragglers.

I was 13 years old in 1925 when I entered Bradfield. With my black hair and darker than average skin, I must have looked pretty exotic to the homogeneous anglo-saxons, all blonds and red-heads, and since my name did not have an English ring, it was decided I must be Spanish. So Jolis was transformed into Don Jolis, then to Don Jolliass, and finally I was known as Don Jolly Arse. This was all good natured, and I took no offense. It was something of a social "plus" to have earned a nickname.

Every boy had his own foot-locker, known as a "tuck box" at the foot of his bed. Here was stored the normal jumble of boys' paraphernalia, sneakers, cricket ball, candy bars, comic books, and so on.

My mother was always convinced we never had enough to eat, and would arrive at the school unexpectedly in a big car, loaded with food for my tuck box, to my huge embarrassment.

School routine was strict and unbending. Chapel, breakfast, classes, lunch. Sports every afternoon were mandatory – Rugby football or track in winter; cricket or swimming in Summer. Boxing, wrestling, fencing, optional. Also once a week, OTC drill and rifle practice. An afternoon class after sports; then a late afternoon meal (early supper). Finally homework. Lights out at 10PM.

OTC (Officer Training Corps) was an important component of school life. This was not a military school by any means, but weekly drill and rifle practice were taken very seriously. Graduating students took with them a certificate entitling them automatically to a commission in the British Army, if and when called up. We were issued World War I kahki uniforms complete with puttees, and performed close-order drill, back and forth across the football field, shouldering Lee Enfield rifles from World War I.

We had a bugle band. As a member of the school orchestra I was given a sympathetic try-out. My efforts to get a sound out of the brass instrument were pathetic. But extra bodies were needed to swell the ranks. I was issued a bugle, ordered to march with the band, hold it to my lips, and under no circumstances ever to blow into it! I escaped carrying a rifle, but not the marching.

The atmosphere was British upper class to the core; much talk about fox hunting, pheasant shooting and fishing. The headmaster, Mr. Beadle extolled the virtues of the British Empire, sang the praise of T.E. Lawrence, and urged us to read *The Seven Pillars of Wisdom*, (just out) which we did. Lawrence of Arabia was our hero. In addition, all of Rudyard Kipling, A.E.W. Mason's "Four Feathers", Baroness Orczy's "Scarlet Pimpernel," P.C. Wren's "Beau Geste" and "Beau Sabreur" were among our standard fare.

1925 was the year of the British General Strike. Overnight the whole country was shut down. It was considered at the time a revolutionary situation. Many Bradfield teachers left to volunteer as train drivers, phone operators, power station attendants, mail men etc. Individuals appeared at the school gates selling the *Daily Worker.* We were, to a man, bitterly opposed to the "bolshies."

The school orchestra occupied an important place. Before leaving home I had been taking violin lessons for some time. I wasn't particularly good at it, nor did I enjoy it all that much. But at Bradfield things changed. Our orchestra was exactly that, not a brass band, not a jazz band, but a real honest-to-goodness orchestra with first violins, second violins, violas, cellos, double bass, woodwind, brass and tympani. We also had a full male choir with trebles, altos, tenors and bases.

I was inducted into the second violins. By the time I left Bradfield I was leader of the first violins. I was still no virtuoso, but I had learned and heard a lot of music. Our director of music was an unforgettable and tragic figure called Mr. Fox. Before the war he had been a brilliant young concert pianist. He lost his left arm in Flanders. Now reduced to hammering a bunch of schoolboys into an approximation of an orchestra, he lashed us and drove us with an intensity, sometimes awesome, sometimes comic, but in truth, tragic. With the full orchestra assembled, together with the school choir, Fox would stand at the piano performing three separate actions simultaneously, shouting instructions, waving his baton, then dropping the baton and filling in passages on the piano, playing both left and right hand with his only one. He would scream at us; his eyes would flash; spittle sometimes foamed at his lips. He was not a lovable person, but we understood his sorrow.

The high point came in 1928 when Bradfield's full orchestra and the choir travelled to Oxford, where, joining with groups from other schools we performed Bach's Mass in B Minor in its entirety, in the Sheldonian Theatre, an 18th century architectural gem. There are moments in everyone's life, rare moments to be sure, when the spirit is lifted beyond the body, moments of disembodied ecstasy – removed from mortal feeling – a soaring into the heavens, into the unknown. Such a moment was mine, the first of others to come, as I played my fiddle under the baroque dome of the Sheldonian while voices of the massed choirs flooded around me and engulfed my spirit.

Bradfield was famous for its Greek theater. This was an authentic replica of an ancient original. An amphitheater carved out of the hillside, with stone tiers seating a couple of thousand persons, stage, proscenium, orchestra alcove. The story went, that an early headmaster, dedicated to the classics, decided to build the amphitheater, and as a form of punishment, obliged wayward students to dig.

Once every three years a Greek play was performed by the senior Greek class. This became a national event. Students and scholars from all over would attend, as well as London drama critics. In 1928 it was *Rhesus, of Euripides*. I was not in the Greek class, and had no acting role. But I was part of the orchestra that supplied musical accompaniement with flutes and lyres. Dressed in a yellow smock, with a fillet around my head, I played the lyre. "Play" is an overstatement. I memorized which strings to pluck and tried to look Greek.

What about sex? What about it to be sure. Girls simply didn't exist, except at vacation time. Sexual stirrings were never far removed. Sexual talk was constant; much empty boasting of sexual prowess. Rumor had it that homosexuality was rampant; probably, again more talk. In any event, I never encountered it. If I had, I would have recoiled, the idea appalled me. It was erotic dreams, girl fantasies and occasional guilty masturbation. The daily cold shower was supposed to keep matters under control. Then when vacations came around, the challenge was to put the dreams into practice. Mostly it didn't work; once in a while it did.

I was not an outstanding athlete, nor was I the worst – sort of middle-of-the-road. I won a few trophies at track, the 100 yards dash and the half-mile sprint. But in the annual cross-country event – 10 miles over fields, streams, ditches, and finally climbing up a waterfall – I made a poor showing. On the other hand I shone at boxing. Don't ask me why, I'm not particularly pugnacious. Nonetheless, I represented Bradfield at the inter-school boxing championships in the under 16 middle-weight class. My favorite of all, however, was skiing. Of course there was no skiing at Bradfield, where winter brought only rain and occasional frost.

No; skiing was a separate chapter.

My father's business was prospering, and around the mid-1920s he initiated an annual Christmas expedition to the mountains for the whole family. My introduction to the slopes took place at the tiny mountain hamlet of Sils Maria in the Engadine Valley of Switzerland, close to the Italian border.

It requires a good stretch of the imagination to draw any similarity between skiing in those days and what prevails today. In the first place there were no ski-lifts, tow ropes, tow-bars, cable cars, or other mechanical means of ascension; not at Sils in any event. Every foot of elevation had to be laboriously climbed. As a result, elevation was jealously preserved. There were no prepared and marked downhill runs, no ski-patrols, no snow-ploughs. "Downhill" skiing as such, didn't exist. Equipment was primitive. Boots did not grip the ankle, but fitted loosely, not the rigid structures of today. Bindings were secured by leather thongs.

A one-hour, two-hour, or three-hour climb was the first phase of every outing. Goat skins were strapped to the ski-bottoms to prevent back-sliding, and it was huff and puff up through the trees of the lower forest during what seemed like for ever, until emerging finally above the tree line.

There the reward was breathtaking; a limitless expanse of rolling snowfields glittering in the sun, surrounded by towering peaks. This was true cross-country, perfect for the Telemark turns in the deep snow. Lunch perched on a rock, and at the end of the day, one glorious downhill trip home.

The Grand Hotel at Sils Maria was full at Christmas time. Swiss, Germans, French, English and Canadian families were regulars. I remember the Eaton family from Toronto, the department store Eatons. They were noisy and clannish; didn't mix. Most of all I remember Brigitte Helm, Germany's leading movie queen at that moment. UFA Films had just released Fritz Lang's futuristic *Metropolis,* in which she played the part of an ice-cold blonde goddess. Now on vacation with a German girlfriend Yuki, she was not at all ice-cold, she was bubbly and friendly. Probably in her early thirties, to me she appeared ageless. It was whispered that she and her girlfriend were lesbians. I had only a very foggy idea what that meant – it didn't seem to matter. At 16 years old, I was totally bowled over, smitten to the core, and followed her around stupidly like a faithful dog. The two women became friendly with our family. Years later, after Hitler came to power, though not Jewish, they fled Germany and came to stay at our house in Wimbledon – Brigitte Helm and Yuki. Though Yuki's name sounded Japanese, she wasn't. I never got her last name.

A memorable episode was the time I dragged my brother and two friends on a hike across the Pyrennees through Andorra. It could have been 1928. In those days there was no road through to Spain from Andorra. We started off on foot from Ax-les-Thermes in France, planning to get to Seo d'Urgell in Spain. Today Andorra is an automobile-clogged duty-free shopping center, swarming with tourists. Then, it was a sleepy mountain valley, not a single auto, not a gas pump, not even a hotel. We were guided halfway across by a local hunter, whose name, believe it or not was **"Chéri le Chasseur."** It was truly his real name. The rest of the trip we made without a guide and a very imperfect map. It was a momentous adventure for three teenagers. When no news had been heard from us for ten days, my mother in London grew frantic. We learned later, she woke up in the middle of the night, screaming "I know the boys are in trouble, they are dying." She badgered my father into initiating a manhunt through the French authorities. We were not lost, though in fact at one point, my brother, Bernard had slipped on some ice, and without a rope or a pick, he was perilously close to a precipice. The trouble was there were simply no phones in Andorra.

Years later, after arriving in the United States, with the Spanish Civil War just ended, the Pyrenees loomed large in my mind. I wrote an unpublished short story about **"Chéri Le Chasseur"** which is reproduced later herein.

CHAPTER FOUR

THE DOOR OPENS

Whether or not I should go to a university had been a matter of debate in the family for some time. It seems hard to imagine such a dilemma nowadays. Everbody goes to university if they can possibly manage it. But in those days there were serious pros and cons. One went to a university for one of two reasons; either to get a degree and be admitted into one of the professions or the Civil Service, or on the other hand, for purely snobbish reasons, "to make the right connections." We are talking of course, only of Oxford or Cambridge. The lesser "red brick" universities were not even considered.

It had always been a given in our family, and I never questioned it, that I would join my father in the diamond business. "You don't need a university education for the diamond business," argued my father, "and the snobbish connections you would make there would do you more harm than good." Mother, probably with better instinct disagreed. She felt strongly that I should go. "He needs the polish," she said, "everyone does, and the friends he makes there will serve him well through life." In the end it was left up to me, and I opted "No."

So, in 1929 I was packed off to Amsterdam to learn the art of diamond cutting. I sat at the bench under the tutelage of the foreman, just as my father had done a generation earlier; but my presence produced no general strike or lockout; – instead, something totally unrelated and far more destructive occurred, the worldwide recession, following the New York stockmarket crash. By 1930, Amsterdam diamond workers were once again on the streets, unemployed, and factories were closing down.

Nonetheless, for one year I lived in Amsterdam and learned about cutting and polishing diamonds in an environment completely Jewish. It was not only Jewish, it was highly civilized. The musical component alone was rich. During the day, as I sat at the bench, the other workers, all men, would sing as they worked. They sang opera. They sang complete operas, each worker singing a role. Tosca, Aida, Carmen; I couldn't believe it.

Weekends saw me wandering through the galleries of the Rijksmuseum, gazing at the wonders of Vermeer, Frans Hals and Ruysdal. And like every Dutchman, I rode my bicycle everywhere; though the windmill-dotted countryside where everyone wore wooden clogs, along the canals which bordered the rich black fields, to the Zuyder Zee which was not yet dammed up, to Haarlem and the house where Rembrandt was born.

From time to time I would be invited to the home of the diamond factory owner, Abraham Soep, for a musical evening, and instructed to bring my violin with me – there to join the family quartet. Papa played the cello, Mama the viola, me the fiddle, and young son Benno the piano. Coffee and cookies followed. On Saturdays I would escort young Benno to the soccer stadium and watch Amsterdam "Blau-Wit" play Rotterdam. Following the end of World War II I learned that Benno and his mother perished in the gas ovens. I'm not sure about papa Bram, he may have survived.

I lived in a one-room walk-up in the Nikolas Maesstraat, (Nikolas Maes was a 19th century Dutch painter – they even gave street names to painters who were not famous) – and continued taking violin lessons, though with less and less enthusiasm. My teacher was Mijnheer Popplesdorf, leader of the first violins in the Concertgebouw Orchestra. It was a signal honor to be a pupil of such an eminent artist. The cause of my flagging enthusiasm was that I realized I would never be a first-class violinist. The more good music I listened to, the more I disliked my own amateur scratchings. The turning point came the evening I first heard Beethoven's Fifth Symphony. I walked out of the Cocertgebouw Hall in a trance, and remained sleepless most of the night. I never played the violin after that.

It was a lonely twelve months; scarcely any social life, and certainly no girls. Time was filled with reading. I would have been better off with girls, and had no doubt of it at the time. No one needed to persuade me that girls were better than books. I told myself Dutch girls were not pretty enough and I did not find them interesting. But come on. Lets be honest; I was too green and too shy to make the approach. Girls would have been better for another reason. I started reading the kind of books that got me off on my political left foot. It took me years before I realized what a mistake that was.

In the 1920s the subject of war was never far from the minds of old and young. Not the coming war whose shadow had not yet appeared on the horizon, but the war just left behind. As youngsters we learned of its horrors through the eyes and ears of our elders. We understood it only dimly, though we were perfectly able to relate to the blue pyjama – clad wounded in the park.

During one summer vacation, my parents took us on a visit to the Flanders battlefields. The trenches outside Ypres were still intact. British helmets, uniform webbing, and mess kits were still lying around. Barbed wire everywhere. Tourists were scrambling for souvenirs. On the road we passed war cemeteries, one after another. White stone crosses for the British, black wood crosses for the Germans. It was a holiday excursion!

Several years later, in 1929, alone in my Amsterdam walk-up, I first read Erich Maria Remarque's **All Quiet on the Western Front.** Gradually the glories of the British Empire, the heroics at the Khyber Pass, Kitchener in Sudan, the Charge of the Light Brigade, and yes, even Lawrence of Arabia; all began to fade. "Onward Christian Soldiers, marching as to war" acquired a deathly hollow ring. In their place I saw the barbed wire and mud-filled trenches; the row upon row of white and black crosses on the Somme, and the wounded cripples in blue pyjamas in the park. It became clear to me that war was the most evil activity ever invented by man.

I read Bernard Shaw, Rupert Brooke, H.G. Wells, Beatrice and Sidney Webb, H.N. Brailsford, and many other left-wing writers. I learned of the Bloomsbury crowd and the Bolshevik revolution. And especially, I learned of the Reverend Dick Sheppard, the pacifist cleric who launched the anti-war movement that culminated in the "Oxford Pledge" – "never to take up arms in defense of King and Country." I tore up my OTC Certificate entitling me to a commission in the British army.

As I explored this exciting new world, it seemed to me quite reasonable to imagine that with enough determination and collective effort, men-of-goodwill could banish war from the face of the earth. If Mahatma Gandhi's campaign of non-violent resistance to the British in India was succeeding, as seemed to be the case, surely the formula would work elsewhere.

I also learned something else. Pacifist views were not held by conservatives. To the extent they were held anywhere, it was on the Left. In 1929, the Left talked Peace. The Right did not talk Peace until 1938, when it was Chamberlain's "Peace with Honor." So I was drawn into the orbit of the Fabian socialists and the Labour Party. The left-wing vista began opening up as an alternative to Tory jingoism and Colonel Blimp.

Socialism as an "idea", was quite new for me. I read about the Labor Theory of Value, public ownership of the means of production and the workers' movement. I even read the Communist Manifesto. Socialist theory as such, met no critical response from my untrained mind, it just sank in. I accepted it because it seemed to offer a utopian dream, even if only in the distant future, of a world without war. As to what was happening in the Soviet Union, my reasoning was simple. I agreed with their utopian objectives, but rejected their methods. I could not accept that the ends justified the means. Communists, despite their professions of "peace" were not men of peace, they were men of violence.

Such were my ruminations and speculations as I walked along the canals, past the pickled herring sellers, or as I waited in the company of hundreds of other Amsterdam cyclists at the Rembrandtplein, before the helmeted policeman directing traffic. The Depression deepened daily. The diamond industry was closing down. Unemployment everywhere. My sojourn in Amsterdam was soon to end. The failure of the capitalist system seemed self-evident. Socialism sounded like a better way to secure peace and social justice. Any doubts I might have had were allayed when I remembered that one of the members of the Amsterdam City Council was a man called Asscher. He was not only a socialist, he was the brother of Joseph Asscher, the man who polished the Cullinan diamond, the largest diamond ever found, now mounted in the British Crown Jewels. The Asschers were the leading diamond family in Amsterdam; wealthy, respected, and by any definition surely capitalist. In such a circumstance, I told myself, socialism couldn't be all that bad.

By the time I returned to London in 1930, little did I realize I was a perfect example of Lenin's "useful idiots," innocently manipulated by the Communist International. I wanted to become involved in the "movement."

While waiting for the diamond industry to emerge from the doldrums, my father thought it wouldn't hurt for me to study accountancy. So I became what is known as an "articled clerk" in a firm of auditors, went to night school, took exams, and in the company of a qualified "senior," visited clients and audited their books. I eventually graduated as a Chartered Accountant, and became a member of the Institute of Chartered Accountants in England and Wales.

But there was a great deal going on besides left-wing politics and chartered accountancy, a profession I had no wish to pursue. I was interested in the cinema and indulged in dreams of becoming a "cineaste" on the order of Eisenstein. I contacted all the movie studios at Esltree and Twickenham looking for an opening as an assistant cameraman. I even got an offer of employment at 2 pounds a week. I felt I was worth more, and that was the end of it.

With it all, a fair amount of time and effort was also invested in having a good time. Indeed, time and effort was the key, and like all investment it was not without risk. Girls did not jump into bed with the alacrity they do today. A great deal of care, planning and applied psychology was the necessary prerequisite. One date; two dates; maybe a theater; a night out dancing; some earnest "talk;" a bit of romancing. And then? And then? Turn-downs were more frequent than not. But when not, how sweet it was.

My sentimental and political lives ran on different tracks. The girls I dated all came from upper class conservative families; they were the good-looking ones. The last thing they had any interest in was left-wing politics; any politics. Left-wing girls, on the other hand, who were anxious to talk politics, were almost invariably plain. With them, I talked politics, that's all.

Many years later, in 1939 I believe, I was reminded of all this in New York. A musical show was running on Broadway, called "Pins and Needles." It was all about the International Ladies Garmentworkers Union and the "Rag Trade." One of the numbers went: "Men seldom make passes at girls who wear glasses." Of course, I said to myself; that's my story. What a shame for those poor girls. Surely, the ugly girls are the true victims of society. They never get the breaks. What we ought to do is form a protective organization for them. How about The League for Ugly Women? I tried this out on a friend. "Dope," he told me, "you'd never get a single woman to join it. Get a better name." Of course, I was ahead of my time. The sisterhood got onto it later. They found better names. Sexist? You bet.

CHAPTER FIVE

BALLETS RUSSES

A brown sedan bearing British licence plates passed through Bordeaux and was barrelling along Route Nationale 10, headed south. It was a Humber (long since extinct) and I was the driver. As passengers, I had my mother, my brother Bernard and a girl cousin, Josette. This region is known as Les Landes, a sparsely populated country of pine forest, occasional vineyards and sandy soil; 150 kilometers of two-way blacktop, almost deserted, but for the occasional red-tiled white-walled farmhouse. It was the summer of 1931 (or was it 1932?) and a hot August sun was beating down.

Then, without notice, the motor started coughing, then sputtering and soon the Humber was reduced to a crawl. No town, no village, no gas station, no vehicle in sight. I was certainly no mechanic – only learned to drive not so long ago. We limped along painfully for what seemed forever until we reached a farmhouse, where, thank goodness, an open barn-door revealed an ancient tractor.

The farmer, an amiable fellow, stuck his head under the hood, and after fiddling for so long, we assumed he did not know what he was doing, he announced with a huge grin and a Basque accent you could cut with a knife: "Carbooratoore – pleing de merde!"

Several hours later, carburettor cleanup completed, we carried on down on N. 10, through Biarritz, and as the sun was setting over the Atlantic, we pulled in to the pretty little fishing port cum beach resort of Saint Jean de Luz, just short of the Spanish border.

Next morning, the beach was almost deserted. Two girls were laying face down soaking up sun. I walked by with a passing glance. How old could they be? Hard to tell; late teens or early twenties;

blonde hair; beautiful bodies; faces hidden in beach towels. This vacation has started off on the right note, I thought. After a while the girls got up and left.

Next morning they were there again. I sat on the sand, not too close, not too far, and improvising a daring opening gambit, I ventured: "Hi!" Not only did I get no rebuff, I was rewarded by the two friendliest smiling and beautiful faces I had ever seen. No need to break the ice, there was no ice.

"Qu'est ce que vous faites ici?" They asked. What are you doing here?"

"I'm from London. Here with my family on vacation. Arrived a couple of days ago. I saw you here yesterday."

"Yes we know. We saw you too."

"How could you with your faces buried in towels?"

"Don't worry. We saw you."

"So, what are you two doing here?"

"We 're dancers with the Ballets Russes de Monte Carlo. The whole company is here with Colonel de Basil. We're here rehearsing.

I had never heard of the Ballets Russes de Monte Carlo, and only learned later that the director, Colonel de Basil was the lover of the famous Diaghilev. So instead of looking properly impressed, I just looked unimpressed. No matter. The girls smiled.

There was not much more conversation, but much concentration on getting tanned.

"Will you be here tomorrow?" I asked when they got up to leave.

"We have to go for rehearsal now. Yes we'll be here tomorrow."

And then they introduced themselves.

"I am Tatiana Riabouchinska" said the shorter one.

"My name is Nina Tarakanova" said the other. Her eyes twinkled as she said it, and my heart jumped.

Then they both walked off the beach, or rather waddled; true ballerinas to be sure.

Riabouchinska later became a famous prima ballerina, and married star ballet dancer, David Lichine. Nina remained in the corps de ballet. It was her I fell in love with.

Nina had ice-blue laughing eyes, a broad slavic face, real ash-blond hair, an infectious grin and a deep throaty laugh. She also had a tantalizing elfin quality. We met every day for the rest of the vacation, often with other dancers from the company, never alone. We never even held hands. Though it took time to blossom, it was my first big love.

At the end of the vacation, she returned to Paris and I to London. We were separated for a whole year. We exchanged letters.

When the Ballets Russes de Monte Carlo opened at the Covent Garden Opera House in London, I became an instant stage-door Johnnie. Every night I sat through the performance and waited for Nina at the stage door afterwards. I became a balletomane, sitting transfixed as she danced her number in "Les Présages" to the music of Tchaikovsky's 5th Symphony. I marvelled at the grace of Alexandra Danilova in Stravinsky's Petrouchka, or the prodigious leaps of David Lichine and Eglevsky, not to speak of the contortions of Woizikovsky. The "Symphonie Fantastique" of Berlioz held me spellbound.

Nina had escaped the Bolshevik revolution as a little girl, fleeing with an older sister across Siberia to Shanghai, and eventually to Paris. Her older sister, more mother than sister, raised her. As a young pupil at the Diaghilev ballet company, she practiced her steps under the watchful eye of those two greats, Anna Pavlova and Nijinsky. She lived with her sister in a comfortable apartment on Boulevard Michel Ange, Auteuil.

As long as the Covent Garden run continued, Nina and I were together whenever she was not dancing. We went everywhere together, ate together, slept together. She was a virgin, I was her first. She became part of my family who loved her, especially my mother. At the same time, I became almost a non-dancing member of "Les Ballets Russes." I spoke no Russian, but everyone spoke fluent French. There was a memorable evening when we celebrated the marriage of David Lichine and Tatiana Riabouchinska. The wedding party was held after the performance in a small Soho restaurant close by Covent Garden. The entire company, including Leonide Massine and Alexandra Danilova toasted the happy couple throughout the night in rivers of champagne and vodka.

Of course the day of reckoning had to come. The London run ended, and the company moved on. With tearful wrenching good-byes, Nina and I swore eternal love. We would surely be together again soon, we vowed. I was broken hearted.

This became the pattern for the next two or three years. Whenever the company was in London we resumed our affair. Even when it was in Paris or the Cote d'Azur, I managed to sneak away for short spells to be with her. But when it was in New York, Los Angeles, Rio de Janeiro, or Buenos Aires, as it was in regular rotation, I despaired.

There was no thought of marriage. It was the last thing to enter my mind, or hers either. We were both too young and both of us had too much ground to cover yet before thoughts of "settling down." But the on-again-off-again affair could not last forever. It cooled imperceptibly. After each three to six months separation, the resumption was slightly less impassioned. It ended without fuss, nor drama, just quietly and naturally; as simply as it had begun. I never knew whether she loved me as much as I loved her. At age 20, I liked to think she did. Today, I suspect she didn't.

Years later, I heard she had married a Cambridge professor and had given up the ballet. I never tried to see her again, though once or twice I toyed with the idea. Much better, I decided, to remember her as I knew her.

CHAPTER SIX

WHAT PRICE PACIFISM?

With Hitler's coming to power and the menace of "Mein Kampf" ringing in our ears, it became more and more difficult to defend the posture of pacifism. Non-violent resistance as practiced by Gandhi against the British in India was successful because the British were, and are civilized. But will the Jews be saved by lying down in the street in front of trolley-cars? I clung to this illusion for a while, recognizing at the same time how massively the evidence was stacked against me. But when the Spanish civil war broke out, I found I could no longer make the case for pacifism.

After exhaustive diplomatic parleys over Spain, not unlike the diplomatic danse macabre over the Yugoslav breakup 55 years later, a Non-Intervention Agreement was signed on October 28, 1936, between Britain, France, Germany, Italy, USSR and Portugal. It proved an utter farce. Only Britain and France observed it; Germany, Italy and the USSR never had the slightest intention of doing so. Hitler supplied Franco with arms and dispatched his Condor Legion, over 5,000 strong. Mussolini, likewise supplied arms and troops. The USSR threw the Comintern into high gear, created the International Brigade, and mobilized writers, intellectuals, fellow travellers, and naive innocents around the world in support of the Republican cause.

Supporters of General Franco, in addition to genuine Fascists, included Monarchists, Carlists, Conservatives, and Catholics, none of whom necessarily had any love for Hitler or Mussolini, but who were united by their opposition to Socialism, and above all, Communism. Supporters of the Republican government, in addition to genuine Communists, included moderate Democratic Socialists, middle-of-the-road Liberals and moderate Conservatives, none of whom were necessarily pro-Communist, but who were united by their opposition to Fascism and Nazism.

What started out as a purely internal Spanish affair, developed into a worldwide struggle between Fascism and Communism, in which those who were both anti-Communist *and* anti-Fascist, conservatives, democrats and liberals alike, were seduced, outwitted, and driven to the sidelines. In the end, one year after Franco's victory, Hitler and Stalin signed their non-aggression pact and, "Hey Presto," the worldwide struggle between Fascism and Communism for which so many died in Spain was off. World War II was on.

None of this was clear to us at the time. What *was* clear was that Jewish persecution had been in full swing since 1932. German refugees were arriving in England in ever greater numbers. "Mein Kampf" was a searing reality and plainly spelled out the horrors to come. A victory for Franco meant a victory for Hitler. There was not the slightest doubt in our minds as to who were the "good guys" in the Spanish Civil War.

Added to that, in my case was my strong tilt to the left. The idea of "going to fight in Spain" kept recurring, and I was indeed tempted. But the Communist Party's juggernaut recruiting methods put me off, and the more strident they became, the less I felt the urge. I had an instinctive dislike for the British Communists (they were the only ones I'd met), and had to remind myself over and over again that they "were on the right side of history." I was still a "useful idiot."

Some have drawn a parallel between Spanish Civil War of 1936 – 1939 to the war in former Yugoslavia of the 1990s. Madrid, 1936, it has been said, is Sarajevo, 1993. In reality there is little resemblance between the two, except for the atrocities. These were committed in Spain by both sides, and were no less horrible than those we have witnessed in Vukovar, Mostar, Gorazde, Srebrenica and Sarajevo. There was no television, but the public was informed. The massacre at Badajoz in which 5,000 civilians were slaughtered by Franco's men; the carpet bombing of Guernica by German planes of the Condor

Legion; the rape and murder of nuns and priests by the republicans. We were fed our daily ration of horrors. There was no need for CNN.

What we did not know, and only learned years later, was the record of torture and murder committed by the Communist Party against its own deviant members and non-communist rivals in the loyalist camp.

But while we prayed for a Loyalist victory and agonized over the battle for Madrid, life at home followed its daily routines, undisturbed. Meetings were attended; jobs pursued; girls dated; vacations taken; family gatherings observed. The good life was still there for those fortunate enough to afford it.

This was the era of "swing" and the music of Benny Goodman had already washed across British shores.

In a short story I wrote in 1936 and never tried to publish, I attempted to capture the flavor of the time. Readers may be pardoned for thinking it stilted, dated and artificial, but I would remind them it was written almost 60 years ago. The full horrors of the twentieth century were not yet upon us; dilletante leftism flourished among Britain's gilded youth. Upper-class radical chic was already fashionable, even when not taken too seriously.

Here it is, unedited.

CHAPTER SEVEN

NON-INTERVENTION — "AS SHE IS SPOKE"

Somewhere on the Cote d'Azur, between St. Raphael and St. Tropez there is a little stretch of beach where the sand is white and the trees grow right down to the water's edge. During the day the sun beats fiercely on the half dozen stucco villas that border the hot tarred road. Most of the cars take the bend too fast. The large sports cars come around with tires screaming. Their bronzed and kerchiefed passengers laugh because its dangerous. The Peugeots and the Citroens, on the other hand, usually overloaded, nearly keel over onto the beach, while their outsize drivers, black-coated and straw-hatted, just sweat because its dangerous. Few ever notice the massive pink hotel set back among the pine trees. Every fifteen minutes the blue streamlined Michelin "Autorail" rushes through, dead on schedule for Cannes, Nice and Monte Carlo, with shrill siren wide open.

During the day, this little stretch of beach is undistinguished. It wears a transitory air, and smells faintly of gasoline. At night time it is different; it is transformed. It becomes the stuff of magazine stories; the sort in which gilded escapists live and love in order to maintain circulation at the million mark. Tonight for instance, it is pure H. de Vere Stakpole. The blue Mediterranean is cleft by a shimmering path of moonlight from the horizon to your feet, as you stand at the water's edge. A scented breeze faintly stirs the pine trees. The air is soft and languorous, bad for clear thinking. Somewhere, you feel, there must be two lovers lying very close in the warm sand.

A few hundred feet along the beach, strains of dance music float from the windows of "La Batterie", and the reflected lights from its terrace dance in the water as it gently laps the white walls. Inside, couples crowd the floor in a stifling atmosphere of mixed perfumes, bleached hair and sunburn oil. Bodies press close; bronzed backs yield under bronzed hands; tanned cheek touches tanned cheek; eyes closed; eyes laughing; eyes roving. The music is bad, but what matter; everyone knows the French can't play "swing." Its the Sun that counts. The Sun makes all the difference. It makes ugly bodies less ashamed, and beautiful bodies more desirable. Unquestionably, the Sun belongs to Café Society – "swinging," trucking, shuffling.

A sleek young Frenchman steps to the mike and strokes it as he has seen a done a hundred times in the movies, and croons joylessly:

"Baby what I couldn't do to you,

"Wiz plenty of money and you-oo-hoo.

"In spite of ze worry zat money breengs,

"Just a leetle feelthy lucre buys a lot of theengs.

"I could take you places zat you'ld like to go,

"But outside of zat I've no use for dough.

"Its ze root of all evil; of strife and upheaval,

"But I'm certain honey, zat life could be sunny,

"Wiz plenty of money and you."

No one is particularly aware of this performance. Over in the corner, two young men lounge on their divan talking. The attention of one is diverted; a dark haired girl is pushed against their table by the crowd. She sways for a moment. The young man's eyes travel up her dress, teasing, provoking; he loses interest in his companion's conversation.

"Alan!" exclaims the other, I wish you'd try and concentrate for a moment. As I was saying, nobody in their right senses believes for a moment that Trotsky worked in league with the Fascist powers for the overthrow of the Soviet U...... Oh God, this is hopeless... What a place to talk politics!" He leans back, abandoning the unequal struggle.

Two dancers leave the floor and approach the table. The girl runs forward, leaving her partner sandwiched between two colliding couples.

"Hello darlings!" she bubbles. "Not politics, I hope? You know that's strictly verboten. I just had to shut Jim's mouth out there on the floor. He started off in the middle of that great "swing" number. Everyone was listening. I gave him a kick in the shins......rather put him off his swing so to speak...ha ha... God, I must have a drink...is this chair taken... didn't it darling?"

"I should damn well say it did," muttered Jim, extricating himself from the melee, "and I wasn't talking politics either. I merely remarked..." he said, grabbing himself a chair. " I merely remarked that this goddam country is getting too bolshie for my liking. There isn't a house between Monte Carlo and Marseilles that isn't plastered with Red slogans. Why, there's even a hammer and sickle painted on the side of the Casino right here. Coming down from the hotel this evening I read on the walls of the houses "Vive Thorez!" — "Vive Blum!" — "Vive Doriot!" —"Vive de la Rocque!" Who the hell are these bastards anyway? What do you know Alan; you're a bit of a Red yourself aren't you? When's the revolution.?"

"What? Oh sorry..." murmurs Alan, still peering after the dark haired girl, "I wasn't listening, to tell the truth."

"Messieurs-dames désirent?" The waiter hovers attentively

"Champagne cocktail for me" chimes the girl.

"Quatre champagne-cocktails s'il vous plaît."

"Tres bien m'sieur." The waiter hurries off.

"Isn't it amazing, that's the cheapest drink you can get here." Jim raises a clenched fist in mock communist salute. "How do you know," he continues " that that oily waiter isn't a budding Lenin, waiting his chance to stab us all in the back?"

"For Christ's sake shut up Jim!," barks Alan. He has lost track of the dark haired girl, and is peeved. "And you might do us a favour, and give up the Continental Daily Mail while we're here...don't want you having a nervous breakdown you know."

"Sorry old boy. No offence or anything," mutters Jim, slightly abashed. Then turning to the others artfully: "There you are, you see, I said Alan was a Red."

Alan is irritated. He bangs his fist on the table, and leaning across: "Now listen here, Jim. I was having a quiet talk with Charles here, before you came butting in. Mildred darling, take him back on the floor and "swing" his bloody head off — theres a good girl."

Mildred giggles.

"Take no notice of him," groans Charles, "Can't you stop leading with your chin just once?...What I was trying to say was this. Just because they've nationalised the means of production in Russia, you imagine the millenium has arrived. Whereas I say that terrorist trials, suppression of individual liberty, an opprerssive bureaucracy, are just as unacceptable whether performed in the name of immediate Fascism or ultimate Socialism."

"Thats Trotskyite bunk!"

"Well, I've read some of Trotsky, and what he has to say about Russia is plenty. I feel his criticism of the way things are going there is sound. Call me a Trotskyite if you wish."

"I'll do nothing of the kind! Why, you're not even a Socialist; something that Trotsky certainly claims to be. You're just a bemused liberal, using Trotsky's criticism of Soviet Russia to reinforce your own prejudice against Socialism in general."

"Darlings!" interrupts Mildred, "*Do* stop talking politics. I want to dance. I'm sick of dancing with Jim. He's got no rythm, and anyway its no fun with your husband."

Jim is far away. Leaning over the back of his chair, he examines with a critical eye every woman who passes the table; from her breasts to her legs, and then back again. He never seems to get around to their faces.

"All right darling" says Alan, soothingly. "I'll dance with you in half a minute. Now look here Charles,... supposeing some of Trotsky's criticisms are justified, and I'm willing to believe some of them may be..."

"Damn decent of you...!"

"Shut up!... The point is this. How do you expect to meet the threat of Fascism by undermining the faith which millions of workers have in the first Socialist experiment in history? You'll only further divide the world proletariat, and weaken the anti-Fascist movement. Besides, don't forget that with all its faults, the Soviet Union is the greatest bulwark against Fascism today."

"In spite of ze worry zat money breengs

"Just a leetle feelthy lucre buys a lot of theengs."

"Yes," ponders Charles, "But I've always been told that Fascism is the Big Boys' answer to Charlie Marx. If Charlie eats too much spinach, the Big Boys will gang up on him and bump him off."

"And" replies Alan, "When the showdown comes, I suppose you'll be doing the proverbial balancing act on the proverbial fence, not knowing which way to fall?"

"Precisely."

Jim is bored. His interest in passing women has evaporated. He decides to liven up the conversation.

"I say," he starts off hopefully, "don't mind my interrupting, but I must tell you people something important. It happened on the beach this morning."

"We most certainly *do* mind" growls Charles. "For Christ's sake why don't you go to the bar?"

"I'm not thirsty" counters Jim. "As I was saying, it happened on the beach this morning. I was sitting alone, and there was a fat woman sitting not far away. All of a sudden, a little Scotch terrier trots up and solemnly lifts its leg against her backside! God how I laughed; the funniest thing since Alan crawled into Susie's bedroom that night in Monte Carlo and found that Charles had got there first!"

Alan and Charles exchange glares.

Mildred chuckles gleefully. "Well boys, you did rather ask for it, didn't you?

"All right" concedes Alan. "We give up. No more politics."

"What a scream though," says Mildred. It must have made a shocking stain on white."

"It did."

"But all the same," persists Alan "I can't leave poor old Charles here balancing on the fence. After all Charles, you're supposed to be a Liberal aren't you? You're supposed to have as much dislike of Fascism as any Communist."

"I have."

"Well that's fine, there's your answer: The Peoples' Front."

"Voila les champagne -cocktails" announces the waiter.

"Thank God."

"But that," argues Charles, " is not the answer either. It does not resolve the fundamental hostility between the two social systems. For me these systems differ only in their property relationships. The methods of maintaining those relationships appear identical; force, terror, and total suppression of individual liberty.

"Wait a minute..." parries Alan, as he gently but firmly guides an overbalanced couple on to the jam-packed floor. "Lets take this slowly. In the first place, don't make the mistake of believing everything you read about Russia. Secondly, you forget that the aims of these two systems are diametrically opposed. One is an attempt to maintain the old class privileges by means of mediaeval mumbo-jumbo and ever more frightful wars, while the other is part of the painful struggle towards the integration of the human race; a struggle for an international classless society, where man can achieve his highest development unhampered by war and hunger."

This is altogether too much for Jim. "Tum-tiddely-um-tum" he beats a tattoo on his champagne glass, "Zing-Boom! But the best part of the story is this," he continues innocently, "no one saw it happen except for myself and the owner of the dog; and was *she* a corker! Oh boy! Cream of the cream. A polish blonde by name of Katia, and I've got a date with her later tonight. And what a voice. Whew! Turns your knees to caviar. Great work for a Scottie – never knew they were that intelligent. I must get one."

"Baby what I couldn't do to you.

"Wiz plenty of money and you-oo-hoo"

The French crooner is back at the mike. An irate Englishman is making a scene over the price of his drinks. Livid in the face, he sends for the maitre d'hotel because the Italian waiter is unable to understand his execrable French.

"That" continues Charles, raising his voice to drown the hubbub, "is an over-simplification, much too romantic. Why must you radicals always reduce everything to formulas. In the light of what goes on today, it seems to me that every time a revolution releases new forces of so-called 'human progress', it also releases hitherto suppressed forces of greed, selfishness and ambition. Sooner or later a new revolution is necessary, just as plausible, just as "Just" as the last, and so on ad infinitum."

Alan protests. "Charles, you're going soft. That's a decadent defeatist attitude; pure liberal nostalgia."

Mildred, who has been sedulously trying to inveigle a young Frenchman into asking her to dance, is considerably piqued when that young man finally gets up, walks straight past her and invites the girl at the next table. "I say you two! she exclaims petulantly, "This is a bit bloody thick. We came on this holiday on the distinct understanding that there would be no politics. I wish to God you'd both shut up. You're spoiling the party."

"Just a minute, darling" says Alan without looking at her, "This is important. I'm just about to deliver the coup de grace to Charles here, and that will end political discussion for all time.... Yes, Charles, the trouble with you is that as long as you enjoy a disproportionate share of the good things of life, you don't like to commit yourself to an open Socialist outlook which your own sense of reason and logic tells you *must* be right. So you take refuge in liberal dream fantasies."

He sits back to let this sink in, and scans for a moment the jostling crowd of dancers.

Charles meanwhile studies the pattern on the table cloth, deep in reflection. At length he looks up and announces with an air of decision: "Well, what of it? Suppose you're right. We only live once don't we? Why the hell should I give up the good things of life? Anyway, how about you? You shouldn't be talking so loud. How, for instance, do you reconcile the world proletariat with all this here?"

"I don't try to reconcile it" answers Alan, feeling that somehow his shot has misfired; "I admit its a duality, but that's not important. I do my share of the donkey work, and when the time comes I shall know what to do."

"What sort of donkey work?" queries Charles.

"Well......" ponders Alan, "Demonstrations, petitions, letter writing, Spain benefits..."

"Why didn't you go to Spain?" demands Charles suddenly.

"Well..." answers Alan, somewhat taken aback, "Why didn't *you,* for that matter? You're an anti-Fascist too.

Jim, who has been "doing a doormouse" for some time, suddenly springs to life."There she goes! he shouts eagerly.

"Who?"

"Katia"

"Who's Katia?"

"Why, I told you just now,... that Polish blonde, don't you remember? Mildred, look! Don't you think she's okay?...For crying out loud, she's going to dance with that lousy dago, I bet he's a pansy."

"No dear," says Mildred softly, "he's not a pansy. I met him in the hotel grounds last night, so I know!"

"Oh you did, did you? Well let me just tell you......"

"Just because I'm anti-fascist, and hate war", says Charles, "Is no reason why I should jump into the very first war that breaks out. But you'll have to think of something else. That answer is no good for you. The trouble with you is that you're bothered with a conscience. An overdose of the 'good things' of life, and then a spot of Party work as a corrective. Its the modern form of penance. I'm willing if you like, to admit I'm decadent, but you are not. You like to think of yourself as a progressive. In fact, you're an incurable romantic, trying to get the best of both worlds with an easy conscience."

Alan wears an injured look. Really, Charles can be most exasperating at times. Its that maddening way way he has of accidentally hitting on a half-truth, and then waiting for your answer to confirm his suspicions.

"Look here, Charles'" he protests, "You know that's not true. Gosh, you ought to know me by now. How many times have I told you that for me its a matter of deepest conviction that Freedom, Peace, Democracy,can only be saved by...... Oh Christ, what's the use? Mildred, lets dance; we've been over this ten million times and we always get precisely to this point and no farther."

"Its ze root of all evil; of strife and upheaval:

"But I'm certain, honey, zat life could be sunny

"Wiz plenty of money and you."

"Why is it?" asks Alan, wedged in the middle of the floor, "that the French can never get hold of a song that's less than two years old?"

"Search me," answers Mildred. "Ouch! Please mind my back, it got frightfully burned this morning. You know, my love," she whispers, smiling into his eyes, "I *do* love you so, when you talk politics, you're so sweet.

CHAPTER EIGHT

BRIEF ENCOUNTER WITH LABOUR

With "non-violent resistance" a fading option, and left-wing politics throwing up more doubts and questions than answers, I was soon to cross the threshold into complete disenchantment; but not quite yet. I had read George Orwell's **Road to Wigan Pier,** a biting satire on corruption and dishonesty in the trade-union-dominated Labour Party. The non-union members of the party, the intellectuals, were in a minority and unable to overcome the union bosses. These were the people it seemed to me, whose commitment to peace and social justice was untainted by self-interest, and whose ideology was not power-driven. Surely, this was the crowd I should get involved with. Or so I reasoned.

The acknowledged leader of this group was Sir Stafford Cripps, an aristocratic intellectual, brilliant lawyer, socialist maverick, and bane of the union bosses. A friend of my father happened to know him, and was kind enough to give me a letter of introduction. This, I forwarded with a personal note requesting an interview. Sir Stafford replied at once, inviting me to his home in Gloucestershire for lunch. The drive down from London took a good three hours.

Nestled in a hollow of rich rolling parkland, amid spreading oak trees and grazing cattle, stood the Cripps home, a patrician gray stone mansion. It was the home of a country squire, not the setting I expected for a leader of the proletariat. The interview took place, over lunch, in the baronial hall, in the presence of Lady Cripps, a friendly and motherly soul. Cripps bore himself with a patrician austerity, quite in tune with his surroundings. He was friendly enough, though, and after hearing my story he offered me a job on *The*

Tribune, the left-wing weekly he had just launched and was bankrolling. I accepted his offer eagerly. The trouble was, as a left-wing ideologue I was a neophyte, and my qualifications were minimal. I was a Chartered Accountant. Not surprisingly therefore, I was given the job of bookkeeper; not at all what I wanted. As consolation, I was invited to write an occasional article and book review.

The managing editor was William Mellor, a rather humorless fellow. The man who sat next to me in the small office off Fleet Street, was assistant editor, Michael Foot, who later became the leader of the radical wing of the Labour Party. He and I struck up a superficial friendship, but it did not go very far. I particularly remember a scruffy-looking Indian who would stop by from time to time, always in a rush, to hand in a manuscript. His name was Krishna Menon, who years later led the Third World Kremlin-orchestrated anti-American chorus at the United Nations.

It was not long before I realized there was a vast difference between holding a set of leftist political beliefs, and becoming involved in the daily "nuts and bolts" routine of the movement. "Bookeeper in The Movement" was not the right career for me. More fun and more satisfying was the time I joined a mass demonstration in Trafalgar Square calling for independance for India, decked out in a white pill-box Gandhi cap.

My stint with *The Tribune* merely added to what was by now a growing disillusionment, and I decided to quit. I wrote Stafford Cripps a short letter, thanking him, and recevied a short friendly acknkowledgement. I never saw him again.

Stafford Cripps became leader of the House of Commons in 1942, and Chancellor of the Exchequer in 1947, and finally, British Ambasador to India, when the latter was granted independence.

CHAPTER NINE

RETURN TO DIAMONDS

As mentioned earlier, it had always been more or less understood by all members of the family, though in my case not so enthusiastically, that sooner or later I would enter the family diamond business. The time had now come.

What was the diamond business? Let us look at it from Jac Jolis' perspective.

When during the 1860s, diamonds were discovered in a volcanic pipe at Kimberley, South Africa, and in alluvial deposits along the banks of the Vaal River, prospectors, diggers and fortune hunters from the world over rushed in, closely followed by grubstakers, scam artists and creative swindlers. The diggers worked small claims and sold their diamond "finds" to the grubstakers or self-appointed "diamond buyers," who were either operating on their own behalf, or for rough diamond merchants in Europe. In the past, the market for rough diamonds had been Amsterdam, where the polishing took place, but this new expanded production from South Africa found its market in London, not unnaturally, as Britain was the communications and financial hub of the Empire. From now on, diamond polishers had to come to London for their supplies of rough stones.

While Cecil Rhodes and Barney Barnato were buying up and consolidating all the small claims at the Kimberley Mine, to create what was to become the nucleus of De Beers, four Jewish brothers from Frankfurt, Germany had emigrated to England, and entered the trade as rough diamond merchants. They were: Ernest Oppenheimer, and his brothers, Louis, Bernard, and Otto. The story of how Ernest Oppenheimer gained control of the subsequent diamond discoveries in the former German colony of South West Africa and made this a stepping stone to eventually controlling De Beers and 80% of the diamond industry, has been fully recounted elsewhere. Jac Jolis built his career in the orbit and shadow of the Oppenheimer family. The Premier Diamond Mining Company where young Jac had been dispatched by his father Bram, some years ago, was eventually incorporated into the De Beers Diamond Syndicate. Jac named his second son after Sir Bernard Oppenheimer, who at one time was his boss, and was associated in partnership for many years with the youngest brother, Otto.

Diamonds, the hardest substance known to man, come in an infinite variety of sizes, shapes, colors and purity. The lowest grades, that is to say, stones too impure to qualify as gems, are used for industrial purposes. And as is normal in the natural condition of the world, fine quality is rare, poor quality is not. A far greater quantity of low-grade industrial diamonds are produced than gem grades.

During the Depression years of the 1930s, De Beers was accumulating enormous quantities of unsaleable industrial grade diamonds. Vaults were bursting, especially with the lowest grade of all, known as bort, suitable only for crushing into diamond powder. Inventory ran to millions of carats. At one point management seriously considered dumping the excess into the ocean. Little did De Beers suspect that only a few years later, new technology would open vast new opportunities requiring the application of industrial diamond, especially the lowest grades. Fortunately, the excess inventory was not dumped. Instead, Jac Jolis, in partnership with Otto Oppenheimer, offered to purchase important quantities, and launched an agressive marketing program. Included in this program was the decision to develop outlets in the United States.

In 1936 I was sent to New York with the mission to lay the groundwork for opening an office. This was to be quite independent of De Beers, and was to be managed jointly by my brother, Bernard and myself. We founded Diamond Development Company of America, Inc, which later was transformed into Diamond Distributors, Inc.

CHAPTER TEN

AMERICA THE BEAUTIFUL

Travelling from country to country in Europe produces little culture shock. To experience real culture shock the European must travel to America. All the oceans of literature, the movies, the popular songs, the stories of immigrants, fail to impart the extent of one overwhelming impression, namely the sheer dimension of everything. Not just the tall buildings, but everything, literally everything; the newspapers, those monstrous Sunday editions, the steaks, the automobiles, the sandwiches, the highways, the bridges, the number of radio stations (no TV yet.) Everything is more and bigger.

When I sailed for New York on the Queen Mary in 1936 I was 24 years old. I found myself in the company of Emlyn Williams and the whole cast of "How Green Was My Valley," on their way to a first New York opening. A lasting shipboard friendship was struck. We vowed to stay in touch. I never saw them again. The Statue of Liberty was ten times larger than I imagined, having only seen Bartholdi's much smaller model on the Pont Mirabeau astride the Seine.

And of course, like millions of first arrivals before me, I spent the first days standing slack-jawed at the curb-side with a crick in my neck from craning up.

Being normally good mannered and speaking faultless English should be an advantage, no? Well, no. Try negotiating a ham sandwich at a lunch counter! Forget your polite English deference. Seated at the counter, shoulder to shoulder with seasoned New Yorkers, while the white-capped counter-man ran back and forth, serving with astonishing speed, my tentative "Er, I say, do you mind...?" ..."Excuse

me, I would like a...".…"Could I please have a..." earned me total
non-recognition. I was a non-person, while my fellow customers
right and left were happily eating and leaving. I got the message.
Next time the counterman passed before me I leaned across and
screamed at him: "Ham on rye" and got an immediate "Coming right
up!"

That was step number one. Step number two occurred on my first
visit to Macy's department store where I made the fatal mistake of
holding the door open for a woman behind me. I was then left
holding the door as ten thousand more women poured through before
I got the message.

Step three came a few years later, when during basic training at
Fort Drum, then known as Pine Camp, I learned that a "limey accent"
was a near fatal liability at the outset of wartime army service.

Meanwhile, my integration process proceeded in a haze of wonder
and pleasure. Brought up in the British tradition of reserve,
circumspection and class-consciousness, I was enchanted by the
general good nature and open handed bonhomie encountered on all
sides. The use of first name on first time meeting astonished me.
Those self-deluded European socialists, looking to the Soviet Union
for the classless society are all wrong, I said to myself. This is truly
the classless society.

On a business trip to the Middle West, a cashier in a cafeteria said
to me as she handed change, "Say, you sure have a funny accent.
Where are you from?"

"I come from London," I answered.

Oh yeah? What? London, Ontario or London, Kentucky?"

I had never heard of either, but really did not feel it necessary to
say so:

"None of those," I said to her, " just London, England."

On another business trip, this time to Lancaster, Pennsylvania, in
the heart of Amish country, I came across a handsome colonial
house converted into a restaurant. The sign on the outside said:

YE OLDE DUTCH KITCHEN
BEST CHINESE-AMERICAN FOOD.
Wonderful!

And of course, in the United States, if they call you a Dutchman, they don't mean you're a Dutchman. They mean you're a German.

As soon as I could, I applied for American citizenship, and was sworn in as a US citizen in the Southern District Court of New York in 1943, just before entering the US Army.

*

There is almost nothing manufactured today that does not require the application of industrial diamond somewhere in the process. In the field of metallurgy, technological advance demands the development of ever harder and ever greater wear-resistant material. But each time a harder substance is developed the tooling needed to work it has to be even harder. The "hardness race" is permanent.

Two technological events in the1930s led to a marked acceleration of this process.

One was the German invention of the hardest metal alloy yet known. It was developed by Krupp, who called it Widia steel. Widia being a contraction of "wie diamant," "hard as diamond," which of course, it wasn't. The process was acquired by General Electric Company, who developed it as Tungsten Carbide and created a subsidiary for the purpose, The Carboloy Company.

The other was the discovery by a Belgian engineer called Neven, that diamond dust could be combined with powdered metal alloy, and fused into a solid mass which could then be produced in a variety of desired shapes. The use of diamond for cutting, grinding, shaping, boring, tungsten carbide work pieces was thus enormously expanded. It couldn't be done without diamond. During the 1930s the main use for industrial diamond was, the dressing of grinding wheels, the shaping of hard metal alloys, the pulling of tungsten wire for filaments, rock drilling, and stone cutting.

In the years preceding World War II, my brother Bernard and I travelled the length and breadth of the United States, carrying a satchel full of industrial diamonds carefully assorted into every known end-use application. Manufacturing plants across the country were visited; in the mid-West, New England, California, even goldmining camps in Quebec and Ontario. In those days, machine-tool operators bought their diamonds loose and mounted them themselves into the appropriate cutting tools. The emergence of a specialized diamond-tool industry producing sophisticated diamond-tipped tools for diverse applications was in its infancy.

Calling on purchasing agents, sitting in waiting rooms, making the sales pitch, getting turn-downs, endless train rides from town to town, seedy hotels, the occasional sale. The life of a salesman. We were totally unprepared for it. But what an education.

Slowly, sales built up; the business was taking shape. We had the benefit of advice and direction from a salty old-timer called Leo Meyerowitz. Leo had his own small diamond tool business and was happy to be of help. In exchange we sold him a few stones at preferential prices. A died-in-the-wool conservative who thought Calvin Coolidge was the greatest, he based his philosophy on one maxim. "Never forget", he would say "The average man is a son-of-a-bitch!"

The overnight Limited to Cincinnati bounces and sways on the uneven tracks. I am stretched out in an upper berth. The long mournful wail of the train's siren and the jolts and bumps make sleep impossible. I have an important call to make in the morning, at the Cincinnati Milling Machine Co, but my mind is restless. Thoughts of the life I left so recently fill my head. What is happening in Europe? It seems like total paralysis in the face of Hitler's aggressions. He has annexed Austria and reoccupied the Rhineland; nobody moved. The Cliveden Set is preaching appeasement. The war in Spain is dragging on; non-intervention is a farce. Chamberlain and Daladier have signed the Munich sell-out.

In a Cincinnati hotel lobby, I fall upon a London newspaper, left no doubt by another itinerant Englishman, and find a rhyme by an anonymous poet signing himself *Sagittarius.* I clipped it, and have treasured it ever since:

ADVICE TO THE AGGRESSOR
Meine Herren und Signori
Clients of the British Tory,

Kindly note that Number 10
Requests your patronage again.
As Chamberlain et Daladier,
Messrs, Hoare Laval, successors,
For doing business with aggressors.
Frontiers promptly liquidated,
Coups d'état consolidated,
Pledges taken and exchanged,
Acquisitions rearranged,
Loans on Fascist risks advanced,
Nazi enterprise financed,
European intervention
Given personal attention.
Have you problems of Partition?
Let us send a British Mission.
Breaking with Geneva's firms,
We offer Nazis favored terms.
Let us lend to back your claim
England's honorable name.
For dirty deals both great and small
Our representative will call.
Orders carried out with speed,
Satisfaction guaranteed.
We obsequiously remain, Daladier et Chamberlain.

The day Hitler's armies marched into Paris in 1940, I stood at a traffic light in Pittsburgh, waiting for the green. Next to me stood a man holding an open newspaper. He was silently weeping.

One year earlier the Spanish civil war had ended. Franco had won. Hundreds of thousands of refugees swarmed across the Pyrenees into southern France. I knew those mountains. Vivid memories flooded back of our youthful trek through Andorra some ten years before. I remembered the cheery voice of Chéri le Chasseur as he guided us part of the way up.

Was it Anatole France who said? "Not to be a socialist at age 20 is to have no heart; to be a socialist at age 40 is to have no head." I was graduating. The Spanish civil war was the real turning point in my political outlook. It cured me of socialism and turned me into a lifelong enemy of communism.

I wrote the story of **Chéri le Chasseur** during my days on the road as a diamond saleman. It reflects my political feelings some 55 years ago. I stuck it away in a drawer.This is the first time it has come out.

CHAPTER ELEVEN

CHÉRI LE CHASSEUR

In the upper slopes of the Pyrenees, above the timber line, the wind blows at times in a thin whisper. In the early mornings it barely caresses the face with it's feathery strokes, and the ear strains in vain to catch the sound of it's faintness. On such days the sky is calm, and the wide grey heavens cast a luminous clarity over the earth below.

On this particular morning, a hunter traversing a rock-strewn escarpment, paused to catch his breath. In these barren regions a hunter is no tourist. He is a man who hunts for his livelihood, a man who knows the high rocky passes and the wooded foothills like the palm of his hand. Such a man was this, now resting at the foot of the rock face. Mountain folk called him "Chéri le Chasseur." From Ax-les-Thermes to Andorra, and thence to the Spanish border, he was known as a good hunter and a quiet genial fellow. Everyone knew Chéri, but few had ever thought to ask him his real name.

Far away below, in the little town of Ax-les-Thermes, the storekeepers were pulling down their shutters, and the café proprietors on the Grande Place were setting out their tables on the sidewalk. From where he stood, Chéri could see nothing of this. Even the roofs of the old town were hidden from view. But the knowledge of their familiar and changeless routine, a daily cycle which he knew so well but never shared, filled him with a sense of order and permanence which he found satisfying. He rested his shotgun against the rock and sat down. From his knapsack he drew a flask of wine and some hard black sausage. Before eating, he listened awhile to the stillness around him. The mountainside fell away steeply and on either side the scrubby grass was dotted with smooth black boulders like that on which he rested. The early morning stillness encompassed him; it flooded him in space, welling up from the valley and descending from the dark crags above. All his life Chéri had sat thus for a brief moment before eating, for he mostly ate alone in the mountains. It was now almost a reflex, and though Chéri had never given a moment's thought to the existence of a Supreme Being, this silent ritual carried with it all the solemnity of a formal grace said at table. As he looked out across the plain toward the faint spires of Tarascon, two large grey birds circled heavily overhead in slow wide arcs. They settled nowhere.

Chéri cut into his sausage and felt at peace with the world. His relationship to society was a simple one. He made no demands of it whatsoever. Indeed, he counted as one of his few achievements in this world his success in finding himself a niche on its fringe, which did not totally exclude him from the warming reach of good fellowship. Here there were fewer problems. A man was free, and yet not quite alone. For Chéri was no recluse. He enjoyed his fellow man. Down in Ax he was a "regular" at the bistros, and his friends would hail him when he came in from the mountains. But he withdrew like a snail into its shell when comradeship showed signs of developing social obligations. His nickname, which others might have resented as a reflection on his masculinity, did not bother him in the least. He earned it in his youth from taunting comrades who watched jealously as the girls vied for his attentions. For although short of stature, his swarthy good looks and insolent air drew the girls like fish to the bait and left his infuriated rivals helpless. But here again, Chéri fought shy of entanglements, and though not one to pass up an opportunity, it soon became apparent that he had no "penchant" for domesticity. "Chéri, c'est un garcon pas du tout serieux," sighed the girls as they turned reluctantly elsewhere for a breadwinner. One girl, however, remained constant, accepted him for what he was, and never tired of his embrace. Adèle worked at the Aubèrge de la Couronne, and whenever Chéri came in from the mountains he shared her bed. She, as self-sufficient and independent as he, always smiled happily when he entered the doorway of the ancient tavern. They made few demands of each other these two. What each gave of themselves was received by the other with gratitude. More was not asked.

Among Chéri's boyhood friends, some had gone to seek their fortune in the "big city", mostly Marseille and Toulouse. Others remained in Ax where they worked in their family bakeries and cafés. A few bold spirits had even ventured as far as Paris, but of these nothing was ever heard again. Others joined the Customs Service which claimed many of the local youths, and not a few entered the Church. Chéri watched all go and envied them nothing. For him life was not acceptable on those terms. He was gently but firmly contemptuous of his friends' docile submission to the unremitting demands of such man-made encumbrances as family, society and the State. It was not surprising therefore, when his time came to present himself for military service for the greater glory of France, that he should turn to the mountains and assume self-awarded "citizenship" in that remote and undemanding little state of Andorra.

There is a special relationship, born out of generations of practice in the friendly and venerated art of Smuggling. The Smuggler and the Customs agent, usually from the same village, strive to outwit each other with skill and ingenuity, but they always retain a mutual respect for the other's right to earn an honest living. Chéri was soon integrated into this fraternity. He was no innovator. Many free souls had trodden the path before him. A hunter after all, must have something to fall back on when pelts are scarce.

Chéri took a pull on his flask and pondered over the ways of men, as he had done before, though never reaching a satisfying conclusion. Men, he reflected seemed unable to escape the web of social entanglements. They ensnared themselves, yes for the most part gladly, in the all consuming trammels of meaningless conventions. Try as he might, he could never understand the allurment which his friends found in the priests' robes, the "douanier's" uniform or the cafe-waiter's apron. Their motivation lay not in their own minds, but in standards set by others. Chéri was unable to analyse these phenomena too deeply. He wondered, found no answer, and followed his own dictates. In later years, many men were to cross his path, bound on errands of seemingly great urgency, and the motives which drove them forward caused him the same puzzlement as when his first friend entered the Church.

Just about ten years ago, he remembered as he cut himself another chunk of sausage, he had been setting some traps not far from where he now sat. Two men appeared below, climbing up the mountainside. As he watched them approach, he noticed they were strangers. By their unfamiliar clothes and painful progress he could see they were no mountain folk.

"Are you Chéri?" they gasped as they drew up close. He nodded.

"They told us in the village we'd find you here, and they said you would be able to guide us over to the other side."

"Why do come here?" Chéri replied, "The easiest way is straight up the road from Ax, past l"Hospitalet. When you come to Bourg Madame, you cross the frontier and you're in Spain."

"No, no," they answered, "we can't do that."

"What's wrong," asked Chéri "The police after you?"

"No, its not that", they answered wearily, "you don't understand. Oh Lord, we thought you were going to be one of us."

"Pardi!" exclaimed Chéri. "Certainly I am not one of you. I've never seen you before, but that doesn't mean I'm against you. For years men have crossed these mountains illegally. Sometimes to escape the police, sometimes military service. But don't worry, its none of my business."

The two strangers eyed him suspiciously. One spoke to the other in low tones.

"This trip has been badly organized," he said "We should have waited and left with the main group."

Chéri spoke again. "Lately," he said, "there has been a trickle of men crossing these mountains. They want to get into the fight over there. Two have already left from my village. If that's where you're going, don't mind me. I never inquire into other people's business. Je m'en fou royalement."

"Listen." the older of the two spoke rapidly. "I am a Belgian; my friend here is an Englishman. We have both travelled across France together. The French won't let us cross the frontier into Spain. We were told you could be trusted to get us over safely. We are going to join the International Brigade. We can pay you for your trouble."

Chéri regarded them for a moment while they eyed him anxiously. "International Brigade?" he said, "That means nothing to me; never heard of it. But if you want to get to Spain the hard way, I'll take you to the border and no one will see you, but once on the other side you're on your own."

"That's all right" the strangers replied eagerly, "they're our people, we have proper credentials."

"Alors bon!" Chéri said, "lets get moving before the sun get too high, its a long hard climb, and as for paying me money, forget it. En avant!"

They climbed all day. The hot August sun beat down steadily, and the two strangers sweated generously. Many times Chéri waited for them to catch up. He taunted them, "Your enemies should see you now! " he laughed "there's not much fight in you like this. Diable!"

When the sun fell behind the mountains the air was sudddenly chilled and the strangers shivered. They dragged themselves forward painfully, grunting at each strain on their unhardened muscles. By nightfall they reached the high defile known as the "Col de Zerbès" and decided to sleep in the shepherd's refuge. They built a fire outside the stone shelter and sat silent and weary. Too weary to eat.

Chéri spoke: "Tell me about this fight" he asked. "What's all the scrapping about, and why do you want to get mixed up in it?"

The two men brightened and answered in turn, one breaking in upon the other.

"Its an international conspiracy" they said. "Its the real showdown with Fascism. There's a guy called Franco over there who has revolted against the Spanish Government. He's got the generals, the reactionaries and the Church behind him, and the whole thing has been engineered by Hitler and Mussolini."

"But my friends" Chéri replied, "What on earth has this to do with you?"

"Its **our** fight," they answered. "The people of Spain are defending their liberties against their own Fascists, but all over the world Fascists

and Nazis are banding together to bring free people under their heel.
My friend here is a Communist, he has fought the Rexists in Belgium.
They are the same kind of people as Franco's people. I am an English
socialist, we too have our fascists. I have fought Oswald Mosely's
followers in the streets of London. I don't agree with the Communists
as a rule, but we must fight together against our common enemy."

"You see," the Communist added eagerly, "Its the People's Front
Against War and Fascism. If we don't stop them now, there will
soon be a greater and more terrible war."

"I understand nothing" said Chéri, deeply mystified. "These names
are foreign, I have never heard them. Who sent you here?"

"Nobody sent us, we came because we wanted to," answered the
Englishman. "My Party urged me to come" added the Communist.
Chéri kicked the embers and they entered the hut.

"Ah mes pauvres vieux," he said as they settled down on their
straw bunks, "politics is a strange language which I don't speak. You
are talking of things I am not ashamed to confess mean nothing to
me. I only know one thing, politics means minding other peoples'
business. Just because someone writes in a newspaper or shouts from
a platform you go rushing out into someone else's fracas to get your
heads knocked off. You look like nice enough guys, but I think
you're both stupid chumps. Good night.!"

The following morning he led them up the steep ascent. The
towering crags of yesterday seemed now almost within arm's reach.
They paused midway across a saddle, a deep trough in what looked
like an immense seismograph. "You are now in Spain." Chéri
announced. He pointed out the rest of the route, shook hands, and
watched them disappear with an "Au revoir et bonne chance!"

*

During the summer of 1936 until the snows blocked the passes,
and then again in 1937, Chéri had more visitors. He found himself
unwittingly on the end of an invisible pipeline that seemed
mysteriously to funnel a trickle of strangers his way. Each was

driven by a slightly different motive than his predecessor, but each was travelling in the same direction. Somebody up the line must have passed the word that Chéri was always there, always willing to help, and that he never talked.

The strangers usually found him on the mountainside. They always approached him in the same half defensive, half hostile manner. Chéri escorted them all to the border, and before they disappeared beyond the final ridge, they usually succeeded in imparting some of the inner motives that drove each of them to fight someone else's battle on foreign soil. Chéri never accepted a penny for his labors, but he developed more than a passing interest in the remarks of his comapnions as he guided them up the precipitous slopes and across the deep ravines.

There was for example, Max the metalworker from Hamburg who burned with a fierce hatred such as Chéri had never known. He found it disturbing, and after Max had crossed over the border, he couldn't forget the supressed fury of his words.

"This is not someone else's fight, my friend," Max declared. "This is our fight. Those brown-shirted swine smashed our trade-union and tortured our leaders. They jack-booted their way into our homes and beat up our families. My sister was married to a Jew, a fine honest man. They looted his baker's shop and paraded my sister through the streets. I am no Communist, see! I never joined a party in my life. When I voted, I voted Social Democrat. All I wanted was a peaceful life, but I'll be damned if I'll let myself be pushed around. In fact that's why I joined my trade-union. Now these bastards want to rule the world and they've got to be stopped. I've seen what they did to my country, now they want to do the same in Spain. I can never return to my home in Hamburg until they're smashed, but smashed *everywhere* – see. I used to try talking to the bastards back home, but talking's no use anymore. You can't argue with gangster-fanatics, you can only kill 'em; and by Jesus I'm going to kill 'em in Spain – as many as I can." Max stopped short and leaned back against the rock face. He had never climbed a mountain before, and his words were forced out between panting breaths. Sweat ran down his face, as he stood quivering with emotion. Chéri waited, not understanding, but moved by the man's intensity.

Chéri knew nothing of politics. When the Popular Front came to France, it stirred only faint ripples in the cafés of Ax-les-Thermes. Occasionally there were heated discussions between a group of youngsters and some old-timers, but Chéri turned away. The subject simply had no interest for him. Of statesmen and politicians he had perhaps heard of Clemenceau and Poincaré, and more recently the name of Léon Blum was roundly attacked and stoutly defended in the cafés. But these mysterious mountain travellers brought with them a host of new names and phrases, a vocabulary from another world; Chamberlain, Daladier, Stalin; imperialism; fascism; working class; ruling class; democracy; power; solidarity and the peoples' struggle. Strange exotic terms. And what fascinated Chéri was the self-intoxicating effect these terms had in the mouths of these intense and passionate visitors.

But they did not all use the same arguments; many disagreed with each other. And it had nothing to do with the countries they came from. Communists, Socialists and Anarchists disagreed with each other violently, even when they came from the same country. But Communists from France spoke the same language as Commuists from America, and Socialists from Holland spoke the same language as Socialists from Italy.

It was all very confusing to Chéri, especially that notwithstanding such violent disagreement between them they were all passionately resolved to kill Fascists. He chided his visitors for allowing themselves to get sucked into other peoples' business and felt comfortably detached with the mountains under his feet.

What remote powers had conspired to direct these crusaders across his Pyrenees to fight the infidel for so many contradictory reasons?

An American lad from a Mid-West university told him: "Russia is the only hope for Democracy. It is the only country helping Spain today. The so-called democracies have failed. Stalin is leading the peoples' struggle against war and Fascism"

A revolutionary socialist from Paris announced: "In 1917 the workers in Europe had a chance and missed it. This time we must turn the anti-fascist war into a revolutionary struggle, and whatever happens, prevent Russia from stifling the workers of Spain with her Stalinist bureaucracy."

Luigi, a dark eyed youth from Milan declared: "The only hope for the Italian people lies in Spain. Capitalism is in decay, Stalin is the counter-revolution, Trotskyism is sterile. Only the Anarcho-Syndicalists can free the workers and bring peace and liberty to the peoples of the world."

Only one person did not fit into this pattern. He was a well-dressed man in his early forties who accosted Chéri on the mountainside without any of the conspiratorial air common to the others. He explained that he came from London and didn't really have to do this sort of thing, except that life in Mayfair was beginning to bore him, "I was a pilot in the last war," he said, "Royal Flying Corps, you know. Some Johnnies in London who said they represented the Spanish Government asked me to fly a plane for the Republicans. I said Why not? Of course they're paying me in good old Sterling, and holding the money for me in London, so its really quite all right. As far as their beastly war is concerned, I couldn't care less, except I think that fellow Franco is a bit of a rotter shipping in those bloody Moors. After all, Spaniards *are* white even when they're Red. I must say, this is a nasty way to travel. I would have taken the comfortable route, except I wouldn't like the French police to find the papers I have on me.

Occasionally a traveller urged Chéri to join the fight and go along to Barcelona, but he refused to get sucked in.

One night, sitting in the shepherd's hut on the Col de Zerbès, a middle-aged professor from a Scottish university explained to Chéri:

"What is going on in Spain today, my friend, is a tragic foretaste of what is in store for the rest of Europe. All the ideologies of the twentieth century are in there slugging it out without the foggiest idea of where they're going. I happen", he said, "to be one of those despised individuals who call themselves a Liberal, and I mean a nineteenth century liberal. I envy you Chéri, you too are a liberal, only you have the great good fortune to be unaware of the fact. A nineteenth century liberal walks the political tightrope. The cross he bears is the balancing pole, and on both ends of the pole sit the irreconcilable fanatics of opposing ideologies. The Liberal is concerned with keeping himself, and the pole, and the fanatics on the tightrope. They on the other hand, through wriggling, squirming and other fiendish manoevers, are interested only in unseating their opponent. That this might send the whole act crashing to the ground is a matter of supreme unconcern to them. I am going to fight the fascists in Spain because I am convinced that today they represent the greatest threat to human liberty, but at the same time I fully realize that if I push them off the pole, I must do the same pretty damn quick to the fellow on the other end, if I'm to retain my balance. In other words, it is this: It is the age-old riddle of Man's society, how to fight the enemies of freedom without, by doing so, invoking forces which are equally bent on its destruction.

*

In the Summer of 1938 very few people crossed the mountains. The mysterious pipeline appeared to have dried up. Chéri began to forget his strange encounters. He roamed the high country from the Col de Zerbès to Andorra, and the valleys from Ax-les-Thermes to Bourg-Madame. He hunted the "isard" and fished in the mountain streams. When he visited the Aubèrge de la Couronne he spent long cool nights with Adèle. Sometimes they talked of the strangers who had crossed Chéri's path, but Adèle dismissed them with summary unconcern. "Ah mon petit Chéri, ce ne sont que des Communistes, t'en fait pas, cela n'est pas interessant."

Adèle, who observed life at closer quarters in the daily forum of the tavern, nevertheless shared Chéri's disdain for politics. Wine-table discussions rarely interested her. She rated the "patrons" purely on their human qualities. If they shouted and stormed, she dismissed them as "des sales brutes." If they were friendly and considerate and sometimes helped with the heavy trays, she approved of them. "Ca alors, ce sont des chics types." Then she would linger by their table and laugh at their jokes and join in the banter. When they squeezed her hand or caressed her a little over-ardently, she didn't mind.

Everyone knew she belonged to Chéri. Neither in his absence, still less in his presence would anyone have dared to make a serious pass at Adèle. Even "la patronne," portly and copious Madame Fernande smiled indulgently on Adèle's lover. Her eyes would moisten as she recalled no doubt her own past loves and sorrows, and she would exclaim: "Ah la belle jeunesse, que c'est beau, que c'est triste."

Then early in 1939, while the snow still lay thick on the passes, a strange thing happened. Travellers started crossing the mountain again. Only this time they came from the opposite direction. One cold February day, two figures loomed out of the swirling mists and stopped short upon seeing Chéri.

"Is this France?" they cried. "Yes it is," answered Chéri. "Just"

"Thank God" they gasped and sank into the snow. They were dressed in the tattered remains of Spanish Republican uniforms and betasseled "gorros." They still carried their rifles. Chéri gave each some wine from his flask.

"The fascists entered Barcelona five days ago," they announced "Everything is lost. Thousands of refugees are leaving Spain by the roads. The frontier is jammed, so we crossed by the passes. We haven't eaten for two days. Back up there it was very cold. Sometimes we thought we couldn't continue. When we started out there were three of us, but the night before last, after our food gave out, Mario finally lost his courage. 'Companeros' he said to us, 'you go on alone, I cannot continue. I will rest awhile, and when I regain strength, I will return to Spain. I am no criminal. What can they do to me? This ordeal is too much for me, and I must not hold you back.' We had to leave him there. Better that two should be saved than three should die. Poor Mario, we hope he does not return to Barcelona, they will surely kill him. He is probably already dead back there in the mists."

Chéri was greatly disturbed by this encounter. So the Fascists had won. This in itself meant very little to him. All along, he had only gathered a sketchy conception of who the Fascists were and what they represented. He saw them only through the eyes of the eager and passionate young men he had led to the frontier two years ago. But though he could never share their hatred of the Fascists, something of the hope, the optimism, and their youth, had caught his imagination in spite of himself. As he contemplated the two exhausted milicianos lying in the snow, he had a premonition that this was going to be a bad business. Somehow, he felt, it might have been better if the Fascists had lost, but he dismissed the thought. "After all, what do I know," he reflected, "au fond ça ne me regarde pas." "Its none of my business." He waited till the milicianos were rested, then he led them slowly down through the drenching mists to Ax.

In the village there was much excitement. "Les espagnols vont arriver d'un moment a l'autre" everyone was saying. "Qu'est ce qu'on va faire?" they asked with ill-disguised resentment. The Spaniards will be here any minute, what are we going to do?

A traveller from Perpignan reported that the road from Puigcerda was already dense with refugees. Outside of Perpignan, he said, huge barbed-wire enclosures had been thrown up, and the beaten Spaniards were being herded into them by French colonial troops. Chéri listened with mounting curiosity. For the first time perhaps, the war on the other side of the mountains was beginning to take shape in his mind. What could this all mean? Where were all those young men so convinced of their cause, so sure of victory?

He borrowed a bicycle and rode to Perpignan. The rain fell in a steady downpour, and he was soaked to the skin. In Perpignan he saw strange and bewildering sights. For days, tens upon tens of thousands of people came down the road from Port Bou. They came singly, in groups, and in columns. Units of the Republican Army straggled in, carrying their arms. Automobiles and trucks groaned under monstrous loads. The streets were jammed. Crowded into the gutters, spilling into the roadway among the troops and the traffic, struggled thousands of overalled workers, women dragging whimpering children, old folks clutching pitiful belongings, pushcarts piled high with household goods, an endless river of wet shivering humanity.

Chéri went to the stockades and looked through the barbed wire. Bodies were huddled together for warmth on the wet soggy ground. Silent men stood in listless groups. At the sight of him a few sauntered over to where he stood. He sensed the look of hopeless reproach in those eyes which regarded him from haggard unshaven faces. They spoke in Catalan, a language close to his. "The French don't seem very happy to have us," one said. "What can you expect," said another "from a Popular Front government which joined with Chamberlain in the farce of Non-intervention? Hey you- Frenchman, do you think this is the right way for a friendly government to receive us" You know *we* had a Popular Front government too. For two and a half years we fought the Fascists – alone, with no help from the democracies, and look at your bastards." He pointed to the black Senagalese troops guarding the camp. "They treat us like criminals."

"I don't know, my friends," Chéri answered, "this is not my doing. I know nothing of politics. Where are those young men who joined the International Brigade? I guided many across the mountains." "Oh them, they left months ago", a Spaniard answered, and spat derisively.

Chéri moved along the wire fence, and the Spaniard called after him, "You watch out, it will be the turn of France and England next! You'll be sorry you didn't help us when the Nazis start bombing Paris."

Farther along, a man stood alone against the wire, his hands thrust dejectedly into his pockets. As Chéri approached, he spoke rapidly. "Hey, Frenchman, help me. Get me out of here."

"I can't, I'm sorry" Chéri replied.

"You must," the Spaniard insisted urgently, "They are after me."

"What do you mean? Chéri asked, "Who is after you?"

The man hesitated, and looked searchingly at Chéri. "The Communists" he answered simply.

Chéri was bewildered. "Diable alors!" he cried, "Ça c'est trop fort. All you Spaniards talk politics. My head swims with your parties, your creeds and your factions. I've heard them all, and I understand nothing. So, the Communists want to kill you? Then, if I've learned anything in the last two years, you must be a Fascist. But 'Sacré Nom de Dieu,' if that's the case, what are you doing here? You didn't have to leave Spain."

The Spaniard laughed softly. "It would take too long to explain," he said "There isn't time, and you probably wouldn't understand.

But listen, my friend, I will tell you a little. All I ask is that you should believe me. If you don't, then forget what I say. For all I know, you may be a Communist."

Chéri listened intently.

"Before the war, I was a peaceful ordinary citizen," the Spaniard continued. "When Franco revolted, I defended my government as best I could. I fought at Madrid, and I fought on the Ebro. But I've seen things during this war that have opened my eyes to much that I never understood before. I've seen the Communists at work. I've seen how their lust for power corrodes their souls; not only their leaders, but little men like you and me. I've seen their Machiavellian use of propaganda to serve their Party ends. I've watched their fanatical intrigues to control every group, every organization where they may have members or fellow-travellers. Listen Franchote, come closer." The Spaniard pressed himself closer to the barbed-wire and spoke with a desperate intensity. "I have no reason to tell you this, I don't know you. If I ever get out of here alive I mean to expose their whole rotten filthy system. Maybe I can prevent other decent democratic anti-fascists from being sucked in. If they kill me here, at least I've had the satisfaction of talking to you. You see, they are fanatics, their minds are closed, frozen against independant thinking. There is no intrigue, no falsification or distortion of the truth at which they won't stop to serve their Party. If you don't agree with their line, you're labelled a Fascist, you're ostracized, vilified and persecuted. If you stand up against them vigorously and fight back on the grounds of simple truth and justice, you're just liquidated. They use the language of Freedom and Liberty to ensnare the innocent, while in fact their methods are no less totalitarian than the Fascists. I declare to you here and now, that they have killed hundreds of Socialists, Anarchists and liberals who believed in true liberty, and refused to be duped. I have seen their secret Party jails. I know their methods of torture and extortion. They have tried to kill me before and they will never cease to hunt me down because they know I've seen too much. They have a world-wide apparatus, and they're determined that none like me shall escape. If you can get me out of here I shall be forever grateful; if not, 'no importa.' I shall not be the only defender of Madrid to have fallen at the hands of Stalin. But just remember this, my friend, if you value human liberty: the Fascists are easy to recognize, they speak openly and make no secret of their hatred of democracy; but the Communists – beware, they speak with honeyed words."

The Spaniard relaxed his grip on the wire and relaxed, and a great weariness overcame him. Chéri shrugged his shoulders because he had no answer, and walked a few paces away. The Spaniard's words troubled him deeply. There was something in them that touched half-forgotten chords in his memory. Suddenly he recalled the words of the Scottish professor that night on the Col de Zerbès. The balancing pole on the tightrope, the age-old riddle of Man's society...... Could it be that the Spaniard was talking of just this?

He was confused and tortured. "Diable!," he thought, "What has all this to do with me? I am outside these things. I have turned my back on such a life as long as I can remember. My world is in the mountains. If other people want to run the world, that's their affair. This is what they get for minding other peoples' business."

Then he remmbered Max the metalworker from Hamburg. All he wanted was to live in peace and not be pushed around. Would he have fought the Fascists *and* the Communists?

"Curse their damn politics!"

Chéri turned and looked across the rain-soaked compound. He saw women vainly trying to shelter their shivering children. He saw old folks prostrate with exhaustion. He saw men working feverishly to kindle a flame, to dry some clothes and heat a few food scraps. He saw thousands of helpless, bewildered, suffering, anonymous figures.

"Merde!" he exclaimed, and suddenly a great understanding dawned upon him. All the discussions and the words he had heard in the summers before; all the passionate phrases of eager young students and workers who had crossed the mountains, and now the words of this Spaniard behind the wire. All this now coalesced in his mind into that vast mass of frozen wet humanity before him. Could this then, be politics? Just the desire of millions to live in peace and not be pushed around? A great pity welled within him "These unfortunates do not live in the mountains. They are not blessed with the immunity of solitude. They live in crowded cities, they work, they struggle. Their problems are not mine. I do not share their needs, so how could I follow their reasoning? But now, I understand.

He walked back to the wire and spoke to the Spaniard. "Listen," he said, "In two nights I will return with a bicycle. I will hide it yonder in the ditch by the road. I'll also slide a wire-cutter under the wire, right here. You can get out in the dark if you listen well for the guards. Ride to Ax-les-Thermes, go to the Aubèrge de la Couronne, and ask for Adèle, She will hide you. I will tell her you are coming. What is your name?"

The Spaniard looked up with a flash of anguished hope, "Felipe" he said.

*

Yes, recalled Chéri, as he completed his breakfast and replaced the truncated sausage in his knapsack, those were the days when new ideas very literally crossed the mountains, back and forth, and only when it was all over was I able grasp some of their meaning. These reminiscences had consumed more time than he was wont to spend on his morning meal, but he was loath to depart. An inertia filled him, and he rested on.

Felipe had duly presented himself to Adèle after Chéri had warned her of his coming. For three nights he slept in the woodshed behind the inn and Adèle brought him his food. Then on the fourth morning, Madame Fernande ventured into the outbuildings on a tour of inspection and found Felipe with his sleeves rolled up, washing his face in a tin bowl. She bustled back to the inn, much perturbed. "Quelle horreur! she exclaimed to Adèle, "Il y a un espagnol qui se cache chez nous. Mon Dieu, appelez-moi la police tout de suite!" ("Horrors! There's a Spaniard hiding with us. Oh Lord, call the police at once.")

Casting subterfuge to the winds, Adèle appealed to Madame Fernande's well known partiality for Chéri. " Madame Fernande," she confessed, "This man is a friend of Chéri. True, he is a Spaniard, and should be returned to the Camp; but Chéri helped him escape; he is a good man, Madame Fernande, and Chéri says, why should these people be held in camps, they've done nothing wrong."

"The papers say they're all, Communists," answered Madame Fernande determinedly, "and I want nothing to do with them."

"Oh Madame Fernande, all they did was defend their governmemt against a revolution. Chéri says that this man is *not* a Communist. Please let him stay. Perhaps he could help saw wood and wash dishes. *Please* Madame Fernande. Chéri feels it is quite important."

Madame Fernande was transparently dubious of Felipe's bona fides, but her tender spot for Chéri prevailed. "Bon, ça va," she consented, "put him to work, but the first time there's any trouble I call the police and he goes back to the camp."

The first time Chéri visited the Aubèrge after Felipe's arrival, he inquired of Adèle as to his whereabouts. Adèle led him to the back of the building where Felipe was stacking fresh-hewn logs.

"Alors mon vieux!" cried Chéri "tu est bien arrivé, non? You got here OK. Good."

Felipe turned and recognized his liberator "Ola compañero," he exclaimed "Es buene verte!" "Good to see you!"

"Thanks" Chéri answered. "You're in good hands here. Don't worry. Tu sera bien tranquille. No one will bother you." Felipe stepped over to Chéri, grasped him by the shoulders and in silent gratitude embraced him with a pat on the back.

That night as they lay together in her small upper room, Adèle asked Chéri: "Who is this man Felipe? Why is he your friend?"

"Ma petite Adèle," answered Chéri, "I am not sure I know. Yes, I suppose he is my friend; though I only spoke to him once through the barbed-wire. He helped me see more clearly many things I did not understand. Perhaps, if truth were known, I have many such friends. It is only by chance that one meets them. He just happened to be the one who stood before me when a great confusion was cleared from my mind. I acted on an impulse. I did not know the man, but I knew I had to set him free."

"You talk strangely" said Adèle, "Je ne te comprends pas."

"I hardly understand it myself," Answered Chéri, "I've heard many strange things these past few years. But it is late, let us sleep

now. We will talk of this more some other time. Dors ma petite." He
kissed her softly. "Sleep, little one."

*

In September, 1939 World War II broke out. Chéri did not learn
of it till many weeks later when he descended to Ax. There was very
little change in the town, except for a company of French conscripts;
"Les poilus" who were stationed on the outskirts. Much learned
discussion went on in the cafés. In the Spanish internment camps
however, there remained only women, children and old folks. All
able-bodied Spaniards had been mobilized into "voluntary" labor
gangs. "Prestataires" they were called. Adèle greeted Chéri with the
news that Felipe had gone too. He gave himself up and joined the
"prestataires," saying he could no longer remain idle now that the
battle against Fascism had been resumed. "He just left" explained
Adèle. "He thanked us very warmly and asked me to tell you he was
sure you would understand." Chéri was mildly surprised, but shrugged
and smiled. "Mon Dieu, I was beginning to understand, yes, but now
that he's gone who is going to explain the rest to me? Ah well,
perhaps we shall see him again yet."

"Even old Madame Fernande," Adèle added with a chuckle, "was
sorry to see him go. In spite of her fears, she took quite a liking to
Felipe. You know how she is."

Chéri remained in Ax for several days. In the cafés he heard much
discussion about the war. The old-timers were drawing generously
on their memories of the Marne and Verdun, and loudly denouncing
the eternal enemy "les sales Boches." Among the younger folk there
was a wider variety of attitudes. Many were dispirited and defeatist.
"What's the use of fighting?" they said. "France always has to bear
the brunt for the rest of the world. We've been sold out by the
politicians. Why should we get ourselves killed? Let the politicians
fight it out."

Some disagreed with this and insisted that the Boche must be
defeated once and for all. "First it is Bismark," they said, "Then it is
the Kaiser. Now it is this madman Hitler. On n'en finira jamais!" A

few youngsters proclaimed this war was no business of the French workers. "Its an imperialist war" they said, "and for the working classes it makes no difference who wins." There was general agreement however, that the war seemed to be following a strange course. No battles, no dramatic reports. The fronts were silent and the boys played cards in the tunnels of the Maginot Line. The tavern experts were baffled. "C'est une drôle de guerre!" they muttered solemnly, "a phoney war indeed."

The night before Chéri returned to the mountains, Adèle lay close to him and whispered: "Chéri, mon petit, this war? Sometimes I am frightened. It cannot go on like this. What will happen?"

"Don't worry little one," answered Chéri. "it will come out all right. "They'll probably settle it without a shot being fired. No one knows what the war is all about and no one is anxious to fight. I can't see it is any business of ours. Its all a long long way away — somewhere in Poland it seems. Diable! What has Poland got to do with us? When they fought on the other side of our mountains here, we had nothing to do with it, and Barcelona is a lot closer than Poland. In any case, before I fight, I want to know what I am fighting for.

Once again Chéri returned to his hunting gounds in the high Pyrenees. The winter passed and the Spring thaws set in. He had forgotten the war and he had forgotten the Spaniards. Sometimes he thought of Felipe and regretted not having known him better.

Chéri did not go down to Ax in the Spring of 1940 and thus it happened he was standing on the steep hillside one day in June when he observed a figure climbing far below. He had to wait before he recognized Felipe. He ran down to greet him "He-la Felipe!" he cried, and the shout came back "Ola Compañero!" The two men embraced.

"Alors mon vieux" Chéri exclaimed. "Je te croyais perdu, I thought you were lost. What are you doing here?"

"Its a long, long story," Felipe replied, "But briefly its this. France has surrendered. France has lost the war. The Nazis are in Paris, and there is a sort of government under Marshal Pétain in Vichy. I've been digging ditches and building roads for months under the mistaken belief that I was helping in the battle against Nazism, but it seems now that France didn't want any real help from the Spanish anti-fascists. When the collapse came I was in the North. Hundreds of thousands of refugees fled from the invader. Cars, trucks, delivery vans, bicycles, baby carriages, any thing with wheels. I joined the flood. For us Spaniards it was desperate; the Nazis are just aching to grab us Spanish "Communists."

"As we approached the Loire, the confusion became indescribable; every town, every village was besieged by frantic fugitives imploring gasoline, begging for shelter, fighting, scrambling, bribing. The Spaniards were being pushed off the road, we received angry looks everywhere as if we were responsible for the disaster. Having nowhere to go, I decided to make for Ax-les-Termes and find Adèle at the Aubèrge. Ax is just overflowing. Crowds mill in the streets all night, seeking rooms. Not a bed to be had anywhere. People sleep in their cars or under them. Adèle put me in the hayloft and I slept there three nights. Then a rumor flared among the Spaniards that the German Armistice Commission would seek out all Spanish Republicans and return them to Franco. Whether this was true or not I can't say, but the threat was sufficient. I had one last refuge; that is why you find me here."

"Sacré Diable!" was all Chéri was able to exclaim. "Eh bien mon vieux, tu reste ici avec moi. On va voir ce qu'on fait. – You stay with me, we'll work something out."

A bright flash illuminated Chéri's mind. Once again he saw the Scottish professor. He was still on his tightrope, struggling to retain his balance. With extraordinary agility the professor had succeeded in unseating the two adversaries on each end of his pole. He was now back in balance on the highwire. He smiled knowingly at Chéri.

Chéri now understood everything. "Felipe, you stay with me in the mountains, you'll be all right. On a compris, nous deux. We have both found the answer."

CHAPTER TWELVE

EVA ORTEGA

There's no way I can write adequately of my 30 years of marriage to Eva Ortega. To deal with it objectively, to plumb the complexities and nuances, to analyze the hopes and dreams, the joys and the miseries, the times of happiness, the disappointments and deceptions, and the erosion of love, is beyond my powers. All I can attempt, is to give some of the facts.

Eva was born in New York of a French mother and a Spanish father, whose family had moved to Cuba at the turn of the century. He was publisher of a Spanish language movie magazine called *Cine Mundial* that circulated throughout Latin America; Eva was an aspiring singer-entertainer, having gotten her start with the Major Bowes Amateur Troupe while still at Hunter College. I met her in 1938 at the St. Regis Hotel in New York, where she was filling an engagement in the "Maisonette Russe." Following that she had the singing lead in Noel Coward's "Words and Music," starring Beatrice Lillie. She was beautiful, sparkling, talented and cosmopolitan. She was "on her way" in show business. I fell in love with her. She was 24, I was 26.

When the Noel Coward show closed, her agent, a good soul called Mrs. Hunter, decided Eva was about ready for the movies. For a few months we had a brief but passionate affair, but Hollywood was calling. So, swearing eternal love and insisting it would be only a short separation, she left me for the West Coast. I was sick at heart. Was this a replay of Nina Tarakanova? It was clear to me that if she had any success at all in Hollywood, I would lose her, despite her protestations to the contrary.

Months went by; I was miserable. Daily phone talks did little to allay my sense of impending loss. She had taken a screen test, but as yet had been offered no contract. On an impulse I decided if I was not to lose her for ever, it was now or never. I bought a used Chevy roadster for $500, and drove to the Coast. I had just finished reading John Steinbeck's *The Grapes of Wrath,* so it was not surprising that I had both Eva and the Okies on my mind as I travelled along U.S.66.

On arrival in Hollywood I made my pitch. After agonizing for two days over my entreaties, Eva decided to abandon Hollywood and instead, pursue her career in the East. Her broken-hearted agent, Mrs. Hunter kissed her good-bye, and wiping a tear, said: "I knew this would happen; it happens all the time, and yes, he *is* a nice young man, but oh dear, what a shame." Eva climbed into my old roadster; I turned it around, and we started back East. It was a leisurely honeymoon trip. We were married by a justice of the peace in Reno, Nevada. Later on, just to be sure, we did it again in New York.

But Eva was interested in more than just show-business. While at Hunter College, she had fallen in with a group of disenchanted radicals; that is to say former Marxists who had become disillusioned by Stalin's political trials, purges, and liquidation of his own collaborators. These people gravitated around two personalities, namely Jay Lovestone and Bertram D. Wolfe. They were known as "Lovestonites." Both these men were former Communists having only recently broken with the Party. Eva took me to some of their meetings. The rhetoric was violently anti-Stalinist, but I did not get the impression it was all that anti-Communist. But it wasn't Trotskyite either. The man most admired it seemed, was Bukharin. Discussion was often bitter and strident, the atmosphere tense. These people still bore the same "Party" characteristics I had encountered and disliked among Communists in England. I did not find them particularly lovable.

Now in all fairness, it must be said that the group was in its very first stages of the disenchantment process that Whittaker Chambers has described so eloquently. In due time they evolved from mere anti-Stalinism into a vigorous rejection of the whole ideology of

Marxism and Socialism. They became stout defenders of traditional democratic free-enterprise principles. Will Herberg went on to write *Judaism and Modern Man.* Jay Lovestone became a close collaborator of George Meany. He organized the International division of the AFL which helped the anti-Communist trade unions around the world following World War II. Bertram Wolfe through his writings, principal among which were *Three Who Made a Revolution* and *Breaking with Communism,* became a leading spokesman in the anti-communist intellectual movement at the Hoover Institution in Palo Alto. Bert and Ella Wolfe became good friends.

The instinctive antipathy to Communism which I had acquired before coming to New York was now reinforced with facts. It became further reinforced when I met Joseph"Pepe" Escuder. Pepe was a Spanish newspaper man who had emigrated to the United States some years before. In fact he was a Catalan from Barcelona. When the Spanish civil war broke out, he returned to Barcelona and became the editor of *La Batalla,* the organ of the P.O.U.M. The civil-war within the civil-war, that is to say the story of how the Spanish Communist Party first tortured and then assassinated P.O.U.M. leader, Andres Nin, and liquidated hundreds, if not thousands of P.O.U.M. members. George Orwell exposed these horrors to the world in his *Homage to Catalonia.* The P.O.U.M. was an anti-Stalinist umbrella group which included left-wing socialists and anarcho-syndicalists. It also supported Catalan separatism. The Communist International, seeking to exterminate all non-communist elements fighting Franco, fraudulently accused the P.O.U.M. of being secretly in league with Franco. Pepe Escuder was arrested by the Communist Party, thrown into a Party jail, and sentenced to death. He survived only because Franco won the war before the execution could be carried out. Pepe escaped over the Pyrenees, starving and near death. His wife, Skippy, who had avoided arrest awaited him in Paris.

When they returned to New York, Pepe and Skippy lived with us for a while until they could get on their feet. I had not yet read Orwell's book, so Pepe's account of Communist Party torture and assassination of non-communist anti-Franco fighters, was the first I had heard of these horrors. It became clear beyond any doubt, that notwithstanding the gushing eulogies which liberals and fellow-travellers were spouting over the heroes of the International Brigade, Hitler and Stalin were made of the same cloth. Communism was as much the enemy of humanity as was Nazism.

If any still harbored lingering illusions that this might not be so, and there were more than a few, it required a supreme act of self-delusion to continue to imagine that Communism was the lesser evil, when Hitler and Stalin signed their non-aggression pact in 1940. Overnight the great anti-fascist crusade was forgotten. Communists and Nazis became instant brothers.

Pepe Escuder regained his health and was thoroughly cured of any romantic socialist dreams. He was at heart an artist. As a serious painter, he shared some of that special Catalan quality found in the works of Salvador Dali and Joan Miro, though he never aspired to their stature. But he had the ability to dash off quick little sketches, cartoons, and childrens' illustrations, "without really trying." He displayed a sure and charming talent, but did not take it seriously. Pepe Escuder became a close and dear friend.

Eva and I lived in a one bed-room basement apartment in a West 74th Street brownhouse. Life was blissful. When I was away selling industrial diamonds on the road, she would take a short nightclub engagement. The only times life was a little less blissful was when her engagement ran on beyond my return. It meant she would return home around three or four in the morning, whereas I had to get up at seven to go to work. This was not particularly conducive to harmonious living arrangements, especially if it becomes a habit, and at such times I began to have misgivings. "Is it always going to be like this?" I asked myself. I had been warned of this beforehand, but had always shrugged it off.

It goes without saying that our circle of friends included many who shared our views on "the world." There were Mac and Sheba Goodman, friends for a lifetime. Sheba, known as Sheba Strunsky was the daughter of Simeon Strunsky of the New York Times. She ran the International Rescue and Relief Association at the time, the forerunner of the International Rescue Committee of which I later became a director.

There was John Dos Passos. "Dos" as he was known, had gone to Spain with Ernest Hemingway under the auspices of a Communist-manipulated propaganda tour. He returned disillusioned and disgusted. Not only did he get first-hand experience of Communist torture and liquidation of fellow anti-Fascists, Spain was the cause of his break with Hemingway. Hemingway excused Communist atrocities and became a fellow-traveller, Dos Passos recoiled and became a committed anti-Communist.

Also there were many occasions when these good friends were joined by Sol Levitas, publisher of the *New Leader,* Suzanne LaFollette, Carlo Tresca, Sidney Hook, Eugene Lyons, Max Geltman and others, in stimulating evenings of good food, drink and vigorous discussion well into the night.

CHAPTER THIRTEEN

RUN-UP TO INDUCTION

When the Ribbentrop-Molotov Non-Aggression Pact was signed in 1939, Hitler and Stalin became allies and partners. The great anti-fascist crusade heretofore masterminded by the Commintern, was called off. Overnight, the Western Allies became "imperialist war-mongers, and Communist cadres and their fellow-travellers around the world became anti-war activists. At the same time the German U-Boat campaign was at its height. The North Atlantic became a graveyard for allied shipping. Arms and supplies desperately needed by embattled Britain were sinking to the ocean bottom. Communist agitators up and down the U.S. Eastern seaboard were inducing merchant seamen from allied ships to desert, and were starting to meet with alarming success. Good paying jobs were available in Detroit and other arms production centers. America was still neutral. The British Allied War Council, deeply concerned, was searching for counter-measures. They found it with the International Transportworkers Federation.

The ITF, a Trade Union umbrella organization covering merchant seamen, railroad workers, bargemen, and truck drivers, from Britain, Holland, Belgium, Norway, France, Italy, Denmark (and Germany too in peacetime) counted among its leaders a genial outgoing Belgian named Omer Becu.

Omer Becu had arrived in London with the Belgian Government when it fled into exile in 1940. It was decided that Omer Becu should go to the United States to look into the merchant seamen desertions and make recommendations. He knew no one there. He had no contacts. One of the members of the Belgian government-in-exile,

Camille Huysmans, former Burgomaster of Antwerp had a suggestion. (You cannot be Burgomaster of Antwerp without having contacts in the diamond industry. Camille Huysmans knew Jac Jolis.) "Go and see Jolis," Huysmans advised Becu.

At that time, my father was in New York, having completed a mission for the British Government in Brazil, the purpose of which was to stem the flow of industrial diamonds, of which Brazil is a producer, to the Nazi war machine.

When Omer Becu showed up, my father told him: "I'm afraid I cannot help you much with the merchant seamen; why don't you talk to my son, Bert. He's the one mixed up in politics. I introduced Becu to Jay Lovetsone. Jay took the matter to George Meany. Soon anti-communist union members of the AFL were down at the waterfront heading off the Communist agitators.

The International Transportworkers Federation played an important role in the Resistance Movements in occupied Europe during World War II. When "Wild Bill" Donovan was putting together his OSS team, Omer Becu, without my knowledge, threw my name into the hat as a potential recruit.

The fall of France and the Battle of Britain were shattering events, profoundly disturbing. I did not escape a sense of guilt at being safe in the United States while all this was going on. I made an attempt at volunteering for the American Field Service as an ambulance driver in North Africa, but was turned down because I was not yet an American citizen.

Our industrial diamond business had expanded; we had added a line of specialized diamond tools as well as graded diamond powder to our line of loose diamonds. Industrial diamonds were essential in all branches of the defense industry. Personnel of Diamond Distributors, (as we were called by then) were entitled to draft deferment.

Eva continued her night-club engagements and this continued to cause me grief. I tried to persuade her, to no avail, to seek roles in the theater, rather than work the night clubs. In the theater at least, one gets home at a more reasonable hour. This 3 AM and 4 AM routine was causing real difficulties in our lives; or I should say, in my life. I don't think it bothered her at all.

I registered for the draft, and did not seek a deferment. When I went for my physical, I was dismayed to learn I would be classified for Limited Service because of a minor breathing defect (Deviated Septum they called it.) I was indignant, demanded full service, and got it.

My 1 A classification arrived in short order. That meant my induction notice would follow any day. Then one day out of the blue, Eva announced she wanted a baby. "Look," she said, "You may never come back, at least let us have a baby." I balked. The vision I had of raising a family, while Eva would still be returning home from her night-club engagements at 3 and 4 in the morning did not strike me as a workable formula. I put it this way: "I have no right to stop you pursuing your singing career even though it makes our life rather difficult. If that is what you want, fine. But in that case I can't see raising a family. You have to decide which is more important to you; your singing career or having children. If you say you must have both, then I don't see how I can go along with you. Its one or the other. I cannot be the one to make all the concessions.

It was not an easy choice for Eva. She hesitated; she pleaded; but in the end conceded. "O.K." she said, "If we have a baby, I promise I will give up show business when you come out of the Army.

By the time I reported to Fort Dix on my day of induction, Eva was pregnant.

I had my basic training at Pine Camp, upstate New York, near the Canadian border. Today, it is Fort Drum. Close-order drill every day. "Hep-two-three-four!" Chow lines, KP, barracks inspection, obstacle course, range and target practice, "Maggies Drawers!" For those unfamiliar with this reference to an article of ladies' underwear, let me explain.

Target practice at the firing range, requires trainee GIs to fire their weapons at targets some 100 to 200 yards away. These are white cardboard signs imprinted with concentric circles, 100 in the bull's eye center; each circle numbered in descending order to the outer rim. Each man fires five or more rounds (I don't remember how many) and is scored on his marksmanship. If a man misses the target completely, another soldier who has been hiding in a ditch behind the target, jumps up and waves a red flag. This is affectionately known as "Maggie's Drawers," and it's appearance is greeted by much ribald jeering, howls and bawdy comment.

The social amenities were not exactly refined, but the excercise was good! Only in the army, and I suppose in prison too, is one thrown into such close proximity around the clock with formless humanity right off the street – in this case, New York City. It is a sobering experience. While the average may be acceptable, it is the lower end that raises the hackles. At Pine Camp it was the Italians from the south, the Calabrese and the Sicilians. I know, I know; "avoid stereotypes; some of my best friends are...." – But, I say, The Hell With It. A cruder bunch of violent foul-mouthed undisciplined "animals" would be hard to find. They just didn't like being in the army and wanted everyone to know it!

In the bunk next to me was a fat Jewish trombone player from Tommy Dorsey's band. He had his trombone under the bunk. Nice guy. How he got classified fit for service is another matter. The Army just wanted him in the band, I guess.

One day the rumor went around that when basic training was finished, our unit would be detailed for Military Police training, and that we would all end up as MPs. What a future!

On a certain morning during close order drill, the sergeant shouted "Jolis. Fall out. Report to the Commanding Officer."

I left the squad and walked over to the C.O's office. "Now what?" I asked myself. "What have I done wrong.?"

Regulation salute – " Sir, Private Jolis reporting Sir!"

The Commanding Officer handed me an envelope. "These are your travel orders, Jolis. You will proceed to New York, by train tomorrow morning, and report to......." He gave me a name and address in Rockefeller Center.

I was greeted at Rockefeller Center by an affable, bald headed gentleman, who introduced himself as Mort Kollender. Wasting no time, he said "Lets go out and have some lunch."

Seated around the Rockefeller rink with the skaters twirling and spinning, my host suddenly shot at me, apropos of nothing: "Jolis, would you be prepared to volunteer for secret and dangerous work?"

I gulped. In a quick flash I saw the alternative; a Military Policeman hauling drunks out of bars when not guarding bridges. "Sure!" I said.

He then proceeded to talk in a roundabout, mysterious way about certain intelligence work, never mentioning The Office of Strategic Services (O.S.S.) – a shadowy organization about which I had heard only the faintest mention. He wanted to know all about my background, although he seemed to know it already. When lunch was over, he told me to go back to Pine Camp, and that I would be hearing about the next step in due course. I never saw Mort Kollender again.

I went back to Pine Camp, but managed to get in a visit with Eva first. Back to basic training. Days went by, then weeks. I thought the whole affair had been forgotten. What I didn't know was that a security check on me was being conducted. Then once again I was called off parade ground to report to the C.O. This time I was handed my travel orders and told to report to Washington, DC.

I said good-bye to Pine Camp and boarded the train in great excitement and much relief.

CHAPTER FOURTEEN

O.S.S.

The Farm was where all new recruits into O.S.S. got their initiation and basic instruction in the arcane mysteries of the intelligence game. It was not a farm at all, but a luxurious estate in the Virginia horse country near Washington, DC

We were quartered in the main house, in conditions not all that different from five star hotel standards.

The "faculty" consisted mostly of British army officers. We were taught secret codes, invisible writing, how to tail a suspect, how to throw off a tail, order of battle, (this includes understanding the structure of the German Army, and how to identify it's component units,) how to fabricate cover, secret contacts, drop-offs and well, everyone has read enough spy novels to know what we learned.

A memorable character was the grizzled sixty-year-old ex-British sergeant, formerly of the Shanghai International Police. He had cauliflower ears, a bull neck and a broken nose. He taught us all about "silent killing" the "rabbit punch" etc., and what to do if someone starts it on you.

Then there was naval sabotage. A particular excercise sticks in my mind because it was beyond my powers to perform. It took place in the swimming pool and consisted of swimming two full lengths under water, the first length with a limpet mine strapped to your back. At the end of the first length, you unstrap the mine, slap it up against the pool wall, where it sticks, and then without coming up for air, you swim back still under water to where you came from. You have now sabotaged an enemy vessel and have returned to safety.

Since I can barely swim one length above water, I was a spectator at this one.

I forget how many weeks I spent at the Farm, but during this period I learned something of what my assignments would be. I was recruited onto the Labor Desk. This division of O.S.S. had been created by William Donovan in order to tap into the intelligence opportunities in the underground labor movement in occupied Europe. The head of this division was Arthur Goldberg, a lawyer from Chicago who had specialized in U.S. labor relations. Later, he was appointed by John Kennedy to the Supreme Court, then resigned his post and became U.S. Ambassador to the United Nations.

Arthur Goldberg was an unabashed liberal. He was not a fellow-traveller; he was just soft on the Communists, and thought "Uncle Joe," being our ally, and fighting the same enemy, needed all the help we could give him. He had no objection to working with Communists in the resistance movements and had in fact recruited American Communists into his division. In this he was hardly different from other branches of O.S.S.

I pointed out to him that the underground labor movement in occupied Europe was divided between Communists and non-Communists, and that Stalin was making every effort to capture the entire underground labor movement for post-war purposes.

I told Goldberg I was prepared to work with the non-Communists but under no circumstances would I work with the Communists. He accepted my conditions. This might sound like a hypothetical abstraction, a superfluous quibble in the safety of a Washington office, light-years from where the action was, but to me it was critical. Arthur Goldberg kept his word, and never crossed me up.

Throughout my OSS service, I remained in contact with Goldberg. He was always unfailingly friendly, and seemed to take a personal interest in my activities. It was he who sent me the cable when I was overseas, announcing the birth of my son Paul.

After the war, Goldberg harbored political ambitions, and invited me to join his "team." How he could have done this, knowing my opinions, I never knew. I disagreed profoundly with his political outlook, and told him so.

Finally the time came for me to ship overseas; destination, North Africa. On a bright sunny morning, the troop train with me and a small party of O.S.S. enlisted men aboard, pulled out of Union Station, Washington DC, and headed south for Hampton Roads, Virginia.

CHAPTER FIFTEEN

EMBARKATION – ATLANTIC CONVOY

It is not the scene witnessed a hundred times in the movies, with crowds waving and cheering at the dockside, bands blaring, and the boys waving farewells from the deck rails to mothers and girlfriends.

It is an empty dockside shed. A long line of soldiers is snaking through the darkened structure and out into a patch of sunlight at the open end. I found myself with the small party of O.S.S. enlisted men near the tail end of the line. The line is strangely silent, in contrast to their noisy exuberance on the troop train from which the men had just climbed. They shift from one foot to the other, adjusting their packs and equipment – removing helmets to ease the weight, replacing them again. Every few moments the line moves forward a few feet, with much jostling and lifting and dumping of heavy barracks bags. At the far end of the shed the line bottlenecks into single file as each man passes the transport officer, giving his name, rank and serial number which is checked off on a roster. Then the soldier crosses the patch of sunlight and staggers unsteadily up the gangplank under his heavy load.

Nobody speaks. Soldiers are rarely silent, except when eating or sleeping. But this is a big moment. Each man nurses his own private emotions. Months of training and camp life are being telescoped into nothing. Each feels he has just stepped out of his home. It is the long awaited moment for some – eagerly anticipated – the big adventure – the great unknown. Some, on the other hand, step forward reluctantly, loath to leave their native soil. Others are retracing the path taken by their parents. In many an ear there rings already the words of greeting and cheer from some grandfather or aunt living in the lands they expect to visit. Some are retracing steps already taken within their own lifetime.

All are aware, some dimly, some acutely, of the significance of what is about to happen; the act of literally stepping off the United States, maybe never to come back. The line shuffles forward. Six or eight Red Cross women move up and down with doughnuts and cold coffee on trays. They are middle aged and not attractive. The soldiers are not interested, but munch pensively. Then suddenly, out of the shed's darkness the air is rent by the blasts of a military band. Strains of the latest hit parade well out in full brass and bass. Well intentioned thoughtfulness of Special Services, no doubt. But somehow, it misses the mark. There are no waving crowds, no girl friends, no mothers. The men hardly respond. A few lighter souls break into a little dance, but its too incongruous, and they give up lamely. The band runs mechanically through one or two "hot" numbers, then packs up and moves off to the next dock where another ship is loading.

At long last it is my turn to pass the transport control and struggle up the steep ramp. There is just time to catch a fleeting glance at the low grey hull of a Liberty Ship. Ridiculously small, it seems. Where have all the men gone? Many are already lining the rails and crowding the restricted decks. We push through and stumble down a greasy companionway into the darkness of what proves to be the forward hold. Hundreds of men are milling about searching for an empty bunk – unable to see by the light of the solitary bulb hanging from the hatch roof.

I never expected a luxury cruise, and was prepared for steerage, but this was even less than I had bargained for. The hold was about 50 feet square and 12 feet high. The center was an open space about 20 ft. square over which was stretched a greasy black tarpaulin. It covered the hatches to additional hold space below, loaded with freight. The central space was flanked on four sides by bunks which rose up the walls from floor to roof in six tiers and extended from the edge of the tarpaulin to the hull plates. Some mathematical genius of the Transport Corps had contrived to fit into this area five hundred and forty steel frames across each of which was laced a strip of canvas. These were the bunks. The tiers were placed so close together that it was hardly possible to pass between them. The lowest bunks rested on the steel deck; the top ones were two feet from the roof – while those on the outside rested snugly against the steel plates of the hull.

By the time our O.S.S. group arrived on the scene, the hold was a seething mass of soldiers with their gear, milling around for the most "desirable" bunks. Of course the "best" had long gone. In fact all had practically gone. I found an empty one on the lowest tier, dumped my gear on it, and reflected on the physical impossibility of wriggling myself into the space between it and the bunk above. The necessary agility and contortions were only developed later in the voyage at the cost of many knocks and bruises.

I got out on deck again as fast as possible. The troops were all on board now, and packing the rails. With little ado, the gangplank was hauled aboard, and the S.S. Betty Zane gave a blast on her siren and was towed slowly out, leaving a small knot of transport officers, a black stevedore and two Red Cross women standing on the dock. A few soldiers cheered and waved, but the dockside group for whom this was daily work did not respond. Only the black longshoreman waved back. We were towed out into open water off Hampton Roads, took our place in a line of about 30 ships, and dropped anchor. Needless to say, nobody knew what to do or where to go. We stood around in silence.

The Betty Zane carried a mixed cargo of troops and war material. Every available inch of deck space was taken up with trucks and jeeps, lashed down with stout cables and wedged tight.

After watching the sun go down over the low lying Virginia shoreline, there was nothing to do but go down into the hold which was to be our collective "stateroom" for the next twenty-two days and twenty-two nights.

Next morning we emerged on deck to find we hadn't moved an inch. We had merely swung around on the tide and Virginia was now to starboard. During the night several more ships had joined us. There were now ships in both directions as far as the eye could see. We counted 45. Many were Liberty ships crowded with deck cargo like ours, with groups of soldiers standing aimlessly on the forward deck. The day passed slowly. We were impatient to get moving. The crowded discomfort made it intolerable to pass one minute not moving towards our destination, especially with the tantalising view of Virginia just two miles off.

The second night more ships joined us. It seemed impossible to fit any more ships into the line.

On the third night I was suddenly awoken in my bunk by a rhythmic creaking and groaning. Five hundred and forty helmets, packs, pistols, belts, and impedimenta, slung from as many hooks from deck to roof, and completely blocking the narrow space between the tiers of sleeping men, were slowly swinging back and forth. We were moving!

I lay awake for a long while. The bunks were uncomfortable. For the man accustomed to sleep stretched out on his back, with arms straight down by his side, there was no problem. Any variation from this position brought you into sharp contact with the metal frame or your neighbor's face. Rolling over in your sleep was out of the question; lying on your side was difficult, but possible with practice; lying on your stomach was possible only when stretched out, with your arms straight down by your side – very difficult!

Additional sleeping problems:

1. Your neighbor in the next bunk would roll over on to your side twice each night and had to be heaved back.

2. Impossible to draw knees up because bunk above too close.

3. Equally impossible to get into even a semi-sitting position. Getting in and out of the bunk had to be accomplished horizontally, like a pole vaulter going over the bar.

4. Due to sag in the canvas, the lowest sleeper, me, had his backside solidly on the steel deck. Reassuring, but cold.

5. There are five men above me. The only way for them to get in and out of their bunks is to step on my frame or my face, on the way up and on the way down. Try that for sleep inducement.

That first night I lay sleepless and stared. The solitary shaded bulb threw a dim strange light on the mass of scaffolding which hid so many bodies. Was it possible that each of the 540 soldiers who had earlier been milling and pushing around the floor had found a perch somewhere up in that monkey cage? The creaks and groans of the ship were mingled with the night sounds of sleeping men – grunts, snores, mutterings, and less musical utterings from the other extremity. The air was stifling.

My mind wandered to the polar extremities of ocean travel. "Just where," I reflected, "would this fit on a scale between a stateroom on the "Normandie" on the one hand, and a slave ship on the other?" Then I remembered we had it better than the slaves, because they were thrown naked into a bare hold and chained to the walls. "And as for the Normandie," I recalled, "forget about it. Its lying on the bottom of New York Harbor." I checked my pampered musings. After all, this is a troopship, and we're not slaves, we're free men going to fight Hitler. Only, it wasn't a troopship, it was a partially converted Liberty freighter, used for troops in one direction and prisoners of war in the other.

The next morning we saw the convoy. What a sight! Over eighty ships steaming slowly in the choppy sea, eleven abreast and eight in a column. All painted grey and not a breath of smoke visible. There were tankers, freighters, Liberty ships, and passenger ships converted to troopships. Clearly visible on the decks, we could see tanks, planes, trucks and bulldozers. Around the periphery we could just make out the outline of the destroyers and destroyer escorts.

Contemplation of this scene was cut short by an order for all men to gather before the bridge. The captain barked at us through a megaphone. "Now listen here, men! We are at sea. These are submarine waters. This is not a pleasure trip. After sundown, any man seen smoking a cigarette or showing a light of any kind will be shot. And I mean just that! And I'll be the one who will do it!"

He turned away. We were properly sobered.

Though the sea was not rough, most of the men felt queasy; some stayed in their bunks all day; some were sea-sick. The feeding arrangements didn't help either. Mealtimes, and you should pardon the euphemism, went like this: Twice daily the men would line up with their mess-kits and file through a narrow room behind the hold which served as galley. For those with weak stomachs, this was the great test. If you could stand in line for thirty minutes, which was average, while the greasy galley smells assailed your nose, with the ship in heaving motion all around you, and still retain your appetite till it was your turn to have the mess sloshed into your kit – then it could be said, you had your sea legs.

Eating in your bunk was an option preferred by those with stomachs of iron. Most scrambled up on deck for some fresh air. But this too was not without peril. It meant making your way up a slippery companionway where, halfway up, someone always contrived to spill his food during a ship's lurch, making this a highly dangerous trip for all. Once on deck, it was still not gourmet dining. If you weren't quick, the wind would blow the food right out of your mess-kit before you could get to it. As for a place to sit, it was either on the deck if you could find a spot, or on the edge of a life-raft or the back of a jeep if you were the first to get there.

Washing and toilet facilities, I would prefer not to remember. For washing, a gutter had been rigged up on the forward deck. Sea-water, pumped up from one side of the ship, flowed into the gutter from a series of faucets, and back to the sea on the other side. Shaving in cold sea-water is a novelty every one should try.

Toilets were rigged up aft. Just a pole to sit on.

Extraordinary as it may seem, everything shook down into a normal routine after a couple of days; faces became recognizable; these were people, with stories and personalities. My O.S.S. companion in the next bunk was a former radio announcer from Detroit, called Guy Nunn. When I asked him what his mission was, he told me he was scheduled to be parachuted into Yugoslavia to join Tito's resistance movement. I told him Tito was a Communist, and we shouldn't be helping him, we should be helping Mihailovich. At that time, my knowledge of Balkan affairs was zero. All I knew was that Tito was Joseph Broz, Stalin's hatchet man in Spain during the Civil War; the man responsible for overseeing the torture and liquidation of the non-Stalinist anti-Franco Republicans from whom my friend Pepe Escuder had barely escaped with his life. I could have saved my breath, Guy Nunn thought the Communists were fine; he was a fellow-traveller from the Middle West. During 22 days and 22 nights I was unable to change his mind.

The most dangerous place to be in a convoy is in the outside column. Ships in the outside column are torpedo targets "par excellence." Consequently, there is a rotation system whereby every ship gets to be in the outside column once or twice during the trip. The night it was the Betty Zane's turn we lay in our bunks listening to distant depth charges.

Towards the end of the crossing, we approached the Straits of Gibraltar. The entire convoy stopped about two miles off, and for two days we heaved up and down on the swell, as eighty ships, one at a time passed through the straits. We suffered no losses.

At long last, it was over. We arrived at Oran, Algeria. Getting off the Betty Zane took as long as getting on. Looking over the rail at the dockside, I couldn't believe I was not back at Hampton Roads, VA. The same G.I.'s manipulating equipment; the same U.S.A. look about everything. We are back home again! Don't you believe it.

Twenty-two days and twenty-two nights of unrelieved unpleasantness which I was fortunate enough not to have to repeat when the war was over.

CHAPTER SIXTEEN

ALGIERS

It is approximately 240 KM between Oran and Algiers – about a three hours drive. The troop train, on which our O.S.S. party had been assigned a box-car, took 24 hours to make the journey. The train stopped every 20 to 30 minutes in the middle of nowhere – we jumped off, and had to scramble back on when it started moving again. Watching the Algerian peasants till their fields with primitive wooden ploughs pulled by oxen, one soldier standing next to me in the box-car opening, exploded: "Just look at those fucking Ay-rabs!" I turned to him; he was a Chinese-American Air Force Captain from Hawaii!

In Algiers, I reported to the Commanding Officer of the OSS station, Colonel Eddy and to my division chief, Gerry Van Arkel. It turned out there had been a mistake, I was not intended for Algiers at all; I should have been shipped to London! Correcting this mistake took many weeks, during which time I was elevated from my enlisted man status and moved into an officers' billet in a villa outside Algiers, on the cliffs overlooking the Mediterranean.

OSS Algiers station was training agents to be dropped or infiltrated into Southern France for tactical intelligence in anticipation of the southern invasion, still in its planning stage. Also in training were German and Austrian anti-Nazis recruited among refugees and prisoners-of-war. While waiting for my transfer to London, I spent time with this latter group, learned their individual stories and their cover. They were intended for deep penetration inside Germany. Evenings were filled with intense political discussion. Among them were Catholics, Protestants, Socialists, Royalists. How many of these men succeeded in accomplishing their missions, and how many survived, I never knew.

Those of us for whom "North Africa" conjured up visions of blazing sun and desert sands, were in for a surprise. In October, 1943, it was cold and damp. Bitter winds and drenching rains swept in from the Mediterranean. Well clad in jump boots and great coats, we hardly noticed it, but I could not fail to notice the number of Arab women walking barefoot and unconcerned, in the streets of Algiers, with children strapped to their backs.

Just before shipping off to London, I received a cable. Eva had given birth to a baby boy on October 30th. I was astonished to learn his name was Paul. Before leaving for the Army, after endless discussion, we had decided to call him Peter. Nothing I could do about that now. My churning emotions were drowned in the booze and hilarity that my companions had improvised in celebration.

The flight to London was made on a DC3. To avoid the risk of enemy action, it had to be a night flight, and no overland flight path. We flew westward over the Mediterranean, and then a wide sweep over the Atlantic, at the upper limit of altitude possible in the unpressurized plane. The flight took hours; it seemed like all night. Seated in opposite-facing bucket seats was a motley collection of passengers – mostly high brass – a few generals, a few colonels, three prisoners of war going for interrogation, four civilians, and two GIs. About 15 altogether. As we gained altitude, the temperature fell, and it got colder and colder in the unheated cabin. The passengers sat shivering with teeth chattering until they could no longer stand it. Finally in extremis, the whole complement got down on the steel floor of the plane under great coats, bunched together for body warmth, prisoners-of-war, generals, and GIs – all.

CHAPTER SEVENTEEN

LONDON

No one walking along Grosvenor Street in London's West End would bother to glance at the doorway of No.10. It bore no name, was quite featureless, was totally anonymous. It was the entrance to O.S.S. London Station.

In November, 1943, Station Chief, Colonel David K.E. Bruce was sitting in his office when I walked in to report. Outside his door, screening his visitors, sat a stunning girl in W.A.C. uniform, and believe me, I mean drop-dead-stunning. She was Evangeline Bell, later to become the second Mrs. Bruce. David and Evangeline became good friends of ours in the years following the war.

While in London, I was permitted to shed my G.I. enlisted uniform, and switch to civilian clothes. George Pratt, Labor Division chief put me to work without delay. I was to handle two French agents in preparation for their upcoming drop into occupied France. This meant spending hours of painstaking time and attention to their cover stories, their documentation, their clothing, the contents of their pockets, and above all, their mission. One of the two was a radio operator. Briefing on radio contact, call procedures, codes, etc. was provided by the communications division. After weeks of rehearsal and repetition, the waiting ended. I escorted the two men to an R.A.F. airfield where I embraced them as they were taken in charge by the British drop team. I learned, after the Liberation that one man was killed in the parachute drop. The radio man survived, and sent regular intelligence messages as called for in his mission.

A fair amount of literature exists on the operations of the London office of O.S.S. and I don't think it is useful to add to it here. Besides, I was very much "low man on the totem pole", and not privy to anything beyond the immediate tasks assigned to me. Joseph Persico and William J. Casey have covered the story extensively in three books: *Piercing the Reich*, (Viking, 1979) and *Casey,* (Penguin,1990,) by Persico, and *The Secret War against Hitler.* (Regnery Gateway, 1988,) by Casey.

One aspect which few writers have alluded to, and which I had occasion to observe, was the fierce rivalry which existed between the various resistance movements in occupied France. This was mirrored at De Gaulle's headquarters, housed at Carlton Gardens, near Buckingham Palace. All factions were manoeuvring and intriguing for position and influence in post-war France. To say that the need to drive out the Germans first was secondary in their minds would of course be an exaggeration, but sometimes I wondered.

Those who most single mindedly pursued this line, and about whom there was no doubt as to their main concern, were the Communists. As far as they were concerned, the war was already won, and all that mattered was power in the post-war. To this end, they flooded us with "evidence" that they were the leading players, if not the only players in the Resistance. Pamphlets, underground newspapers, broadcasts, reports of actions and "coups" poured in. It is a fair question how much of this was fabricated exclusively for our benefit.

Nowhere was this rivalry more acute than in the underground labor movement. The bane of my existence at this time was a young man called Patrick Walberg. He was the French-born son of a Los Angeles dentist, and an avowed Communist. Arthur Goldberg had recruited him into O.S.S. especially to maintain contact with the Communist trade unions. Except for being a Communist, Patrick Walberg was an amusing, entertaining intellectual; a friend of Louis Aragon and André Breton, and a poet in his own right. He pursued his pro-Communist activities within O.S.S. with exuberance and gusto, never expecting to meet any opposition. Normally, this would have been the case, because most everyone in O.S.S. (as well as elsewhere, for that matter,) found nothing disturbing about the idiotic "we're all fighting the same enemy" policy. It was my great pleasure to surprise him. One of my duties was to maintain liaison with the non-Communist trade union representative attached to the Free French establishment. His name was Albert Guigui. Though he was waging an unequal struggle against his rival, Louis Saillant, leader of the Communist labor underground, he was able to furnish me with plenty of evidence of exaggerated Communist resistance claims, which in turn I fed back into O.S.S. past Patrick Walberg's nose!

Once I was ordered to proceed to Belfast to recover a coded message from a seaman on an allied freighter. During the entire trip I was followed at every step, and kept under close scrutiny by a very suspicious British Security.

Buzz bombing of London was a daily feature. First there had been the V.1s. Now it was the V.2s. The sirens would go off as the flying bombs were sighted over the coast. We heard the engines as they approached London. Everyone waited anxiously for the moment when the engines stopped. Then there was silence – which seemed eternal, and then the roar of explosion. It was during that moment of silence that everyone froze. The OSS girls at Number 10, Grosvenor Street, sat silent and rigid at their typewriters, fingers in arrested motion over the keyboards. I admired their cool.

One night I was thrown out of bed when a bomb fell on the next building. Was I scared? Yes. On another occasion, a group of us went up to the roof during a night bombing raid to watch the aerial dog-fights. It was a spectacular display, which held us spellbound until, with a whining "zing" a piece of shrapnel whizzed past my ear and embedded itself in the brick chimney against which I was leaning, only inches from my nose! I decided this was no spectator sport and retreated down below.

As the time approached, all talk centered on the expected allied landings; when, where, who? An O.S.S. detachment was being organized to go in with the landings, attached to General Omar Bradley's First Army. I was to be part of the unit, my mission being to obtain tactical intelligence via contact through the lines with the underground labor resistance.

CHAPTER EIGHTEEN

NORMANDY – SAINT LO

To have been bit player in such a vast human excercise as the Normandy landings is to have experienced a range of emotions never before or since imagined. The anticipation, the excitement, the waiting, the boredom, the confusion, the rush of adrenaline, the pit of fear, the awe-struck wonder, the mind-numbing dimensions of it all, and then more waiting, and more boredom. Those who have read Cornelius Ryan's *The Longest Day,* and seen the movie, have enjoyed a vicarious experience of that moment in history, and that is how it has remained ever since, in the public mind. But, as I discovered as an English schoolboy, reading that witty satire on the teaching of history, *1066 And All That,* "history is not what you learn, it is what you remember." In retrospect, now some 50 years later, it all merges into an ageing tapestry, and though the collective popular image is implanted in our minds, it was not that either. Each man had his own story, and each was different.

Let me see what I can remember.

First there was the 1st Army staging area outside Bristol. A huge encampment of tents; miles of tents, row upon row. How long were we there? Days? No, not days. Weeks? Yes. Nobody was allowed off camp. Three times we had embarkation drill, during which we boarded a ship lying in the Bristol Channel. Then came the fourth time, only this time we were told this was no drill, this is the real thing! We boarded the boat (another Liberty ship!), found our bunks, and the ship pulled out into mid-channel, where we rode on the tide all night. Next day, we disembarked. It had been a feint to fool the enemy! This happened twice. The second time, tensions ran really high, nerves were on edge. To cool things down, the camp commander gave us one evening time off base; each man got a pass into town, which meant Bristol. I heard a group of southerners shout in mock seriousness: "Come on! Let's get into town! Let's go kill us a nigger!" I had never heard this before; it shook me. In the same vein, on a later occasion once we got to Normandy, chatting with my jeep-driver on a long trip, I asked about some girl friend he had mentioned. "How is she?" I asked: "Well, he answered; "not all that beautiful, but O.K. to take to a nigger ball-game." Although I found it funny, it put me off. Some things are funny; some things are funny-sour. It has nothing to do with "political correctness," which, thank goodness, was unheard of at that time. It was just instinctive. The army was segregated in those days. Colored troops were in separate units.

In the end we didn't even sail from Bristol, we sailed from Southampton, which we reached by road in an all-day truck convoy.

At dockside, again a Liberty ship! Boarding procedures were the same as at Hampton Roads, VA. Only this time there was real tension. It was palpable. The line inched forward in silence. Then the silence was broken by the third man ahead of me who broke into hysterics. He started laughing, shouting, crying, shivering, and had to be carted off by the MPs. Was it fake? Was it real? Who knows?

Conditions were a repetition of the crossing to North Africa, both on board and all around us. A huge flotilla of ships lay at anchor, each with a barrage balloon attached. After an all night assembly, the armada moved out across the Channel. The whole operation took three days!

This was not D Day. Just how many days later, I don't remember. The beachead had been secured, and an enormous quantity of men and material was being poured into the salient. We moored a half mile off Omaha Beach, and disembarked into landing craft. Rope netting was thrown over the side of the ship, and each man climbed down the netting into a landing craft below. Sounds simple? The ship is rolling at anchor, the landing craft is heaving up and down on the swell, the distance down the ship's side seems endless, each man carries all his equipment with him; barracks bag, weapon, and in my case, in addition, a suitcase containing civilian clothes. It was a perilous trip, simple no doubt, for trapeze artists.

The beach itself can best be described as "order out of chaos." Pathways and duckboards had been layed between the minefields. Every man and vehicle was scrambling up the dunes with orders to "get off the beach fast." MPs were screaming orders through megaphones: "Move your ass! Get the lead out! Move that Jeep! Get the hell off the beach!" Planes are flying overhead; mines go off in the distance; sounds of gunfire.

The first building I saw, as I scrambled up the sand-dunes, was a farmhouse, one side of which was covered with an enormous painted sign. It was a helmeted German soldier in full battle gear, ten times life-size in heroic pose, weapon aimed – and underneath, in large letters were the words: "DEUTSCHLAND GEGEN DER KOMMUNISMUS" (Germany against Communism)

I swallowed hard; goddamit, sons-of-bitches. I'm against Kommunismus; this is psychological warfare; they scored a point, the bastards. On the other hand, the point was probably lost on 99% of the GI's struggling up the beach.

The O.S.S. detachment under Colonel Ken Downs spent its first night on a country lane between high hedgerows. We slept on the ground under our vehicles. Next day we moved into an apple orchard between Isigny and Carentan, and pitched our tents.

The Allied landings had secured a beachead salient stretching from Bayeux to Sainte Mère Église along Route Nationale 13. Extending the salient inland was rendered slow and difficult because of the narrow lanes, high hedgerows, known locally as "bocage" country – very difficult for tanks and armored vehicles. The battle to break out of the salient had been raging for two weeks, at a very high casualty cost for General Omar Bradley's First Army. The key to the break-out was the little town of Saint Lo.

O.S.S. agents, previously parachuted behind the lines, sent regular intelligence reports by radio, of German troop and equipment movements. Our mission was to link up with these agents, get their latest information and give them new intelligence targets.

Writing in his book, *The Secret War Against Hitler,* William Casey says this:

"With the fall of Cherbourg to Allied forces, the O.S.S. was directed to concentrate on the development of intelligence in the area bounded roughly by Avranches-Domfront-Periers-St. Lo....... It was here that we mounted our best intelligence operation from Normandy. It was called the Helmsman plan. Overrun FFI resistants (Free French Forces of the Interior) were briefed on tactical intelligence targets and flown over to England, whence they were parachuted back into France at points about fifty miles behind enemy lines. These agents then had the job of recruiting sub-agents, briefing them on required tactical intelligence, and sending them back to the Allied lines with what information they could pick up on the way.

Jack Hayes, and SOE (British) organizer, parachuted into the Avranches region, succeeded in sending back 28 sub-agents just before the St. Lo breakthrough, and provided excellent reports on German artillery placements, tank units, troop dispositions and condition of strategic bridges.

O.S.S. officers like Bert Jolis and John Mowinckel undertook the hazardous missions of going forward into towns like St. Lo, not sure whether they would be dodging German or American artillery fire, in order to contact FFI leaders, get their reports, and assign intelligence tasks."

John Mowinckel, an amusing and talented American of Norwegian descent, was my partner as we moved up forward by jeep to the front line a mile from St. Lo. on the afternoon of July 12, 1944. Our O.S.S. special passes allowed us free movement in the combat area. We were informed American troops would enter the town at 5 am next morning, and we were free to accompany them. Meanwhile, we should lie low. The first imperative was to dig foxholes, one for each. An intense American artillery barrage had been in progress since morning, and continued throughout the night. Sleep in the foxhole was out of the question, with water seeping in below, and artillery shells whistling overhead every thirty seconds.

At 5 am we joined forward elements of the 29th Division and proceeded on foot into the town. We were armed only with 45's. The artillery barrage had stopped. The Germans had retreated. There was an eerie silence as we moved cautiously down the narrow street. Mowinckel and I each had a prearranged rendezvous with an agent. Mine was awaiting me in the crypt of the church, whose spire I could see at the other end of town.

It suddenly became evident the Germans had not retreated very far; they had simply moved back to the high ground beyond the town, from which they now started raining mortar shells into the town center. This halted the American advance. But before the order could be flashed back, more troops moved in, and in no time at all, the narrow streets were filled with milling men. A very dangerous situation. As mortar shells fell indiscriminately into the crowd of GIs, causing countless casualties, and amidst screams of "Medic! Medic!" Mowinckel and I decided to go for shelter. We ducked into a doorway which turned out to be a hay-barn beneath a house. Hay was stacked to the ceiling. It was dark inside except for the light from the door. Crouched in a corner was a solitary GI quietly eating his K ration breakfast. He had mindlessly lit his spirit lamp to heat the coffee! Men poured through the doorway behind us, seeking shelter from the mortars. Of course, it was only a minute before someone kicked over the spirit lamp, and in no time at all, the barn was a blazing inferno. There followed a desperate struggle between those trying to get out and those trying to get in. In extremis, Mowinckel and I regained the street, preferring to take our chances with the bombs rather than getting burned to death inside.

That same day, the American forces withdrew from St. Lo despite the fact that the world had been informed of it's liberation. The American artillery barrage was resumed, accompanied by massive aerial bombardment by waves of Flying Fortresses, some of which dropped their bombs short, killing hundreds of GIs.

The next day we moved back into St. Lo. This time the Germans had really withdrawn. St. Lo was liberated, and the world never knew it was a day later than announced. I made my way down the main street to the church. The steeple had been blown away. There was nothing but a mountain of masonry. The entrance to the crypt was all but hidden by the rubble. Robert Ehlers, French railroad

worker, a "cheminot," was lying motionless. After enduring days
and nights of incessant bombing from both sides, he was in shock, he
couldn't speak, and he couldn't hear. His eyes lit up in recognition as
he handed me a scrap of paper on which he had scribbled what I took
to be tactical information. All I could do for him was to call a medic
and have him evacuated to a field station. I learned later that he
survived. A brave man. The scrap of paper was duly handed in and
passed up through channels. I was unable to decipher whether it had
value, but the intelligence maxim was "never overlook anything."

The battle for St. Lo lasted five days, and cost 11,000 American
casualties.

*

Some incidents remain vivid, even after 50 years.

One day, before the break-out from St. Lo, a farmer stopped my
jeep on the Nationale 13 highway and addressed me in great agitation.
"Come with me'" he said "it is most urgent, I must show you
something." He led me to a large barn, swung open the double doors,
and said "Voila! Just look for yourself." What I did not recognize
until he explained, was that the barn was filled from floor to roof
with butter! Tons upon tons of butter. "You Americans have ruined
me," he said. Before the landings, this good farmer shipped his
butter daily, by rail to Paris. But now the rail lines were cut. I looked
at this monstrous mountain of butter and remembered how Americans had been carefully briefed on the deprivations of the French
citizenry. We were not to take food from the people, we were told;
we would bring food to the people. This evidently did not apply to
Normandy which was literally groaning under accumulated dairy
products unable to reach market. What the farmers wanted was that
we should take their food, and of course, pay for it.

While parked in the apple orchard, a collective foxhole had been
dug in front of each tent. It was a slit trench, long enough and deep
enough to hold ten men in case of German air raids. The O.S.S.
detachment, happy to oblige the local farmers, filled up on Camembert
cheese. Every man bought his own supply, and brought it into the

tent. Since there were ten men to a tent, the stink soon became too much, even for us hardened characters. There were no German air raids, the Luftwaffe had disappeared; the obvious solution was to dump all the Camembert into the trench, which we did. That solved the smell problem. But, against all odds, the fates willed that we should have an air-raid. The alarm went off, it was midnight; everybody jumped in the trench! It proved to be a false alarm, but we spent a couple of hours deep into that smelly mess, and nobody felt like eating any Camembert cheese from then on.

On another occasion, again before the break-out I was called back to London by George Pratt for consultation. Armed with the proper travel orders, I went back to Omaha Beach to hitch a ride on the first vessel available. The beach was crowded with German prisoners awaiting shipment back to Britain. I remember one young Luftwaffe officer, Hitler's ideal Nordic blond, arrogant and defiant. The captain of a prisoner-of-war ship invited me to share his quarters during the six hour crossing. There were six hundred prisoners in the hold below. Soon the sounds of mass singing voices were heard on the bridge. It was the prisoners singing "Wir fahren gegen England!" Hitler's invasion of Britain song! "We're sailing against England."

Before the break-out from Normandy, I received a battlefield commission, as 2nd Lieutenant. I peeled off my staff-sergeant's stripes and pinned on my gold bars.

CHAPTER NINETEEN

PARIS – SAINT GERMAIN-EN-LAYE – 1944

After Normandy, the O.S.S. detachment was transferred from Bradley's First Army to 12th Army Group. By the time we reached Paris, it had already been liberated for a couple of weeks. But the delirium still prevailed. Our motorized column came in from the west. As we rounded the Rond Point de la Défense, (no tall modern buildings yet) the distant sight of the Arc de Triomphe at the far end of the Avenue de la Grande Armée triggered a cheer which no one could suppress. Both sides of the avenue were thronged with cheering, waving crowds.

I remember thinking at the time: "What an extraordinarily lucky fellow I am! But for the throw of a dice, I might now be sitting in a foxhole in some Pacific island jungle, or guarding an airfield on the Aleutians. But no – here I am at the most exciting place at the most exciting moment of the war. What have I done to deserve it?

Our mission from now on was no longer to gather tactical intelligence for immediate battlefield use, but to develop long-range strategic intelligence through deep penetration of Germany itself. During my quick trip back from Normandy to London, George Pratt had informed me I would be put in command of a special unit of the Labor Division after the liberation of Paris. My mission was to recruit agents and develop intelligence missions for the purposes just described. This was now implemented. Ten O.S.S. men possessing various skills and talents, flown over from London, duly reported to me. O.S.S. headquarters was established at 79 Champs Elysees, where the Biarritz Cinema stands today. Here, I was assigned an office and a WAC secretary.

In addition, we acquired a villa at St. Germain-en-Laye (just outside Paris,) where I and my team were to be housed. This was a large residential villa set in its own grounds behind wrought-iron gates, secluded, discreet and anonymous. It not only served to house my unit, it also became a staging area, where agents could be briefed and debriefed, or where they could be held pending their mission. This was my base for the rest of the war, interrupted when the occasion demanded, by missions to the front, sometimes to recover and debrief an agent, sometimes to put an agent through the lines.

The recruitment of agents having the necessary talents, motivation, physical characteristics and temperament to enable them to function successfully inside Nazi Germany was not an easy task. The screening of anti-Nazi refugees, displaced persons, German prisoners of-war, White Russians, and other potential candidates required infinite patience and wary attention. How can one be sure of an agent candidate's bona fides? One can never be sure. In the last analysis it has to be a hunch. But the better you know the individual, the better are your chances. That is why we brought candidates to our base. We lived with them for days, sometimes weeks, getting to know their personalities, their strengths, weaknesses and hang-ups, if any, before activating their mission. This was a rough-and-ready procedure, not up to the strict standards of the professional spy business, but the best we could do under the limits of resources at hand and shortness of time. We had to improvise. U.S forces were approaching the Maginot line, and were pausing before Metz. The Seventh Army had landed in Southern France and was moving up the Rhone valley.

Fierce German resistance slowed down the Allied advance, and it came to a halt on a line stretching from Maastricht in Holland to the Vosges mountains near the Swiss border. The war was by no means over, and though there was no doubt about ultimate victory, the question was how long, and at what cost? I was constantly reminded of the enormous efforts being exerted by the Communists to exploit their role in the Resistance for post-war political advantage. With the Red Army advancing from the east, there could be no doubt as to the Soviet Union's post-war aims. Whatever territory the Red Army conquered, would be irretrievably communized, and local Communist

Parties would seek to dominate as much of the rest of Europe as possible.

There was little doubt in my mind that whereas the West was concentrating all its efforts and resources on the one exclusive objective of defeating Hitler, the Soviets on the other hand, were engaged in fighting two wars, one against Hitler and the other against the West. None of my colleagues appeared concerned with this problem; their view being, lets get the war over as soon as possible, and the more help we get from the Russians and Communists wherever they are, the better.

This attitude was a constant source of concern to me, and in one particular case it influenced my choice of intelligence target, over which we were allowed a fairly wide discretion provided it fell within the definition of "deep penetration of the German heartland." It was known as *Mission Ruppert,* and Joseph Persico has described it in his book, *Piercing the Reich,* published by Viking. The mission succeeded in infiltrating an American agent, not only as far as Berlin, but into the headquarters of the Sicherheitsdienst, the ultra-secret, elite Nazi intelligence service.

Here is the story as I remember it:

CHAPTER TWENTY

MISSION RUPPERT

We did not enjoy the luxury of long lead time in the selection of intelligence targets and the planning of missions. Opportunities were snatched and missions implemented as circumstances and pure chance dictated.

One day, a member of my team brought in a young White Russian man in his early twenties. Speaking fluent French, German, and some English, his polished appearance and upper-class manner was but a thin gloss covering what was clearly a street-smart, fringe-of-society nature. His name was Youri Vinogradov, and without further ado he quite simply and bluntly offered his services as an American agent. I was instantly inclined to show him the door, but didn't. "Is this man a crank, a crook, or a double?" I asked myself.

Youri told me his story. His parents had fled to Germany after the Russian Revolution, and he had been born and raised in Berlin. His explanation of how he managed to avoid being drafted into the German Army sounded highly dubious to me, but I let him go on. With the Red Army advancing in the East, and Paris liberated, he explained, it was clear to him how the war would end, and he was determined to finish up on the winning side. He worked out a plan.

As a White Russian living in Berlin, it was not unnatural that he should have contacts among representatives of the various nationalities seeking independence from the Soviet Union, Ukranians, Tatars, Uzbeks, Kazakhs, Kirghiz, Armenians, Georgians, etc. The Nazis had exploited these elements as their armies advanced into Soviet territory, encouraging them to believe they would gain full independence after a German victory. They were grouped under the auspices of the Ostministerium, headed by Alfred Rosenberg, member of the German cabinet. They were also closely monitored by the Sicherdienst, known as the SD, the German Secret Service, a select, elite formation, enjoying greater power and prestige than the Gestapo.

One of Youri's friends, representative of Soviet Georgia, by the name of Michel Kedia, was employed by the SD as a "consultant" (informer, agent). He had access to the SD and was on intimate terms with some of it's members. With the help of Michel Kedia, Youri managed to get himself recruited by the SD for a special intelligence mission. His objective was to make his way to France – the SD would help him of course – and then glean information on Allied strategies and intentions, both short-range and post-war. He was then to bring this information back to Berlin, and was left to his own devices on how to get there.

It all sounded to me, as Youri described it, pretty amateurish. The SD must have been getting desperate.

But Michel Kedia and Youri had another secret purpose, unknown to the SD. It was to seek Allied help in saving the ethnic leaders from capture by the advancing Red Army.

Youri was now proposing himself as an American agent; he made no bones about it, a double agent.

After listening to his story, I didn't believe a word. It was just too outlandish. It didn't hang together, and Youri's cocky self-confident manner only encouraged disbelief.

Then I began to reflect. My OSS instructions in the selection of intelligence targets, was "deep penetration inside Germany." How much deeper could one get than SD headquarters in Berlin? What a target! The OSS had not a single agent in Berlin at that time. Sure, he's a double agent, I said to myself. But what of it? He won't get any information from us worth a damn to the Nazis.

I decided to take a closer look at this character, and told him we would examine his proposition. The first step was to move him into our villa base at St.Germain-en-Laye.

There I observed him for the next several days. He was sophisticated, intelligent, and obviously daring and resourceful. I rated him a cold, non-ideological survivor. There was no way I could check on his story, and certainly I did not trust him. But what finally persuaded me to take him on, was the fact that nothing obliged him to go back to Berlin. He could simply have disappeared and survived by his wits in the French black market.

The fact that he didn't, and was willing to take enormous personal risk, suggested to me he did not just want to find himself on the winning side at war's end; he wanted some honor and glory to go with it. I never doubted that his motives were self-serving and cynical, but I felt on balance we could take a chance with him.

Then began the preparation for his mission. It was to be called **Mission Ruppert.** I arranged for Youri to be received at Supreme Allied Headquarters (SHAEF), where he was supplied with a stack of "intelligence" information. This sounded impressive and genuine, but carefully selected so as to cause us no harm.

Once back in Berlin, Youri's mission was to gather whatever information he could concerning Nazi "last ditch" plans, including their Bavarian mountain redoubt. He was to keep at it as long as possible, and when he saw the end approaching, and before the Red Army entered Berlin, he was to arrange the escape of Michel Kedia along with the other Russian ethnic national leaders. They were to make their way to the Swiss border and cross over as refugees. I told Youri I would meet them there. Youri was then to make his own way back through the American lines, and report back to me.

The problem of communications was a tough one. I considered it too dangerous to give Youri a radio. The Germans would pick this up immediately. In the end we devised a system of classified advertisements to be inserted in two daily newspapers. If I wanted to send a message to Youri, I would place a coded innocent-sounding classified ad in the *Neue Zuricher Zeitung,* which I could do through the OSS office in Switzerland, and which was available on Berlin newsstands. If Youri wanted to contact me, he would do the same in the *Berliner Morgenpost,* which was available in Switzerland. Both of us would scan these papers daily.

Working up coded messages to cover all eventualities, and in Youri's case, memorizing them, was a long tedious task.

What about money? Youri was not at all sure the SD would keep him on the payroll after he delivered his report. He would then be on his own. He would need money to live on, without attracting attention. He would need money to spirit the ethnic leaders out of the country, and eventually himself. We could not risk his being found carrying large amounts of currency in the event of search. I had the answer – diamonds.

The diamond district of Paris is located between the Rue Lafayette and the Marée. A few non-Jewish diamond dealers were still around – expatriate Armenians and Lebanese. It did not take me long to negotiate a purchase of $10,000 worth of polished diamonds, which were then carefully sewn into the hems and linings of Youri's clothes; very carefully, you may be sure. No tip-off bumps or lumps.

It was the wildest long-shot, but the prize was tempting.

We were now ready to go. The next step was to infiltrate him through the lines. After conferring with OSS specialists in the matter, it was determined that the best point of infiltration would be in the Seventh Army sector in the Vosges mountains. Here in the Fall of 1944, the Seventh Army had been stalled by stubborn German resistance, and intractable mud, just short of the German frontier near Epinal.

                                         *

On October 31, 1944, I accompanied Youri to the OSS Seventh Army detachment at St. Dié, in the Vosges. Putting an agent through the lines poses a double risk. He must be passed through our own lines undetected, and then through enemy lines, also undetected. OSS officer Jack Nyle needed a couple of days to complete the preparations. On November 2, we climbed into his Jeep and proceeded toward the front lines. Youri was disguised as an American soldier wearing an army greatcoat over his civilian clothes, along with a helmet. Soon we left the blacktop road and made our way up a narrow winding mud-filled lane.

I remember the scene vividly. It was late afternoon and raining. Darkness would shortly set in. Moving up toward the front lines were files of American infantry slogging through the mud on foot, in silence, pressed against the hedgerow. The center of the lane was crammed with US Army mechanized equipment also moving up – artillery, half-tracks, tanks, armored personnel carriers. And on the opposite side, moving down returning from the front, pressed against the other hedgerow was a mounted column of Moroccan troops, a unit of the French 1st Army. Known as Goums, they were Berber tribesmen wearing turbans and rain-soaked capes. Those not riding horseback were leading pack-mules. I stared, spellbound. The scene was unreal. Horses? Mules? "Beau Geste" outfits? Is this a Hollywood scene, or are we back in World War I? Youri was lost in his thoughts. Jack Nyle made no comment.

The point selected for the infiltration was in the French 1st Army's operations zone. At battalion headquarters, we were stopped by a French MP and told the enemy had just commenced shelling the road ahead, and that no vehicles could proceed further. We left the Jeep and continued the last two miles on foot. The road was under enemy observation, but three American soldiers on foot aroused no enemy interest. We stopped a few times for the shelling.

The infiltration process consisted of passing the agent through three "safe houses" with the cooperation of courageous French farmers. Youri would move forward each night from house to house under cover of darkness, and leave the last house at daybreak for the final walk through the German lines. Nyle and I accompanied him to the first house. The farmer let us in without a word. I took Youri's greatcoat and helmet, grasped his hand, embraced him in silence, and we left.

The rest of the story I only learned later.

On the third day, Youri left the last "safe house" and walked toward the German lines. He was challenged by a German sentry hidden in a blockhouse. He gave the SD password and ordered the soldier to direct him to the nearest intelligence officer. The soldier sent him on to company command post. There he was questioned by the officer in charge, but Youri refused to give him any information. He insisted that he could not speak with anyone at company level, and demanded transportation to division headquarters. He was evidently convincing, for an army major accompanied him in a staff car headed for division headquarters at Strasbourg. On the way their car was strafed by an American warplane. The major was mortally wounded, but Youri and the driver were unscathed.

The SD officer at Strasbourg was dubious of Youri's bona-fides and ordered him to report directly to Baden-Baden where SD headquarters for Western Europe was located. Here the SD men interrogated him in fine detail. They wanted to know all about his visit to Paris, dates, times, places, means of transportation. They were especially interested in the location and movements of Allied units in the area he had just crossed. Youri was ready for them. The OSS Seventh Army unit had provided him with stale but accurate information which he was free to divulge.

Youri was then presented to the chief of the SD for Western Europe, Standartenfuhrer Bichler, who greeted him warmly. Youri found himself something of a celebrity. He was the first presumed SD man to return since the fall of Paris, and his colleagues were anxious for news of the French capital. Youri told them what he knew they wanted to hear, namely that since the departure of the Germans, France was being taken over by the Communists.

Standartfuhrer Bichler invited Youri to remain in Baden-Baden as a guest of the SD, which he did for three days. During this time he became privy to internal SD gossip which could have vital intelligence value.

*

In Bern, Switzerland, OSS officer, Gary Van Arkel sat scanning the German daily, **Berliner Morgenpost.** In the classified section he fell upon a classified ad for a furnished room. Recognizing the coded reference, he rushed to the communications room and flashed a message to me in Paris. Youri was in Berlin. It was eight days since I had left him at the first "safe" farmhouse.

On arrival in Berlin, Youri rented a room at Eisenacherstrasse 10. The next day, before being able to report to the SD, he was picked up by the Gestapo for questioning. An acquaintance had spotted him, and knowing he had just returned from "out-of-town," reported him. While Youri protested that he be allowed to contact the SD, the Gestapo held him on the pretext of checking his story. Rivalry between the two services caused this process to be unduly prolonged.

Eventually, Youri made his report to the SD. They were impressed with the Allied "intelligence" he supplied. They were especially pleased to hear his account of conditions in Paris, and the degree to which rampant Communism was taking over French life. He deliberately exaggerated this, knowing it would enhance his value in their eyes. It worked.

The SD enrolled him as an agent for its Soviet espionage section. It was planned that Youri would eventually return to Paris to spy among Russian emigrés in the West. He was issued an SD identity card and permits to carry arms and wear an SD uniform. He spent the next several weeks training for his return to Paris, all the while losing no opportunity to learn what he could about the internal workings of the SD, its organization and its personalities.

Youri was given a bonus in Reichmarks, equivalent to $500 for the Allied "intelligence" and information on conditions in France. In addition, the SD put him on the payroll at a salary equivalent to $50 per month. Such a pittance left him well short of the standard of living to which he thought he was entitled. Youri soon had recourse to the diamonds sewn into his clothing. In short order, he became a thriving operator in the Berlin black market. The SD did not seem to mind.

His orders to return to Paris were delayed, and this allowed him to pursue the information gathering aspect of his US mission. He cultivated profitable sources, including a woman named Maria Frankenstein, who was a close friend of Hermann Goering's wife, and who also frequented highly placed figures in Heinrich Himmler's SS headquarters. During this period he was denounced on more than one occasion by people who remembered pro-Allied statements he had made before leaving for France. In each case, his friend Michel Kedia, the Georgian leader, came to his rescue and vouched for his pro-Nazi loyalty.

After being activated twice, and twice inexplicably cancelled, Youri concluded that his second mission to France would not take place. Months had gone by. It was now March, 1945. The Red Army was advancing remorsely on Berlin. The leaders of the ethnic movements were becoming more and more agitated at the impending fall of the city. Youri decided the time had come to execute the final phase of his mission. He summoned his friend Michel Kedia and told him to assemble his group, and start moving to the Swiss border. This would not be too difficult because under the patronage of the Ostministerium they enjoyed a form of pseudo diplomatic recognition with relative freedom of movement.

For Youri it was not so easy. He was under SD orders and needed a travel document. Once again, his friend helped him. Michel Kedia enjoyed other contacts with the Abwehr, the German Army Intelligence. On April 8, 1945, without notifying the SD, Youri left Berlin with an Abwehr ID card and travel document. Before doing so, he placed a coded classified ad in the **Berliner Morgenpost**, as we had agreed.

*

The agreed rendezvous point was Geneva. As a military combatant I was not allowed legal entry into Switzerland. OSS had foreseen such impediments. An OSS staging base had been established at Annemasse, a village on the French side close to the border. I reported there in uniform and changed into civilian clothes. The residing OSS officer, Paul Mellon carried a diplomatic passport and his car carried diplomatic plates. At his invitation, I climbed into the trunk of his car and he slammed it shut. It was not more than a five minute drive to the frontier, but in my cramped position I had time to reflect that after the war, I might write a piece for a travel magazine on the exotic modes of travel you might enjoy in the OSS if you are lucky; first the slave ship across the Atlantic; now this. The frontier guards waved Paul Mellon through, and we drove into Geneva.

In the quietest of quiet streets, Paul stopped the car, opened the trunk and I climbed out, a bit stiff. He bade me good-bye, wished me luck and was off in a split second.

I had no idea where I was. I was not familiar with the city. I had no identity papers on me. The rendezvous had been arranged at the Hotel d'Angleterre, a faded but still elegant establishment on the lakefront. As I stood for a moment trying to get my bearings, I heard the unmistakable sound of marching boots approaching. There was nothing in sight. Then, suddenly, they came around the corner, a block away. An instant glance at them, and I froze in horror. A squad of German soldiers. "My God," I muttered, there's been a horrible mistake. I shrunk into a doorway as they got closer. By the time they came abreast, I relaxed. They were not German, they were Swiss. But the same grey uniforms, the same stewpot helmets, the same marching gait, not exactly goose-step, but enough to have me fooled. They paid me not the slightest glance and marched right on by.

I found my way to the Hotel d'Angleterre and entered it's imposing lobby. Gilded ceiling, ornate chandeliers, and a broad staircase leading down into the reception area, it was nothing if not Victorian. Hotel guests and patrons were sitting around, taking tea, conversing, and socializing. The only name I had was that of Michel Kedia. I rang his room on the house phone, and he eagerly announced in German that he and his friends would be right down.

"No, No!" I shouted, horrified. "Let me come up, its not good to meet down here." The Georgian would not hear of it. He insisted that he and his friends would meet me downstairs. I was devastated at the thought of having to conduct this meeting in public. I fumed and fretted at the foot of the stairs, trying to figure out who to blame for this idiotic failure of advance planning. I concluded it must have been me. Then the elevator at the head of the stairs opened, and I stood aghast. Of the seven members of the delegation, only one wore western clothes. The rest were attired in an assortment of fezzez, flowing robes, pantaloons and kaftans. They marched solemnly down the staircase, looking right past me, searching for the reception committee.

I had no idea what Michel Kedia looked like, but I approached the one in western attire. It was the Georgian, a large blond muscular man in his middle forties. As I introduced myself, he looked at me in obvious disappointment, but quickly recovered, broke into a broad grin, pumped my hand and bowed deeply. The rest followed suit and crowded around me smiling and talking excitedly in languages I could not recognize. A few spoke German.

The concierge, the bellmen, the waiters, all no doubt working for Swiss intelligence looked on with much interest, not to speak of the patrons and guests.

I whispered into Kedia's ear, "We have to get out of here" He seemed perplexed, but finally agreed, and we all retreated upstairs and crowded into his room.

It was then that I got my first direct exposure to the Soviet nationalities question which figured so prominently in my life some forty-six years later.

These ethic leaders would be considered Nazi collaborators by any definition. Yet they didn't see it that way. They were not Nazis, they knew nothing of National Socialism, they were politically unsophisticated. They only knew that they hated Soviet imperialism and wanted independence for their people. Germany had promised them this, albeit half-heartedly. They understood that with Germany now defeated, and the Soviets victorious, the United States was their only hope. Furthermore, they were convinced that the United States and the Soviet Union would be at war in the immediate future.

In this context, they took it for granted that I was a special envoy, at least of General Eisenhower, if not the US President himself, empowered to commit the United States on their behalf. I had the greatest difficulty disabusing them, and doubt I succeeded. Bringing them down to earth was painful. They were well aware that had they remained in Berlin it would have meant certain death. But now, what plans did the Allies have for them and their movements?

Alas, I could not give them much hope. I laid out the realistic alternative. They could remain in Switzerland where they would be eventually interned. Or they could remain inconspicuous for a few days, while I arranged for their transfer to the US Army interrogation center in occupied Germany, where their knowledge of the Ostministerium, the Sicherheitsdienst, the Abwehr and other Nazi organizations would prove valuable in the final prosecution of the war.

Their deception and disappointment were palpable. I felt sorry for them. They asked me if I could not at least deliver a letter on their behalf to General Eisenhower. I said I would gladly do so. At this moment their spirits revived and the atmosphere became charged with exuberance. In a babel of tongues they set about drafting their message. There was heated debate and concentration over each phrase. Michel Kedia struggled to keep the process on track. It was finally finished, and each leader affixed his signature. I promised that the document would reach General Eisenhower.

Following this tragi-comic episode, I reported personally to Allen Dulles, Chief of OSS Station Switzerland. Dulles was anxious to get these ethnic leaders out of the country at the earliest possible moment, not wanting to have complications with the Swiss authorities. I tried to persuade him that these men were a valuable asset; that we should not allow them to be used only for short-range interrogation, and then be discarded.

I urged that he recommend they be transferred to the United States, so that their long-range potential could be preserved, and not allow them to be dumped into Germany, where an uncertain fate awaited them. Alas, Allen Dulles was less than enthusiastic. He expressed no more interest in the post-war scenario than the others.

This being within his jurisdiction, he had the authority. I was too junior to prevail.

Frustrated and disappointed, I felt that an extraordinary opportunity was being casually thrown away.

*

I remained in Geneva for a few days, while OSS staff under Allen Dulles' direction, made arrangements for the extradition of the ethnic leaders to Germany. One day, John Clark, one of the staff members, seeing me sitting around with nothing to do, invited me to "take a little ride in the country." It turned out to be a drive from Geneva to Bern. In Bern, he drew up in a quiet secluded street and told me to wait in the car while he ducked into the doorway of a nondescript house. About ten minutes later he emerged. "Everything's OK," he said, "we can go back to Geneva now."

Properly mystified, I asked "What's this all about?"

"Oh," he replied, "We have a radio operator on the top floor of this house. "We've just sent a message to Wally, our OSS undercover man in Milan, for transmittal to General Karl Wolff, commander of German troops in Northern Italy. The message contains our terms for German surrender."

"Is that all?" I gasped, stunned at the enormity of his information.

We drove back to Geneva in silence. I was nursing my unhappiness over the treatment of the Russian ethnic leaders. "What's the matter with Allen Dulles, the acknowledged star performer of American intelligence?" I asked myself. "Can't he see the potential value of these men. What a waste. The war with Germany is over, for God's sake. You don't have to be a genius to know the Soviet Union is going to be our number-one problem from now on." These ruminations did me no good; they only fuelled my exasperation and rubbed in the truth – which was that there was absolutely nothing I could do about it.

After a few days, with extradition formalities completed, the ethnic leaders were transferred to a Red Cross camp in the city of Hoechst, Germany, now occupied by the US Army. There they underwent routine US Army interrogation. Despite strenuous efforts on my part, I was never able to obtain further information concerning their fate, and can only surmise they were eventually caught up in the Soviet repatriation dragnet and shot.

I left Switzerland the same way I entered, that is to say in the trunk of Paul Mellon's car. Back at Annemasse, I shed my civilian clothes, got back into uniform and drove back to my base at St. Germain-en-Laye outside Paris.

*

On April 15, 1945, I received a message from Ninth Army G2 at Maastricht, Holland. They were holding a man who claimed to belong to my unit. Youri Vinogradov's luck had held, but barely. He had managed to travel west as far as the American lines. But there he ran afoul and faced the greatest danger since he first penetrated Germany over six months earlier. As he approached the American lines, the password I had originally given him proved ineffective. Edgy GIs simply blazed away at him. Miraculously, he escaped unscathed and was eventually able to surrender. But the G2 intelligence officer refused to accept his story, and he was clapped into a prisoner-of-war cage, where he spent two days in the rain without food.

After finally managing to convince Ninth Army to send me a message, he arrived at my St. Germain-en-Laye base. He was unrecognizable. Instead of the cocky self-confident "operator" I had known, I now saw a frightened haggard individual. I did not press questions upon him, but gave him two days to come around, to rest, to eat, to sleep. Then we sat down and conducted a long, detailed debriefing. This took several days. He had much useful information to give us.

When it was all over, I asked Youri what he wanted to do. If he wanted to go to the United States, I said I would help him. But he had no desire to go. He wanted to stay in France.

This brash, cocky street-smart fellow, for whom I had such early misgivings, had accomplished a dangerous and difficult mission. He did exactly what he had promised to do. He wanted to finish up on the winning side, not just as a survivor, but with a little honor thrown in. I felt he had earned it. I recommended him for a decoration. I don't think he ever received it.

Youri hung around with us at our OSS base for a couple of months. Then one day, he left without a word, and melted into the Paris scene. I never heard from him again.

CHAPTER TWENTY ONE

TOVARICH AND THE RUSSIAN BABE – L'AMOUR SLAVE

In late September 1944, the road from Metz to Verdun was a shiny tape of two-lane blacktop, snaking across rolling fields between an endless avenue of poplars. My jeep was scudding along in a dull steady rain. An occasional truck convoy moved west in the opposite direction, their windshields bearing drivers' names like Pfc. H. Kovacs, T/5 Richard Parenti. Some of the trucks were loaded with G.Is. who lolled and dozed as their vehicles bounced over the ruts and potholes. At intervals a large sign appeared at the roadside: 'ROUTE MILITAIRE —INTERDITE AUX CIVILES." I needed to reach Verdun before 12.30. The transient officers' mess closed at 12.45. A jeep bearing the sign 'COURRIER. DO NOT DELAY' bounced and skidded past me over a half-filled shell crater.

Verdun, bearing the battle scars of 1917, 1940 and 1944, was teeming with troops and convoys. The officers' mess at the Hotel Vauban offered tepid C rations, meat, beans and coffee.

Beyond Verdun, the road was quiet. The rain had stopped, and the familiar after-rain smell was rising from the shiny pavement. Coming over a short rise, the highway again stretched away in a straight black ribbon until the flanking trees merged at the horizon under a vast grey sky. It was deserted, but for two civilians just discernible, walking under the trees half a mile ahead. As I passed them I noticed a man and a woman carrying suitcases. They did not turn with that shy but hopeful "give us a ride" look, common to all civilians immediately after the Liberation. They were just plodding along steadily, looking at the ground. "just two more civilians," I thought, gassing the jeep up to 55. But the burst of speed failed to dampen my conscience. The highway stretched away endlessly. Wherever they were going, they would never get there by nightfall.

I slowed down and looked back. They had shifted the suitcases to their shoulders, but were still plodding along, ignorant of the offered ride. "Want a ride?" I yelled. They stared uncomprehendingly. "Voulez-vous monter?" I repeated. Still no response. Then the man walked over slowly. He wore an overcoat with the collar turned up and a cap with a shiny black peak. I pointed to the back seat and then to the two of them. He nodded vigorously and called the woman over. They climbed in and off we went.

I heard them talking quietly, but their language was strange. It wasn't French. It wasn't German. "Polski?" I ventured, They shook their heads. "Russki" they answered, which effectively silenced further conversation for the next five hours. We stopped once or twice; it was cold and damp. I broke open a K ration, and their eyes popped at the chopped ham and eggs and powdered bullion.

The man was young, probably middle twenties, small eyes, broad peasant face, and a grin that showed strong regular teeth. The girl was mousey and non-descript, probably also in her middle twenties. Slightly built and shy, she wore a grey astrakhan fur cap with ear flaps tucked up. It was the only clue to her origin. They both eyed me with a mixture of friendliness and suspicion, alternatively grinning and whispering furtively to each other. Eventually they uttered a few halting words of German. "**Russiche lager**'" they repeated several times. Having no idea where to find a Russian camp, or indeed if there was one, I could only shrug my shoulders and drive on.

As evening approached, I skirted Paris and made for my base at Saint Germain-en-Laye. What to do with these two? Dump them back on the open road? It was the easiest thing to do. Then I remembered Private First Class, Jacques Gourevitch. Jacques was a member of my St. Germain team, a recent immigrant of White Russian parents. Jacques of course, spoke fluent Russian, a rare accomplishment for which a grateful army had elevated him to the rank of Pfc. I should get Jacques to talk to these two. Who knows?

Intelligence information often comes from the most unexpected sources.

I pulled the jeep into our wrought iron gateway and climbed out. The Russians looked at the villa with terror in their eyes and didn't budge. I made signs of eating and told them to follow me, which finally, after whispered discussion they did with much hesitation. On the front steps they stopped again, and were afraid to go further. Trying to reassure them, I coaxed them into the house and got them to take their coats off. Sounds from the mess room indicated the evening meal was in full swing. This did nothing to reassure my guests, it only scared them more. I threw open the door of the mess hall. Ten hungry men paused at their chow and looked up. "Fellows," I announced "A couple of guests are going to eat with us." All eyes were focused on the Russians in the doorway, or more precisely, on the girl standing timidly behind him. For a moment they stood bewildered and hesitant.

I waved them to two empty chairs at the end of the one long table, but they didn't move. Then slowly; at first imperceptibly, and then with an infectious deliberateness, as the plain facts dawned upon him, a huge grin spread across the boy's face. He stood thus for a moment, surveying the assembled faces, and then with a sudden happy gesture, he raised his right fist in the Communist salute, and walked to his seat, followed by the girl. Ten astonished GIs watched them sit down, and then resumed their attack on roast pork chops and corn fritters. Not a word was spoken.

After dinner, I called Jacques over. "Take these birds into the next room and get their story."

An hour later he came back and reported authoritatively that the boy's name was Mischa and the girls's was Sasha. Hardly an intelligence scoop. But wait, there was more.

Mischa had been a sailor in the Red Navy, serving on board a submarine. During the siege of Leningrad he had been ordered to shore duty, to help man the city's defenses. One night on reconnaissance patrol he was captured by the Germans. After sojourn in various prison camps he was shipped to the Western front in a prison labor gang, where for the last four months he had been hauling ammunition on the Siegfried Line. He was able to supply us with some useful information during careful interrogation; gun emplacements, thickness of bunker walls, types of ammunition, communications systems etc. This, we duly passed on up through channels.

Sasha came from a little village with an unpronounceable name in Eastern Ukraine. When the Germans overran the village, they seized several hundred women and shipped them back to Germany. After working in several forced labor camps she was sent to Metz as an untrained nurse in a Russian prisoner-of-war hospital.

Sasha and Mischa met for the first time in a Russian prison hospital in Metz. They were homesick. They liked each other. Perhaps they even fell in love. They knew the German armies were retreating in France. They knew Paris had been liberated. They talked of escaping, and decided that if they saw a chance, they would take it together. Then, almost before their decision had been reached, their chance came. With complete surprise, General Patton's armored reconnoissance units swept into Metz. The Germans were unprepared and disorganized. It was several days before they recovered sufficiently to take advantage of Patton's strained supply lines and push us out again. Once they recovered, they held on to Metz for many grim long weeks. But for several days, all was confusion, and Sasha and Mischa simply walked down the street with their suitcases through the American lines.

They had no idea where to go or what to do. They wandered along roads crowded with troops and convoys. Without a word of French or English, they couldn't ask directions, and even if they could have made themselves understood, they wouldn't have known what to ask for. For two weeks they wandered back and forth just behind the American lines, hopelessly lost. They slept in barns, and farmers occasionally gave them food. American troops, taking them for French civilians, ignored them. Once, a black Engineers battalion took them in, housed them and fed them for three days, and asked them not a single question, in fact never said a word to them. But the Engineers moved on and they found themselves back on the road again.

When I picked them up, they were walking to Paris, about a hundred and fifty miles away, because they had heard of a Russian repatriation center, the "**Russiche Lager.**" I decided to let them stay over in the villa. Meanwhile we had the opportunity of watching the two of them thaw out. While Mischa and Jacques were poring over maps and drawings of the Siegfried Line, Sasha remained in her room and only showed up for meals. Both ate voraciously. In a few days, color had returned to their faces and they lost that scared look. Mealtimes were a constant source of wonder for them, and a reminder they were still in fairyland, and the Americans harbored no dark or malevolent intentions toward them.

Meanwhile, I had ascertained that there was a Russian repatriation center at Versailles, called Camp Beauregard, where the Soviets were rounding up all their displaced persons, escaped prisoners of war, and others, whom Joseph Stalin had lumped together as "war criminals." Stalin demanded that all such persons found in areas liberated by the Western Allies, be forcibly repatriated, and to their eternal shame, the western Allies complied.

After a couple of days, in response to their earlier request, I asked Mischa if he still wanted to go to the **"Russiche Lager."** The mere suggestion produced vehement protests from both of them.

"Oh no, not to the **Russiche Lager**, please!"

"But why not? Don't you want to go back home to Russia?"

"Well..... yes. But not yet. We're frightened. You see, we were taken prisoner by the Germans and we don't know what they will do to us for that."

Russian prisoners and displaced persons, even those who had not voluntarily worked for the Germans had good reason to express such fears. Rumors of the fate which awaited them had been filtering back.

"Well, what do you want then?"

"We'd like to stay here with you," they stated emphatically.

This was a poser. To throw them out immediately after the services Mischa had just rendered would indeed have been churlish. On the other hand... a liberated Russian P.O.W. and his girl friend, a little irregular, to say the least...... Army establishment... Regulations...

Aw, the hell with it. Stretch a point. Let 'em stick around for a while. Won't do any harm.

The happiness and relief that spread across their faces was palpable.

For some time, Mischa had been demonstrating a boundless interest in our vehicles. Once, we caught him alone with his head under the hood of a jeep. A reprimand produced only an apologetic grin. A few days later, thinking himself alone again, we found him driving a jeep around the yard at some speed. Pretty soon, dressed in G.I. coveralls and a fatigue hat, he was indistinguishable from anyone else in the motor pool and performing admirably first echelon maintenance.

Sasha gravitated to the kitchen, and was soon lending a hand with the dishwashing and general housework. In fact, Mischa and Sasha were accepted as regular members of our civilian complement. They lived together in their own room, worked their respective jobs, showed up regularly for meals, and once sure we were not going to throw them out, appeared to give no thought to the future. They were happy.

To the rest of the boys, Mischa was "Tovarich." Responding to the greeting of "Hi-ya Tovarich!" he would pause in washing down a jeep, look up grinning, and raise his fist in a happy Communist salute. Sasha was known simply as "the Russian babe. She never said much, and clung very close to Mischa. Occasionally, in moments of expansiveness, she would smile shyly and say: "Amerikanski — sehr gut!"

In the evenings before going to bed, they would invariably go to the radio and tune in to Moscow. They sat glued to the box, straining to catch every word against the babble of voices in the day-room. As the speaker announced sweeping Red Army victories, their faces would glow with pride. Sometimes, when the radio was tuned to the BBC or the American Forces Network, they would catch words from the announcer like Zukhov, Stalin, or Molotov, and their eyes would light up in recognition.

*

One night, I came home late and found the day-room empty, everyone having gone to bed except Sasha. She was sitting alone by the radio, weeping quietly.

"What's the matter Sasha?" I asked. She looked up with tear-stained red-rimmed eyes. In response to a pat on the shoulder, she attempted a wan smile and shook her head as if to say "Its nothing." But she wept nevertheless, and the next day I called her in and had Jacques Gourevitch interpret for me.

"Is something wrong?"

"No," she replied.

"Anyone been bothering you?"

"Oh no,....... not that. I guess I'm just homesick. I was thinking of my home in Russia. It seems so far away. I just cried a little."

"Why, Sasha, you don't have to be homesick. You know you don't have to stay here with us. We thought you wanted to. We can take you over to the Repatriation Center and you can be with your people right away. They are starting to ship people back to Russia already. You could be home in quite a short time."

"Oh no... please don't do that. We are happy here. We want to stay as long as possible. Amerikanski, sehr gut. Only...... I don't know,. We're such a long way from home."

"Yes, we know how you feel. We're a long way from home too. It won't be long now, though."

I glanced at Jacques. Our efforts at consolation had gone somewhat flat.

Mischa, on the other hand, showed absolutely no signs of home-sickness. On the contrary, he showed a disturbing sign of taking permanent root. Once or twice he confided in Jacques. In fact, Jacques was the only American he could talk to. All this food! At first he thought there must be some ulterior motive behind it. Were these our regular rations? On being informed they were, he shook his head in wonder. Back home he had never heard much about the Americans. They were foreigners. Allies, sure... still foreigners all the same, and they didn't really hate the Germans, not like the Russians did.

He couldn't say exactly why he was scared the first time we brought him in. He wasn't scared of Germans; he'd killed Germans.

But he was scared of us Americans that first night. He and Sasha had a feeling all Westerners really hated the Russians more than they did the Germans. However, it was different now. He had never dreamed Americans were like this. When he got home he was going to tell all his friends.

"But your officers," continued Mischa. "The way your soldiers behave with their officers; we would never dare to act like that."

"Why not?" queried Jacques.

"Well... I don't know. It wouldn't be right; its never done. We'd be punished."

"I guess its just that we're democratic," suggested Jacques with a sly smile.

"I don't understand. It is we who have the most democratic army in the world," replied Mischa. "After all, it is the Army of the Revolution, the Peoples' Army.... only we couldn't possibly take the liberties with a Red Army officer that you take with yours."

"Oh, I don't know about that." replied Jacques, "We think our officers get all the breaks."

"When I get back to Leningrad..." continued Mischa

"You want to go back?" interjected Jacques

"Want to go back? Sure I want to go back, why not? I'm a good Russian. My mother and father live in Leningrad."

"But you said you didn't want to go to the Repatriation Center; I don't see how you can go back otherwise."

"Well that's different. I want to go back, and yet I don't want to go back. I couldn't help being taken prisoner. My friend next to me, he was killed, but they were on top of me before I could do a thing."

"But there's nothing wrong with being taken prisoner" said Jacques.

"I don't know." replied Mischa dubiously. "In all the camps I was in, there were rumors that all prisoners would be shot when they returned to Russia. Maybe these were only rumors spread by the Germans."

"But that's ridiculous" said Jacques. "You don't really think they'd shoot you do you?"

"I don't know what to think." answered Mischa. "Maybe not, although many prisoners think so. Maybe a forced-labor camp in Siberia, or the N.K.V.D. on our backs for the rest of our lives."

"Whew!" whistled Jacques, while I swallowed.

*

One day my sergeant came up to me and said:

"Say, Lieutenant, don't you think we ought to get rid of those Russian civilians?"

"Get rid of them? Why?"

"Well, I mean... before they cause any trouble, like."

"Trouble? They won't cause any trouble. They're good workers; besides, I've taken rather a liking to them. Let 'em stick around a while longer."

"OK" said the sergeant. But I didn't like the way he said it. It sounded like "Don't say I didn't warn you. What does he know about it? I said to myself. He's just too hooked on regulations, that's all.

Two evenings later, I came home and was greeted by the sergeant with an odd gleam in his eye.

"Lieutenant," he said, "The Russian Babe is sick."

"What do you mean she's sick? What's the matter with her?"

"I don't know. She hasn't been down all day. Looks like its bad."

"Well go and get Tovarich, and send in Jacques."

"Mischa, what's the matter with Sasha?" He didn't know. He guessed it was the same trouble she had before, but he didn't know what it was. The Germans had given her injections, and it had gone away in a few days.

"Jacques'" I said, "go up and see how she is and let me know right away."

While he was gone, we stood around waiting. Mischa did not appear much concerned.

Soon Jacques returned and reported that Sasha was in great pain. She could only breathe with difficulty, and seemed very weak.

"She was moaning a lot," said Jacques "and kept pointing to her heart. She said "picure" (injection) several times."

"Oh Shit!" said the sergeant.

All we had in the villa was a first-aid kit. The nearest Army hospital was twelve miles away. We couldn't take her over there, and the chances of dragging out an Army doctor that distance to see someone who wasn't even Army personnel were too slim to attempt. Something had to be done. We couldn't just let the girl lie there. Mischa was not helpful. He stood at the window with hands in pockets, staring absently into space.

"Say, there's a French barracks about a mile down the road," suggested someone. "They must have a doctor there."

"OK" I said. "Lets go." Mischa went up to the room he shared with Sasha.

On the way over to the French barracks, I wondered how best to explain our irregular request. Better just tell the truth, I thought, that the woman is part of our civilian help, and that we don't have a doctor around. That's pretty near the truth anyway. The barracks were occupied by a unit of General Leclerc's armored division. The medical officer on duty was a young Jewish captain who agreed to come over right away. "Just one of our civilian help'" I explained. The French officer needed no explanation. He pointed to his leggings, his O.D. pants, his field jacket, and helmet liner. "All American," he smiled. "Now I can do something for you"

In the jeep he recounted how he had left France after the collapse and joined Leclerc in North Africa. He was at Lake Tchad and Tripoli. Then he went to England and landed in Normandy with Patton's Third Army.

Back at the villa, I led the way up the narrow stairway to Sasha's room. The doctor followed. Sasha was lying in one of the two iron beds, breathing with difficulty and looking very pale. Over the mantle shelf, a large portrait of Stalin had been clipped from a magazine and tacked to the wall. But the doctor was not looking at Stalin; he was looking over my shoulder with a fixed and fascinated look. Mischa, unconcerned with the doctor's arrival, was in process of undressing for bed. His shirt was flung across the bed, and as we entered he turned around. I had never seen Mischa stripped before; he was broad chested and muscular. But it was not his physique that was hypnotizing the doctor. I stared also. There across his chest was imprinted the most fabulous piece of tattoo art I ever hope to see. It was nothing less than the Russian Revolution in majestic and heroic proportions. All the agonies, the suffering and the triumph were woven and interwoven in blues, reds and purples, and the masterpiece was surmounted by the Red Flag and approximate likenesses of Lenin and Stalin. No one moved in this moment of awed silence. Then I pointed to the other bed. "Eh... la voila, mon Capitaine." The doctor walked over, and I closed the door and went down to wait.

After a while, the doctor came down. "I gave her a shot," he said. "Its her heart. She'll be all right in a day or two. That's to say, as all right as she'll ever be. She's in pretty poor shape. She's had typhus and didn't get the right care. Now she's got complications. What with under-nourishment, strain and overwork, she should go to a sanatorium for six months if she wants to live more than a few years. We only count the ones they kill," he added bitterly. "We forget the ones who will die when this is all over. Ah, les salauds." He picked up a pebble and hurled it against the iron gate with a resounding clang.

I thanked him, and as he left, he shot me a broad wink: "Civilian help. Eh?"

The Russian babe recovered and was back washing dishes in a couple of days. Life returned to normal. Mischa washed jeeps, checked oil and gas and chopped wood. Sasha helped in the kitchen, swept floors and listened to the radio. We would ask them how they liked G.I. jive. They giggled. "Funny music," they said. When we sat around the radio listening to Jack Benny or Bob Hope, they would stare in uncomprehending amazement.

Once again the sergeant pinned me down one morning as we crossed the yard.

"Hey, Lieutenant, when are we going to get rid of those Russians? Don't you think its about time?"

"Well, maybe," I replied. "There's no hurry though. You might check up on the location of the Russian camp though. It won't hurt to know where it is."

That evening the sergeant got what he wanted. All through dinner, he looked at his plate and said little. A half-smile played around his lips. It boded ill. A smile of triumph, I thought, looking down to the end of the table. Mischa and Sasha were both taking second helpings of corn beef hash and talking together. Nothing wrong there, I thought.

After dinner the sergeant followed me into my office. "The Babe's pregnant," he announced flatly.

"She's what?

"I said she's pregnant."

"How do you know?

"She told me"

"Since when did you learn Russian?"

"She just pointed and made with the hands. No mistake about it."

"Oh yeah? Sergeant, go fetch the Babe and Tovarich, and bring Jacques with you."

"Yessir!" The sergeant moved off with a self-satisfied smirk.

In a few moments the four of them trooped in.

"Sasha, is it true you are pregnant?"

She nodded shyly.

"How long?

She wasn't sure. Maybe three months, maybe four. Mischa stood with his hands behind his back, quite impassive.

OK that settles it. You'll both have to go to the repatriation center. We can't have any babies born here.

Mischa's face clouded over. "Comrade Lieutenant, Sascha go to the Russiche lager. I stay with the Amerikanski, yes?"

"I don't know," I replied impatiently. Turning to the sergeant, I said "How come nobody could see she was pregnant?"

"Search me," said the sergeant, "What did I tell you Lieutenant? Should have got rid of them when I said."

"OK, OK, we'll get rid of them," I countered a bit testily. "Not this week though, we're too busy. We'll do it next Monday."

*

For the next episode I was mercifully absent, but the sergeant was happy to fill me in when I returned from Dijon, two days later.

The sergeant was alone in the villa. The others were all at work, when all of a sudden frantic screams came from the Russians' bedroom. The sergeant tore up and found Mischa with a death grip around Sasha's neck. She was turning purple in the face. After a struggle, the sergeant managed to pull the Russian away, and Sasha fell prostrate to the floor. It took about two hours to revive her, while Mischa sulked by the window and refused to lend a hand. That evening only Mischa showed up for supper, but sat and sulked in his plate.

It was useless to hold another inquest. The reason was obvious enough. But what we hadn't figured on was the degree to which these two characters could pass off mayhem as no more than mild throat irritation. They both showed up for breakfast the following morning, hand in hand, smiling lovingly at each other, with Mischa's finger marks still livid on her throat.

"As long as he doesn't kill her before Monday," murmured the sergeant.

On Monday, we packed them into the back seat of a jeep, and set off for the Russian Repatriation Center, at Versailles. When we were about two miles away from the place, they started talking rapidly to each other and tapped Jacques on the shoulder.

"What's up?" I queried.

"They say," replied Jacques "They don't want us to drive them to the gates."

"Why not?" I said, although I understood perfectly.

"Well, they're scared of what will happen to them if the Russians find out they spent five weeks with an American Army unit. They say they'll have enough trouble anyway explaining where they were."

"Sure, sure, but we're still two miles away; I'll let 'em off a bit farther down."

But the two in the back got more and more agitated. "Bitte! Bitte!" they pleaded, in German.

So they piled out and were too nervous to linger over good-byes. We watched them walk away, each with the same suitcase they carried when they walked out of Metz. Though the sun was hot, he wore his overcoat and the cap with the shiny black visor. She walked at his right side, her frail figure close to his bulky frame. Her grey astrakhan fur cap with the ear flaps turned up, barely reached his shoulder

I had few illusions about the fate awaiting them, although at that time I was unaware of the full implications of the vast forced repatriation program underway, and our own complicity in that monstrous crime. I just felt sorry for them. She truly wanted to return home, even though scared. He did not wish to return at all, in spite of being homesick, but he went because of her. It was a sad little story - "L'Amour Slave."

Well, Jacques and I agreed, "That's that." I had more serious and pressing matters to attend to.

But it wasn't quite over yet.

About four mornings later, as we sat just finishing breakfast, the door opened and in walked Mischa grinning an amiable "Good morning Comrades!" to all.

"Tovarich! Goddammit, how the hell did you get here.?"

"I walked all night," he explained through our translator.

"So? What's wrong?"

"Nothing is wrong. The camp is fine. Lots of Russians. In the day we drill, and the women clean and wash clothes. In the evenings we sit around and sing songs. No, there is nothing wrong, only well... could the Amerikanskis let me have some food – the camp isn't feeding us all that well.

So we packed him up some food, but wait! "You don't want to take American rations with you. Thought you were worried about that kind of thing.

"No problem," grinned Mischa "Black market!"

As he was about to leave, he paused in the doorway with a worried look. He called to Jacques and they spoke for several moments. "Lieutenant," said Jacques, "he's got something on his mind, you'd better come over."

"What's the trouble, Tovarich?" I asked.

"Comrade Lieutenant," he replied anxiously. "It's the things I've been hearing in the camp. They talk about it in the mess every day. I couldn't believe my ears. It reminded me of the Nazi propaganda programs in Russian which we used to hear on the German radio, only this time its our own people, the Russians saying it."

"What are they saying, Tovarich?"

"Well," replied Mischa, "they're saying that the Americans now want to fight the Russians! I tell them it isn't true, but they look at me in a funny way. Its better not to argue, so I shut up. But tell me, Comrade Lieutenant," he looked at me anxiously, "Is it true?"

"No, Mischa it isn't true."

He looked greatly relieved. "Good," he said. "That makes me happy. I wish I could tell them in the camp what you told me – but it would be too dangerous. Its enough that I should know it." As he walked out through the gate, he turned and with a large wink, snapped us a clenched fist salute. "Take it easy, Tovarich!" We shouted after him.

Two months later a battered envelope arrived, bearing a Marseilles postmark. It was addressed in a thin spidery hand in purple ink. Inside, a crumpled letter, written in very bad German:

"Dear Friends, So far, things are well with us. We are waiting for a ship to take us home. I am the only woman among all these soldiers. Mischa and I, we often speak of you, and want to thank you for all your goodness. We are glad to go home, but also very frightened. How can I explain? Amerikanski sehr gut! Love, Sasha. (I still have this crumpled letter.)

*

Only after the war was over did I learn of the full scope and significance of Stalin's program of forced repatriation of Soviet prisoners and displaced persons, all of whom were automatically considered traitors and spies for the West. I was ignorant at the time, of the fact that my own government, along with the Western Allies had agreed to comply with Stalin's demands, and were prepared to assist in this evil crime.

CHAPTER TWENTY TWO

GEORGE ORWELL

In September, 1944, not long after the liberation of Paris, I was sitting in my office at OSS headquarters, 79 Champs Elysées, when I received a phone call from the American Embassy. My caller wanted to know if I could spare any transportation.

"What's the problem?" I asked.

"We need a jeep and a driver for a few hours. Can you help us out?"

The American Embassy had only just re-opened, and being chronically short of vehicles, was obliged to beg and borrow from the military.

"OK." I said. "I can send a man down. Where do you want him, and what time?"

"Send him down right away. Its to pick up a British newsman. Name is Orwell.

"Did you say Orwell? What's his first name?"

"First name? What the hell difference does that make? Tell your driver he's waiting in the lobby. He can't miss him. He's a tall lanky Brit."

"Look feller," I insisted, "do me a special favor, will you? I really would like to know his first name."

"Godammit, I don't have it any longer; threw it out; I'm duty corporal here, not the vice-consul. OK wait a minute, while I try to fish it out of the trash. Here it is – name is George."

OK, Thanks," I replied, "The driver is on his way."

And in case you had any doubts, the driver was me.

There he was, the famous George Orwell, waiting in the Embassy lobby; a tall gangling figure, in an ill-fitting British War Correspondent's uniform, at least one size too big.

"Mr. Orwell, I'm Lieutenant Jolis, its a pleasure to meet you. I understand you need a vehicle."

"I say! Awfully good of you to come yourself. Are you sure you have the time?"

"Mr. Orwell, I've got all day."

"That's splendid! Here is what I'd like to do, if you can manage it. It has been years since I was last in this city. What I had in mind was, perhaps we could go and visit some of my old haunts, you know, the ones I wrote about in *Down and Out In Paris and London.;* that is to say, of course, if you ever read it."

It had been published in 1933. Of course I had read it.

And that is exactly what we did. It was one of the more memorable days of my life.

We combed the narrow streets of the Left Bank, the Quartier Latin, the Rue de la Montagne Ste. Genevieve, Place de la Contrescarpe, Rue Mouffetard, Le Panthéon. We located the run-down hotel where he lived in the early thirties, l'Hotel des Trois Moinneaux, in the Rue du Coq d'Or. His old landlady, Madame M, rushed to him with a squeal of joy: "Oh, Monsieur Orwell, quelle joie de vous revoir apres tant d'années!" And Orwell embraced her and gave her a buss on each cheek.

We found the site of the Aubèrge de Jehan Gothard, where he worked as a "plongeur" (dishwasher), but it was under different management, nobody remembered him.

After climbing I don't remember how many steep staircases, seeking out former landladies, and while he re-lived those early days, we found ourselves at St. Germain-des-Pres. I suggested a beer. Parking my jeep on the Boulevard St. Germain, we sat at the terrace of the Café Flore. Orwell stretched his long legs, fatigued but happy.

"Jolis, you can't imagine what this is doing for me. All these memories. You really are a frightful sport."

"Don't even think about it," I said, "you can't imagine what this is doing for me."

And we sat at the terrace and watched the girls go by. Hardly any traffic in the streets; a few military vehicles; not all that number of men either. Mostly women; the girls clip-clopping along on high wooden platform shoes, or on bicycles, with short skirts blowing in the breeze. Many were young and pretty; a heartwarming sight. The war seemed a long way off.

Orwell knew I was with OSS, and he knew what OSS was all about.

"I say, Jolis," he said, after a silence. "Do you think the Communists will take over France when this ends?"

"Hard to say," I replied, having asked myself the same question more than once.

"You know," he said, "If they do, we'll have to ask ourselves what this war was all about."

In *Homage to Catalonia,* which was published in 1938, Orwell had clearly stated his condemnation of Communist behaviour in Spain, but he had not yet gone quite so far as to equate Marxism and Nazism as twin evils of the same stripe. He did this later in *Animal Farm* and *Nineteen Eighty Four,* but these two books did not appear until 1945 and 1949 respectively; consequently, on this memorable day in September, 1944, as we sat at the terrace of the Café Flore, it was a discovery and a joy for me to find someone who shared my own views on these matters.

At the end of the day we parted and vowed to stay in touch; a wish that had to wait for the war's end to be fulfilled. Then we met many times either in Paris or London. We became good friends. I visited his home at Hammersmith, at the entrance to Kew Gardens, London's botanical gardens. I met his wife Sonia. He was astonished when I explained I was born only a few blocks away, at Chiswick. He had trouble believing me, but it added an element to our relationship.

We had countless discussions, particularly over the betrayal of the Left, the mirage of socialism, La Trahison des Clercs, the Treason of the Intellectuals, and above all, the unadulterated evil of totalitarianism, both Nazi and Marxist.

The caustic tone he adopted when discussing the Left had a very personal quality. He spoke almost as an injured party. He gave the impression he felt he was the victim of a monstrous fraud. I had no trouble agreeing with him. I felt the same way.

In his biography, **George Orwell, A life,** (Secker & Warburg, London), author, Bernard Crick writes: "Orwell was unusually reticent to his friends about his background and his life; his openness was all in print for literary and moral effect; he tried to keep his small circle of good friends well apart – people are still surprised to learn who else at the time he knew – he did not confide in people easily."

I did not find Orwell reticent about his background or his life. He talked freely about his schooldays at Eton and his early days in India. Among the subjects we particularly discussed, was the need for an international organization to help victims of Communism. There were many organizations helping victims of Hitler, but victims of Stalin were ignored. The International Rescue Committee in New York, of which I was a director was an exception. We talked of expanding it in association with a British-based group he wanted to initiate. I was enthusiastic, but though I felt rescue and relief of victims was badly needed, I did not think this answered the need for a political counter-offensive. Orwell agreed.

When Orwell's collected Essays and Letters were published many years later, I learned quite by accident, that he had referred to these discussions in a letter he wrote to Arthur Koestler dated March 16, 1946, in which he mentions a certain: "Bert Jolis......who is very much of our thinking." I had not met Arthur Koestler at that time, but met him on several occasions in 1948.

Tall and gangly, wearing size twelve boots, clothes ill-fitting, Orwell always had an awkward look about him, except when sitting down. He had a sickly air and spoke in a soft voice, due to a throat wound suffered in Spain. This made it hard sometimes to catch his words. But the effort it took was never wasted. He never failed with a caustic comment or original slant on whatever was being discussed. His accent was flat middle-class English, not the upper-class "Mayfair" tone you might have expected him to acquire at Eton.

The last time I saw George Orwell was at his home in 1950, shortly before his death. He was sick, and propped up in bed. He did not want to discuss his sickness; told me it was "nothing." I did not know what was ailing him, but did not press him on it. I had no idea he was dying. He had just published **Nineteen Eighty Four** and I told him what a masterful piece of work I had found it. He smiled and thanked me. We did not have much conversation, he was not up to it. I told him about some of the gains the anti-Communist Left was making in France; in the trade-unions for example, and particularly how the Communists had been ousted from control of the Paris daily, **Franc-Tireur et Partisan,** and the role of my friends Daniel Benedite and Charles Ronsac in that operation.

He nodded in interest, but spoke little. As I left, wishing him a quick recovery, I remember looking out through his window at the massive wrought-iron gates of the Botanical Gardens at Kew, and somehow those gates and Orwell's frail features have merged into a faded collage in my memory.

He died at the tragically young age of 47. His insights were genial. "**Some are more equal than others – Big Brother is watching you – Newspeak,** just to mention only a few of his deathless inventions, have become part of our language. We use these phrases as if they had always existed, without thinking. Had he lived a normal span, who knows how many further brilliant concepts he might have formulated in defense of freedom. He had so much more to tell us. What a loss.

CHAPTER TWENTY THREE

LYDIA TOLSTOY, VLASSOV, AND THE RED ARMY TANK OFFICER

When we landed in Normandy, we encountered thousands of displaced persons wandering in the liberated areas. These were ex-slave laborers who had been employed by the Germans for work on the "Atlantic Wall" fortifications. Among them were large numbers of Russians. Though not part of my mission, curiosity impelled me to inquire about these people. Fast moving events and language difficulty were such that only superficial contact could be made. Enough though, to learn that certain Russians had been engaged in combat on the side of the Germans against the Soviets.

After arrival in Paris, I looked into this matter further. Pfc. Jacques Gourevitch, a member of my team, had contacts with the White Russian Community. Among them was Princess Lydia Galitzine. This lady proved to be not only a valuable source of information, but a gallant and courageous freedom-fighter in her own right.

At the time I met her, Madame Galitizine was in process of divorcing the Prince. Shortly thereafter, she married Ivan Tolstoy, the youngest grandson of the great Leo.

Lydia Tolstoy furnished me with extensive information on the degree to which Russians fought with the German armies against the Soviets. She was particularly familiar with the story of Major General Andrei A. Vlassov and The Russian Liberation Army – Russkaia Osvoboditelnaia Armiia (ROA.)

This was the first information we had on this phenomenon, and I considered it an intelligence plum. But because it had little impact on the immediate prosecution of the war, it met with only tepid interest higher up. I felt this was a mistake. After the war I furnished the information to George Fischer who incorporated it into his book, *Vlassov... Soviet Opposition to Stalin,* Harvard University Press, 1952.

Even today, though the facts are now known, there is little public awareness of this extraordinary facet of World War II.

In 1987, on the 70th Anniversary of the 1917 Bolshevik Revolution, I wrote an article on the subject for *Politique Internationale,* an abbreviated version of which follows:

*

When the German armies capitulated in the Spring of 1945, among the hundred of thousands of prisoners captured by the Allies, there were found to be large numbers of Russians wearing German uniforms. Thousands of such Russians had already been captured in the Normandy Beachead and the Battle of France.

The presence of these Russians in the service of the Germans was remarkable enough, considering that Germany was waging a war of annihilation against the Russian homeland. All the countries occupied by Germany produced their local brand of "collaborators", but of all the principal powers taking part in World War II, with the exception of the Balkan armies, only the Soviet Union suffered large-scale military defections.

It is true that the Germans recruited "Anti-Bolshevik Legions" in the occupied countries of the West, and made great propaganda of the various units of Frenchmen, Belgians, etc., who volunteered to fight for Germany on the Eastern front. Their numbers, however, were insignificant compared with the thousands of Russian nationals who provided real additional fighting strength for Germany.

Russian effectives were organized along three principal lines:

The first category was organized along national and religious lines into small units serving with the Wehrmacht. These were mostly Trans-Caucasians, Tatars and Kirghizians. They manned anti-aircraft defenses, supply lines etc., and worked in auxiliary units such as the Organization Todt. They were commanded by German officers.

The second category, more homogeneous, were the Cossacks from the Don, the Kuban, and Terek. These were organized as Cossack units up to the level of regiment, and were commanded by Cossack and German officers.

The third category, and the largest and best organized, was General Vlassov's Russian Army of Liberation, known as the ROA.

Soviet authorities and their apologists in other countries have succeeded in shrouding in deepest mystery the story of their wartime traitors. While all the world knows about Quisling, Petain, Laval, Degrelle, Mussert, and others who collaborated with the Nazis, the Soviets would have us believe that no Soviet citizen was capable of such treachery. The myth assiduously broadcast by Stalin, and parroted by fellow-travellers all over the world, that the Soviet people stood shoulder to shoulder as one man in the face of the Nazi invader was not borne out by subsequent revelations.

When Hitler launched his massive invasion of the Soviet Union on June 21, 1941, his armies met little resistance except for temporary checks, until they were held in November on the Moscow-Witebsk-Kiev line. Lack of preparedness and faulty deployment of troops on the part of the Russians are only part of the answer to this phenomenal advance.

The Russians were *psychologically* unprepared. Throughout the period of the Nazi-Soviet pact which preceded the invasion, the Soviet government had forbidden all public criticism of the Nazis. Nazi ideology was represented as being closer to Communism than the "bourgeois" philosophy of the Western democracies, (which indeed it was.) England, America and France were regarded as "imperialist war-mongers." While American communists were beating the anti-war drums in the USA, Moscow was organizing exhibitions of Nazi culture and Nazi military glory. Hundreds of Wehrmacht officers moved freely around Moscow in uniform, and German victories in the West were hailed as "just retribution" for British, French and Norwegian "war-mongers."

Victor Kravchenko in *I Chose Freedom* tells us the following about this period:

"It took months of direct experience with German brutality to overcome the moral disarmament of the Russian people. They had to learn again to detest the Nazis, after two years in which Hitler had been played up as a friend of Russia and a friend of peace. Let it not be forgotten that in the early weeks entire Red Army divisions fell prisoner to the enemy almost without a struggle."

The motives for collaboration were varied. Though there were probably extremely few who favored Nazi ideology, there were unquestionably a number of Germanophiles. Some hoped to advance the cause of national separatism, particularly those from Ukraine, Belorussia, and the Trans-Caucasus. Plain opportunism can account for a further segment. But the strongest motive for collaboration was the widespread belief that the German invasion provided the one opportunity for establishing a new social order on a non-Stalinist basis. The people, rightly or wrongly, believed the German armies would withdraw at the conclusion of the war. The best proof of this was that when the true vision of German aims became apparent to the population, practically all collaboration ceased. Many groups of partisans fought both the Russians and the Germans.

During the early days of the invasion, the number of Russians serving with the Wehrmacht swelled daily. They served as interpreters, in liaison groups, police detachments and even in armed formations.

Where populations were evacuated to the rear by Soviet authorities, groups of peasants would hide out in the forests, waiting for the Germans. Intellectuals and workers in the towns hid in cellars until the Russian troops withdrew.

For the most part this widespread desire on the part of the Russians to assist in the overthrow of the Soviet regime remained unorganized and uncoordinated, and this remained true until the emergence of Major General Andrei A. Vlassov.

A veteran of the Revolution of 1917, Vlassov fought in the ranks of the Red Army throughout the Civil War. He commanded the 61st Division in Crimea during the storming of Perekop in 1920. A graduate of the Frunze Military Academy, and Communist Party member, he established for himself a brilliant military career. He was one of the few top-ranking officers in the Red Army to escape the purges following the Tukachevsky affair.

After the German invasion of Russia, Vlassov was placed in command of the Second Assault Army. By personal order of Stalin he was directed to replace the defense of Moscow, and played a decisive role in checking the enemy's advance on the capital. He received the Order of the Red Banner on January 2, 1942. Vlassov then received orders to raise the siege of Leningrad. His army broke through the German lines, but was encircled before it could relieve the city. After desperate fighting, the bulk of his army was annihilated. Vlassov was captured by the Germans early in 1942.

The motives which prompted Vlassov, brilliant Soviet General, defender of Moscow, to join the growing movement bent on overthrowing the Stalinist regime, can best be understood from the writings of others who turned in bitter hatred upon the regime they once so ardently supported; writers such as Barmine, Kravchenko and Krivitsky.

The Russian anti-Soviet movement took on significant proportions in the summer of 1942. Vlassov's headquarters were established at Dabendorf in the suburbs of Berlin. His staff of high ranking Red Army officers included Generals Troukhin, Malishkin and Zhilenkov. It also included a group of Soviet scholars and economists who set to work developing the political program for the movement.

At the end of 1942, the German High Command started showing signs of nervousness at the growing response to the Vlassov movement, in which they saw an implied threat of resurgent Russian nationalism. The "master race" theories of Alfred Rosenberg, chief of the Ostministerium prevailed over the Wehrmacht's more intelligent approach, and German troops in Russia engaged in sadistic brutalities against the "untermenschen aus Osten" (eastern savages.)

Unable to account for this switch in policy, Russian collaboration with the Germans dwindled sharply. In many cases acts of open resistance occurred. These were greeted by the Germans as proof of the "ineradicable Bolshevist strain in all Russians," and resulted in even more savage reprisals against the population. Eventually all collaboration with the Germans ceased and the invader was regarded with universal hatred.

To those who regard the invasion of Russia as the mistake which cost Hitler the war, it is pertinent to ask whether Alfred Rosenberg's master-race policy might not have been the real and fatal blunder.

With exception of three divisions, the Russian Army of Liberation was never permitted to organize above the battalion level. These battalions were dispersed throughout the German Army and attached to regular Wehrmacht units. In the tug-of-war which took place between Vlassov and the German High Command, the one point which the former always strove for and which the latter never conceded was an independent homogeneous Russian Army.

Nevertheless, in their moment of greatest desperation, when German defeat was no longer in doubt, the Wehrmacht consented to a tentative operation by an independent force of Vlassov's ROA. As the Red Army approached the River Oder, an ROA Russian force under the command of Colonel Sakharov fought a successful engagement, during the course of which Red Army units passed over voluntarily to his side. Upon surrendering they declared they did so solely because they were faced by troops of General Vlassov. This astonishing incident at the very close of the conflict when the Red Army's victory was certain, was reported by Russian prisoners.

Vlassov and his generals who had sought refuge in western Germany, were turned over to the Soviets by the Americans. On August 2 1946 Pravda announced that twelve individuals had been hanged for high treason and collaboration with the enemy; they were: A.A.Vlassov, V.F. Malyshkin, G.N. Zhilenkov, F.I. Trukhin, D.E. Zakutnyi, I.A. Blagoveschienski, M.A. Meandrov, V.I. Maltsev, G.A. Zverev, V.D. Korbukov, N.S. Shatov, S.K. Buniachenko.

The war-weary Western Allies were disinclined to draw distinctions between collaborators of one stripe or another. Quisling, Petain, Lord Haw-Haw and Vlassov, had all cast their lot with Hitler; that was enough. No one was interested in looking into the real significance of the Vlassov movement.

One may reflect that this ill-fated quixotic tragedy can rank as one of the great "might-have-beens" of history.

*

IVAN, THE RED ARMY TANK OFFICER

For the purposes of this true account, we'll call him Ivan. He was not a member of Vlassov's army. He was a 1st Lieutenant in a Soviet armored division; a tank officer in his early twenties, who was taken prisoner by the Germans during the siege of Leningrad. After serving time in various prisoner-of-war camps inside Germany, he was drafted into a labor gang and shipped to Normandy for construction work on the fortifications. From there he escaped.

In order to avoid recapture by the Germans, he made contact with one of the resistance groups in Brittany, as it happened, a Communist group, and he fought with this underground unit prior to and during the Allied landings.

After the liberation of Paris, Ivan made his way to the capital and reported to the Soviet Repatriation Mission, just then in process of setting up shop, and whose purpose was to round up all Russian nationals and ship them back to Russia. The Mission was short of manpower. Ivan had excellent credentials, having fought with a French communist resistance group, which he was able to document. The commanding officer of the mission took a chance; he reinstated Ivan in his rank of 1st Lieutenant and recruited him onto the staff of the mission.

One day, Ivan was designated as escort officer, and ordered to accompany a special group of ex-prisoners and displaced persons by air back to Moscow. On the day of departure, the thirty or so individuals were assembled at Camp Beauregard, the Russian staging area near Versailles. Under Ivan's command they proceeded in two vehicles to the Allied military airfield at Le Bourget.

The airfield was all confusion. Planes landing and departing; French and American military personnel scurrying on errands; military freight parked seemingly everywhere. No one visibly in charge. At long last, Ivan succeeded in locating the Soviet plane. It was parked at the far end of the airfield – way off in a corner, almost out of sight. It was getting dark, it was misty and raining. As Ivan watched his prisoners debark from the vehicles and mount the steps into the plane, he suddenly decided he didn't want to return with them to Moscow. As the last prisoner entered the plane, Ivan made a dash for the nearby fence, jumped over and crouched in the ditch on the other side. No one saw him, and he was not missed.

It seemed an eternity before he heard the plane start its motors and lumber off onto the runway. He waited till he heard the takeoff, and only then picked himself up. Now, what to do? This was totally unplanned. He had acted on an impulse. He had no place to go. He was in Red Army uniform – he certainly couldn't go back to the Mission. He started wandering. As he wandered in the vicinity of Le Bourget, he struggled with the impossible. Fortunately it was dark by now. His uniform was not too evident. Where to get a change of clothes? Where to sleep tonight? Where? Where? Where? After fruitless hours, he was exhausted, and now committed his second ill-considered act. He entered a café, sat at the bar and ordered a drink.

One drink led to another. Other patrons were also drinking. They had noticed the Russian uniform. Voices were raised in heated discussion over "the Russians." Ivan sat and paid no attention. Then one of the patrons, under the influence, staggered over to Ivan, poked him in the chest and started berating him. It was clear he didn't like the "the Russians." Ivan poked back. Others joined in. It soon developed into a melée. Ivan was bounced off the "zinc," flung across the room, gashing his head on a table corner and falling unconscious to the floor.

The French gendarmes were called. They saw the Russian and wanted no part of him. They called for instructions, and were told to contact the Repatriation Mission. So Ivan was picked up by two Red Army MPs and taken back to Camp Beauregard, where he woke up in the hospital annexe. Not only was he a deserter, he was now a recaptured deserter. There was no question he would be shot.

His injury was not serious, not more than a day, possibly two, in the hospital. He thought furiously. His only possible chance was to confide in the doctor. He had nothing to lose. This time it was the right decision. The doctor, a Red Army medical officer, a Major, agreed to help. The toilet had a window to the outside. The Major told Ivan he would hide some civilian clothes behind the toilet and give him the signal when all was clear. He added, he was only sorry he couldn't go along too!

Lydia Tolstoy was helping Russians escape forced repatriation. At great risk to herself, she was hiding Russians in her house at Auteuil. More than that; she was helping them get false identification as Poles, Serbs, or Bulgarians. I forget the circumstances, but somehow she picked up Ivan and was hiding him too, when one day she brought him to my attention.

At that time we were looking for an agent to accomplish a mission in southern Germany. Allied forces had not yet crossed the Rhine. There was a group of Russian war prisoners working in a salt mine south of Stuttgart. They had smuggled out a message to say they would be able to stage an uprising, create local confusion, and disrupt communications behind the German lines, if the operation could be coordinated with the Allied advance into Germany. What they needed was a radio operator. This message had come to the attention of OSS Bern, who in turn asked us if we could supply the agent.

The plan was to infiltrate the agent into southern Germany via Switzerland. He needed two cover stories; one for the journey from the Swiss border to the salt mine; the other as a Russian war prisoner, once inside the mine. He needed to be competent in radio transmission and understand procedures for maintaining contact with OSS base station.

I thought of Ivan. It would be worth investigating whether he was capable of such a mission. So Ivan left Lydia Tolstoy's house in Auteuil and moved into our base at Saint Germain-en-Laye.

Ivan's personal story was fairly straightforward. His father had been a Party member and an early Bolshevik activist. In time, he became disillusioned with the Revolution, and turned bitterly against it; but only internally. That is to say, he avoided being purged, by keeping it to himself and drinking himself to death. Ivan saw his father die, hated the Stalinist regime, and refused to return to his homeland. But he was nonetheless a patriotic Russian, and listening to the radio, he would glow with pride at the Red Army advances. Above all, he wanted to go to America. Somewhat mixed up? Yes, but young and still with ideals.

Was he right for the mission?

On the plus side he was motivated and courageous. On the minus side he had shown evidence of impulsiveness bordering on the reckless. But there was no time to engage in a leisurely appraisal of his personality and character. We had to move fast. We had no one else. We decided to take Ivan. He was a fast learner, and the time soon approached for the mission to be activated.

Ivan was smuggled into Switzerland in the trunk of a car from the OSS base at Annemasse on the French side of the border. (The same route I had taken in Mission Ruppert.) OSS Bern took him in charge and waited for the appropriate time to activate the mission. But it failed to happen. Something went wrong. Did the Swiss get wind of it? I never knew exactly. In any event, OSS Bern decided security was not good enough, and the mission was scrubbed.

Ivan returned to Paris and we had him back at our base at Saint-Germain-en-Laye. Here, he became restless, no mission, nothing to do, time on his hands. It was hard to keep him under wraps. One day he asked whether he could go into Paris and visit Lydia Tolstoy. With some hesitation, we agreed.

We never saw Ivan again.

After he arrived at Lydia Tolstoy's house, Lydia excused herself for an hour while she went out on an errand. Ivan climbed the stairs to the small room he had occupied before, and waited for Lydia's return.

Neighbors reported seeing a car pull up. Four men jumped out and forced open the door of Lydia's house. Shortly thereafter, they came out again dragging a struggling screaming individual. The car roared away. When Lydia returned she found Ivan's room ransacked, the walls, the staircase, the entrance hallway spattered with blood. She was in a state of shock, and did not call me right away Call the police? Useless.

Later that night, she walked her dog on the street outside. A man drew up alongside of her, hat pulled down over his face, and addressed her in Russian. "Lydia Tolstoy, we've had you under surveillance for some time. We know what you are up to. But now its finished. The boy was today. Next will be your turn." Then he vanished.

She phoned me next morning after a sleepless night. KGB? GRU? Either one, it didn't matter. I rushed to the American Embassy. With the help of the political officer, we got Ivan and Lydia Tolstoy out of France and into Portugal next day, and eventually to the United States.

CHAPTER TWENTY FOUR

ERNEST LEMBERGER – PRIVATE "NOWATNY"

It probably looks as though all I was involved with during the war was Russians. Not so. Ernst Lemberger was a Jewish refugee from Vienna, who emigrated to France when Hitler annexed Austria in 1938. He was active in Austrian emigre politics, and during the German occupation he fought with the French resistance under the name of Commandant Jean Lambert.

In early 1945 the Germans were in retreat on the eastern front. The outcome of the war was no longer in doubt; the only question was when? The Western allies had no plans to occupy Vienna. It was tacitly understood the Soviets would liberate the city and be the first occupants. An underground resistance movement had flickered, notwithstanding fierce Nazi repression. As eventual German defeat became daily more evident, the resistance became emboldened, and had created an underground organization called the Provisorische Oersterreichische National-Komite, (POEN), the Provisional Austrian National Committee. Ernst Lemberger volunteered to go to Vienna to establish contact with the POEN, and report back to the Western Allies.

It was planned that he would be infiltrated into Austria in the uniform of a German soldier, with a cover story properly documenting him in his "Soldatenbuch" as Private Nowatny. The trouble was that Lemberger had been outside Germany for some seven years, and his unfamiliarity with current idioms and local gossip would certainly endanger his cover. So I decided to have him spend a few weeks in a German prisoner-of-war camp near Compiegne. For this, he needed another cover story: – where he saw service – where he was captured – where he was recruited – what campaigns he fought in, etc.

Lemberger spent three weeks as a prisoner-of-war learning current German lingo, slang and "soldier gossip." When he came out he confided to me it had been one of the most terrifying experiences of his life. The camp was divided between unregenerate Nazis, heartened by the Battle of the Bulge then in progress, and those tired of war who were ready to collaborate. The diehards had introduced a reign of terror into the camp against all defeatists. Beatings, kangaroo justice, and occasional killings by the Nazis created an atmosphere of permanent shock. For Lemberger, it was a nightmare preserving his cover.

When Lemberger arrived in Vienna on February 25, 1945, as Private Nowatny, he knew exactly how to conduct himself as a German soldier.

While in Vienna, he established relations with the POEN, and gathered much useful information which he memorized, including recent data on the vital Ploesti oil fields in Romania and fifteen military targets as yet untouched by Allied bombers.

On March 3, Lemberger prepared to exit from Austria and regain Switzerland. Armed with the necessary travel orders, and in uniform, he boarded a train in Vienna headed west. Soon, a German military policeman entered his carriage, and started examining every passenger's papers. Lemberger sat perfectly still, very worried. Would his papers stand up under scrutiny? This could be fatal.

The MP examined Private Nowatny's papers, while Lemberger inwardly quaked. They were of course, expertly forged. The MP found them in order and took a look at Nowatny, found him fairly responsible, and said: "Look soldier, this train is horribly crowded, I'll never get through all the checking. Come on, give me a hand, there's a good fellow." So Lemberger accompanied the MP through the train, checking all papers and identities. He gathered a mine of information, which he memorized. This was an intelligence coup of no mean proportions. It covered German troop movements, including the locations and shifts of various infantry, tank, and artillery units.

On March 4, Lemberger re-entered Switzerland, reported to Allen Dulles, and a few days later arrived in Paris.

Ernst Lemberger, Jewish refugee, posing as a Nazi soldier, had proven himself, a brave and resourceful agent. He had accomplished a successful mission. I recommended him for the Silver Star.

After the war, Ernst Lemberger became Austria's first ambassador to Washington. We remained in friendly contact for a few years. Then when he was reassigned, I heard no more of him.

*

CHAPTER TWENTY FIVE

NOEL FIELD – SOVIET AGENT – FRIEND
OF ALGER HISS

In 1949 an American Communist named Noel Field defected behind the Iron Curtain, and never returned to the West. He was a Soviet agent who had succeeded, during the war, in penetrating the highest levels of the OSS, where he rendered valuable service to the Kremlin. He was a friend of Alger Hiss, and defected in order to escape a subpoena in the Hiss investigation.

But in 1940, very few people knew Field was a Communist, let alone a Soviet agent. Those who knew, were not believed. Just as no one believed, or wanted to believe Alger Hiss was a Communist agent, no one believed it of Field either. He was the perfect suave, urbane, upper class "Wasp", and like Hiss, he was so obviously part of the "establishment," he "couldn't be a Communist."

I happened to be one of the few who knew Field to be a communist, and I had known it since before the war. I didn't realize though, till much later, the extent of his involvement with the Soviet apparatus.

It came about through my association with the International Rescue Committee, (known in those days as the Emergency Rescue Committee.)

In 1940, tens of thousands of refugees were flooding into southern France to escape the Nazi invasion. The Emergency Rescue Committee had opened offices in Marseilles, to provide relief and help resettle the victims. Two men ran the operation, an American called Varian Fry, whose subsequent book, *Surrender On Demand* describes this experience, and Daniel Benedite, a Frenchman who later became a good friend of mine. The guiding principle governing this operation was that aid was given to refugees from and victims of totalitarianism, that is to say, both Nazi and Communist.

Other relief organizations had also set up branches in Marseilles, Catholics, Jewish, Evangelical, and among others, also the Unitarian Service Committee, a branch of the Unitarian Church whose headquarters were in Boston. Noel Field was in charge of the Unitarian office. He was also in charge of another operation in Toulouse where the Unitarians had opened a hospital, ostensibly to provide care and medical assistance to Republican refugees from the Spanish Civil War. In fact the hospital served as a staging area, where Spanish Communists were provided with new identities, new cover, and in some cases, new faces. Reports we received from both Marseilles and Toulouse, left not the slightest doubt that both Unitarian Service Committee operations were part of the international Communist apparatus.

Noel Field had managed to insinuate himself into the good graces of Allen Dulles, head of the OSS mission in Switzerland. In fact, they had known each other before the war. He persuaded Dulles that due to his work with the Unitarian Service Committee, he had unrivalled knowledge of anti-fascist and anti-Nazi refugees, and he further convinced Dulles how these sources could be exploited for intelligence and agent recruitment purposes.

Field did more. He persuaded Dulles to hire his adopted daughter, Erika Glaser, a German national and a dedicated Communist party activist. She became private secretary to Gary Van Arkel in the Bern office of OSS, and had access to all classified material.

Even before the Battle of Stalingrad, the Soviets realized that the German armies would be unable to survive the combined allied onslaught on two fronts, and would ultimately suffer defeat. They lost no time in preparing the post-war European scenario. It was a scenario in which direct Soviet rule would apply in all territories occupied by the Red Army, and indirect Soviet rule via local Communist surrogates would prevail in those countries liberated by the Western Allies. Germany was the prime target.

Among the high-ranking German officers captured at Stalingrad were two generals, von Seydlitz and von Paulus, who agreed to collaborate with the Soviets in setting up the framework for a post-war German government. They created the "Freies Deutschland Komite" or Free German Committee. Headquarters were established in Moscow, and branches in the West were set up in London, Stockholm and Paris. In France the organization was known as Le Comité pour L'Allemagne Libre à l'Ouest, (CALPO.) Intense recruitment for the organization was conducted among German refugees, and prisoners-of-war.

Noel Field recommended to Allen Dulles, who in turn recommended to General Donovan that OSS should avail itself of the good offices of the Free German Committee to recruit anti-Nazi Germans as intelligence agents for infiltration into Germany. Donovan accepted Dulles's recommendation, and it became OSS policy.

I learned of this quite fortuitously one day when Commander Tom Cassady, at that time in charge of the OSS Paris station, called me into a meeting at OSS headquarters, 79 Champs Elysees. As I entered his office, I noticed Noel Field. He was expounding to a group of OSS staff members, the advantages of accepting the offer extended by CALPO to furnish OSS with lists of candidates to be recruited as agents for infiltration behind enemy lines in Germany.

"These are all proven anti-Nazis," he was explaining. "We are the most qualified to assess their bona-fides. We would not recommend anyone about whom we were not absolutely sure."

I sat in silence.

After the meeting, I went in to see Tom Cassady. "Do you realize, Sir?" I said, "Noel Field is a Communist, and all the candidates he will recommend to us will also be Communists. Do we really wish to ensure that the whole of Germany become Communist after the war? Cassady was a naval officer. Previously he had been US Liaison with Vichy. He listened to me sympathetically. "Look," he said, "I don't make policy. We have received instructions to work with CALPO and use them as a source for agent recruitment."

"But sir," I protested, "This is utter madness."

"Look, Jolis," he replied, "As I said, I don't make policy. And for that matter, let me remind you, nor do you. These are orders."

I shifted uncomfortably. " Sir, with all due respect, I can't see myself going to CALPO to recruit Communist agents. I just can't do it. I won't do it. I'd rather resign from OSS."

"See here, Jolis," Cassady replied, " I don't wish to get into a political discussion on this matter. Even if I agreed with you it would make no difference. Orders are orders, and I should remind you that an officer on active duty does not enjoy the option of resigning, and that a refusal to obey orders can well lead to a court martial. I advise you to be careful."

I left Cassady's office badly shaken.

What to do? An idea slowly took shape in my mind. Would it work? It might be worth a chance. What is there to lose?

Out at our base at St. Germain-en-Laye, I was holding a young German Social Democrat in preparation for a mission. Some Social Democrats, though not all, were bitter opponents of the Communists. Hans was one of them. I now needed him for another mission.

"Hans," I instructed him, "You will go to the offices of CALPO in Paris and say you have heard they are recruiting anti-Nazi Germans for missions inside Germany, and you wish to volunteer. Don't tell them you are a Social Democrat, even though they may find out in time. Learn as much as you can without raising suspicions, and come back and report to me."

The Paris office of CALPO was under the direction of a woman called Herta Tempi, a Communist apparatchik, who had previously worked for the Unitarian Service Committee. She was Noel Field's mistress. Hans presented himself at the CALPO office and told the receptionist he was an anti-Nazi refugee and wished to speak to someone about volunteering. The receptionist told him to wait while she went to get Herta Tempi from the next room.

There was no on else in the outer office. The receptionist had been typing. Her desk was covered with sheets of paper. Hans looked more closely; they were lists of names! Making sure no one was returning from the next room, he quickly snatched up all the sheets from the desk and dashed out of the office into the street.

What he brought back to me proved to be lists of names of candidates who had been interviewed and were to be recommended as potential agents. What a fantastic piece of luck!

I went back to Tom Cassady and presented him with the list. "Here are your secret agents Sir. What kind of security will their missions enjoy, where anyone can walk in off the street and come away with their names?"

That was enough. Cassady took the list, smiled, "You're right'" he said. "Terrible security, we couldn't possibly risk our missions with such a sloppy show." I'll report back to London and Washington. He gave me a wink, and shook my hand. OSS Paris Station never used a single CALPO agent.

Unfortunately London and Stockholm did. American interests were not served.

*

If there was anyone else concerned about Communist penetration of OSS, or about the wisdom of doing Stalin's bidding in the prosecution of the war, I did not meet them; with the exception of one, namely Bill Casey. He was the only person I was able even to raise the question with. Bill understood the problem, and agreed to a great extent with my concerns, but he was shouldering huge responsibilities and was under massive pressure. Allen Dulles enjoyed unrivalled prestige and was considered well-nigh infallible. Bill Donovan listened to him. Moreover, the entire military and political establishment of the West had bought Joe Stalin's line. "We can do business with Uncle Joe, and any price is worth paying if it will shorten the war by one day."

If there was one other person who might have agreed with me on all this, it was James Jesus Angleton, but I never met Jim. He was in the counter-intelligence branch of OSS, known as X2. He understood the problem, and for that, in later years he was hounded and derided as an obsessive "kook" to the point of resignation from CIA by the establishment anti anti-Communists.

I too was considered a kook, constantly looking for Communists under the bed. This turned out to be more than a mere jest on one occasion.

Somewhere along the line I had been promoted to 1st Lieutenant, and now proudly wore my silver bar. But I always had higher ranks under my command. London had shipped over another officer to join my team. He was Captain Richard Watt. Dick Watt was a handsome "all American" college type from Chicago, in his middle twenties; an intelligent, likeable fellow. Before being transferred up to the Ardennes, he stayed in our base at Saint Germain-en-Laye, and occupied the cot next to mine in our crowded quarters.

One night, we lay awake talking into the early hours, discussing possible outcomes of the war. It was clear by now that somewhere, at some point, the United States Army would come face to face with the Red Army. We speculated as to "What Then?" Would it be peaceful? Would it be confrontation? All of a sudden, Dick Watt sat up in bed and said: "Bert, I'm terribly worried. If the U.S. and the Russians ever came into conflict, I don't know what I'd do."

"What do you mean, you don't know what you'd do?"

"Well, what I mean to say is, I'm not sure what side I'd be on?" answered Dick Watt.

"What!!" I shouted, and jumped out of bed. " Richard Watt, Captain United States Army, you don't know what side you'd be on? Do you know what you're saying? You're talking treason, my boy. Pretend you never said it."

I was deeply troubled. Here in truth was a case not of Communists under the bed, but on the bed! Useless to talk to anybody about it. Nobody had time to listen, and as I just said, I was not taken seriously on the subject.

The matter was passed over, but not forgotten. Dick Watt was pretty naive talking to me that way. I figured he was just a college radical, who would in time grow up. But its not the end of the story.

Following the end of hostilities, OSS set up a German headquarters at Wiesbaden, West Germany. Dick Watt joined the Wiesbaden complement. Erika Glaser, Noel Field's adopted daughter whom he had infiltrated into OSS Bern, now got herself transferred to OSS

Wiesbaden. As a German Communist this gave her unrivalled opportunity to advance Soviet interests. She was young and attractive. She spotted Dick Watt, and knew exactly what to do. As I just said, Dick was pretty naive. They had a flaming affair for exactly as long as it suited Erika, during which time she had every opportunity to serve the Kremlin well, and I am sure Dick Watt was happy to help her.

After Noel Field defected behind the Iron curtain, Erika followed, she was an integral part of his apparatus.

In 1965, Flora Lewis wrote about Noel Field in **Red Pawn** (Doubleday). She had this to say: "Thirteen years after the war, Nikita Kruschev could joke in Washington with CIA Chief, Allen Dulles, that they both used the same intelligence agents who were paid twice, so 'Why don't we get together and save money.'"

*

V.E. Day came and went. The war was over. When would I get home? One day I was summoned to a meeting of OSS "Washington top brass" in Wiesbaden. Present were, Richard Helms, Frank Wisner and Milton Katz. They wanted me to stay on and join the OSS postwar operation in Germany. I told them I wanted to get home, I had not yet seen my newborn son. They said OK, take a month's leave and then come back. I said no thank you. They said, half in jest, its your patriotic duty. I said, let me be the judge of my patriotic duty. They said, we need you here. I said, this Wiesbaden station is penetrated by the Soviets, I don't want any part of it. They raised their eyes to the ceiling. The meeting was over.

Had I agreed to go to Wiesbaden, I would probably have ended up in the CIA. But I am glad I didn't, and despite what some have assumed in subsequent years, I was never a member of the Agency. On the other hand, I was from time to time involved with it as an "outsider."

I maintained ongoing contact with Frank Wisner during 1949 and 1950 on a number of matters, notably, Soviet defections and repatriation of Soviet prisoners. I ran errands, carried cash, delivered messages, in the preparatory stages of The Congress for Cultural Freedom, which was about to be held in Berlin.

During the 1950s I had correspondence and discussions with Lyman Kirkpatrick in an effort to obtain Agency support for an African political leader from Ghana, Dr. K.A. Busia. This man was the leader of the opposition to Ghana's president, N'krumah, for which he had been driven into exile. He was anti-Communist and pro-West; he enjoyed significant support inside Ghana.

N'krumah, was being manipulated by the Soviets; he was drumming up support among Africans for Patrice Lumumba in the Congo; he was the leading spirit in the anti-American propaganda campaign in the Third World, which reached it's climax at the Bandung Conference in 1955.

I felt that anything that would reduce N'krumah's power and influence was in America's interest, and that consequently Dr. Busia deserved support. I knew Kirkpatrick from OSS days; he was a co-team mate in the Normandy beachhead. "Kirk" listened sympathetically to my story; we had meetings, real interest was expressed, we corresponded, we discussed, but in the end there was no help for Dr. Busia.

*

In later years, when returning from various business trips in Africa, having met with one or another African leader I would, from time to time, be interviewed by an Agency staff person. All pretty routine.

On one occasion though, at the Agency's request, I agreed to provide cover for one of their men as an employee of our mining operations in the Central African Republic. He was taken on as an accountant-bookkeeper. All went well at the outset. The man worked diligently for us, while at the same time maintaining secret contact with the station chief at the Embassy. No one in my company was aware of his identity. Then, one day, the foolish fellow went and blew his own cover! Instead of having his mail from home addressed to him care of our company, which was the normal practice for all company personnel, he had it addressed to himself care of the

American Embassy! We all ended up with egg on our faces, and I decided never to repeat such an exercise.

*

As I sit writing these words in 1994, the fiftieth anniversary of D Day is being celebrated in an unprecedented hoopla extravaganza. I watch the news clips of the landings and remember my own experience. I cannot help thinking of my two elder sons, Paul and Jack who saw service in Vietnam twenty-some years later. Paul was a 1st Lt. in the Green Berets, and Jack was a 1st Lt with Military Intelligence, working with the H'mong tribesmen, the Montagnards. They risked their lives fighting a totalitarianism just as evil as the Nazis. They were not given a hero's welcome when they returned. Why not? Because public opinion in the United States had been manipulated into believing it was a wrong war. It wasn't, it was the right war. The anti-war movement was masterminded and orchestrated by the Soviet apparatus using the same methods that were used during the Hitler-Stalin pact. At that time it was called The Keep America out of War Movement. But on June 22, 1941 when Hitler invaded the Soviet Union, World War II became overnight a "good war."

Any war against Communism, whether it be VietNam or Central America, was ipso facto a "bad war," and America's Fifth Column tele-guided by the Kremlin worked tirelessly for America's defeat.

That is why Paul and Jack were not given heroes' welcomes when they returned from Vietnam.

Just as, so many people could not bring themselves to accept that Alger Hiss was a traitor, and by the same token Noel Field also, until he defected, so do most of those who dodged the draft and protested the Vietnam war refuse to accept the possibility they might have been duped and manipulated. President Bill Clinton not only rejects such a possibility, he reaffirms, even today, his opposition to the Vietnam War, and hardly anyone dares remind him publicly that as a draft dodger and a war-protester he gave aid and comfort to the enemy. Watching him preside over the fiftieth anniversary celebrations of the D Day landings in Normandy, sickened me. I switched off the TV.

*

Receiving a Bronze Star Medal is very gratifying, though I was never sure what it was for. Nor do I feel I deserved the Croix de Guerre Avec Palme, but when, to my astonishment it arrived via The War Department in 1946, signed by French Premier, Georges Bidault, I was mighty proud, and have treasured it since.

CHAPTER TWENTY SIX

"WILD" BILL DONOVAN

I did not get to know General William J. Donovan well during the war, though I met him several times in the field. I was too low in rank. But as soon as I got out of uniform in 1946, I went to see him at his law office in New York, to voice my concern at the Communist penetration of OSS which I had encountered. The widespread recruitment of Communists as OSS agents in Italy, Greece and the Balkans, as well as Noel Field's plan for Germany, all of which had received Donovan's personal approval, had opened the door for Communist infiltration into the innermost workings of our intelligence establishment. I had no knowledge at that time of a fact I learned fifty years, namely, that in 1941, Donovan established a relationship with Milton Wolff, Commander of the Lincoln Brigade in the Spanish Civil War, and a dedicated American Communist, for the purpose of recruiting American Communists for intelligence purposes. This was revealed in a book published in 1995 by Yale University Press entitled The *Secret World of American Communism*, by Harvey Klehr, John Earl Hynes, and Fridrikh Firsov. What I had learned from personal experience was enough, I told Donovan I felt this was a disaster.

He listened to me with sympathetic interest, and I wondered if anyone had talked to him in this fashion before. In 1946 the Cold War had not yet erupted into the open, and in common with the prevailing sentiment of the time, Donovan had not been overly concerned with a post-war Soviet threat. It did not take long however, for him to see things differently. He caught on fast, and appeared grateful for what I told him. He told me to write and express my thoughts to Allen Dulles, which I did. But Dulles seemed impervious.

Donovan evidently liked me, and a warm mutual friendship developed. His law firm, Donovan, Liesure, Newton & Irvine became our corporate lawyers, and in a subsequent chapter, I describe how he helped us with our diamond problems in Africa.

I have always considered Bill Donovan to be the Billy Mitchell of World War II. During World War I, General Billy Mitchell had the greatest difficulty persuading the military hierarchy of the efficacy of air-power. They wouldn't listen to him. Bill Donovan had similar problems with Washington's top brass in World War II, trying to persuade them of the importance of "irregular" warfare; guerilla tactics, covert operations, behind the lines resistance, etc. The military establishment was not convinced, and Donovan was obliged to wage a continuing struggle in Washington on behalf of OSS.

Both men were vindicated only after their deaths, in the wars which followed; Billy Mitchell in World War II, when air power was decisive, and Bill Donovan during the Cold War when "covert operations" became the crucial weapon, so hated by the fellow-travellers and the anti-anti-Communists.

The story goes that Donovan earned the "Wild Bill" nickname during World War 1, when he became a national hero as Colonel in command of the "Fighting 69th," New York's own "Rainbow" division. The "Wild" had nothing to do with battlefield exploits, for which he earned the Medal of Honor. The "Wild," it seems, was more closely related to boudoir exploits. Whether or not this is apocryphal, I found Donovan, in his mid-sixties, somewhat rotund, with the bluest of blue eyes and a deceptively soft voice, a man of enormous Irish charm.

When I was living in Paris, Donovan would drop in for a visit when he was passing through, and my son Jack may remember the occasion, around 1952, when as a four year old, the General dandled him on his knee. This may have been the root of the youngster's hankering after the military life which he developed thereafter.

Donovan always travelled with his pretty blonde daughter-in-law, Mary. So much so, that it gave rise to a certain amount of whispering, for which there was not the slightest foundation. The family was beset by tragedy. He treated his daughter-in-law as a daughter, no doubt as a substitute for his own daughter, Patricia who died in a road accident aged 22. And Mary's own little daughter, aged 7, died from accidentally drinking a cup of silver polish which a maid had momentarily left unattended. Mary herself, became unhinged after this and committed suicide in 1955. Serial tragedy indeed. When Bill Donovan used to bring Mary to our apartment in Paris, she seemed a happy, charming and friendly girl.

If ever a man had earned the right to head up America's post-war intelligence establishment, it was Bill Donovan. But both Presidents Truman and Eisenhower thought otherwise, and I never knew why. It was a deep disappointment for him. Instead, Donovan was offered the ambassadorship to Thailand, which he accepted. Before taking up this post, always "soldiering on," he served with the War Graves Commission.

One night in Paris, I was awakened out of bed by a phone call from Bill Donovan. It was past midnight. He was calling from London.

"Bert," he said, "I need to talk to you. Could you hop over and have breakfast with me in the morning. I'm at the Claridge."

"Why sure, General," I replied, without thinking how on earth one could perform such a feat, given the late hour. I always called him General.

Without much sleep that night, I took the very first flight out of Paris, and arrived at the Claridge Hotel, in Brook Street, in time for breakfast. Announcing myself at the desk, I was invited to go up. There I found Bill Donovan standing in the middle of the room, in his pyjamas, with the floor all around him littered with scribbled and crumpled sheets of paper.

"Hey, Bert, am I glad to see you. I'm due to fly to Brussels in a couple of hours. From there have to drive to Bastogne and dedicate a new War Grave. I can't get my speech right. Give me a hand, there's a good fellow."

So we sat down and worked out his speech together. Of course he could have done it without me.

Bill Donovan died in 1957. I was able to visit him one last time at Walter Reed Hospital in Washington. He was too ill to speak or recognize me. He is buried in Arlington National Cemetery, the only man ever to win the four highest medals for gallantry and public service. Anthony Cave Brown, could not have found a more apt title to his biography of the general, ***Wild Bill Donovan, The Last Hero.***

CHAPTER TWENTY SEVEN

ALLEN DULLES

I never got to know Allen Dulles as well as I knew Bill Donovan, but I did have a number of meetings with him both during and after the war. He was a pipe-smoking, tweedy man with a ready laugh and an affable nature. He looked and behaved like an Ivy League college professor.

On most occasions, the topics we discussed had to do with my views on the Communist post-war threat, which he unfailingly pooh-poohed. But to be fair, he always did it in the most pleasant and friendly manner.

"Bert," he would say, "I think you're a bit too obsessive about this. I don't think the threat is nearly as great as you do. If and when the time comes, we'll be able to deal with it. Let us get the war over first, then we'll see. If you want my opinion, the Russians will have such a colossal task putting themselves back together when the war is over, they won't have time for anything else."

That conversation took place in April, 1945 when I was in Geneva trying to save the Russian nationalities leaders. Two months earlier, in February, Roosevelt and Churchill had handed over Eastern Europe to Stalin at Yalta, and though I was unaware of the terms of the Yalta Agreement, I knew Dulles was being far too sanguine. On the other hand, since he had his hands full with the German surrender in Northern Italy at the time, I could understand his insistence on "first things first."

The trouble was that all my conversations with Dulles reflected the same lack of concern with any Communist threat or Soviet post-war aims. He was a member of the East Coast liberal elite who considered anti-Communism to be rather primitive and excessive. It reflected above all, ignorance of Marxism-Leninism and a disinterest in it's tactics and methods. And when one realizes that this state of mind was shared by almost the entire Roosevelt administration, it is easy to see how a man like Noel Field, whom Dulles already knew socially, could insinuate himself into his confidence. It was the same state of mind after all, that refused to believe Alger Hiss was a traitor, even after the evidence was in. He had such an impeccable background, these people reasoned, it was just not possible.

Nevertheless, the defection of Noel Field behind the Iron Curtain in 1949, must have come as a rude shock to Allen Dulles. I was not in touch with him at that time, and do not know how he reacted. It surely must have shaken him. I suspect that if he had not already started to see the reality of the Soviet threat, this must have hastened the process. By 1951, in any case, it was brought home to me that Dulles was fully aware.

By this time, though not yet head of CIA, but nonetheless an active member of the intelligence establishment, he was focusing his attention on defections from the Soviet Bloc.

On one occasion, during a stopover in Paris in 1951, Allen Dulles called on David Bruce to discuss the topic. I was back in private business after a stint with the Marshall Plan, where I worked for Bruce. We had remained in friendly contact. Bruce invited me to join the discussion. The three of us sat in Bruce's office at the American Embassy.

Dulles was interested in devising a Defectors Program, a project that would encourage defections from Iron Curtain countries. This was a subject close to my heart. I told Dulles I thought our policy of Containment was not conducive to the success of such a program. Individual defections, yes; they would continue to occur from time to time, as they already had; but a Defectors Program, such as he was thinking of, implied a steady stream. Serious political defectors, I said, have only one aim, the liberation of their countries from the Soviet yoke. Our policy of Containment, I argued, means we have accepted the Soviet conquest of East Europe. For the people of East Europe, this means the United States has become an accomplice in their subjugation. With all hope lost, any defections, with rare exceptions, will have lost their political component, so that even if a "steady stream" did occur, it would do little to advance American interests.

The alternative to Containment, I argued, is not preventive war, it is a combination of great military strength in **defensive** posture with great moral and political strength in **offensive** posture.

Dulles asked me to set my thoughts down on paper, which I did in a letter addressed to him in Washington, dated January 11, 1951. (See Appendix No. 1)

Later that same year, I had further contact with Allen Dulles concerning Soviet political and strategic gains in Africa. Again, he asked me to put my thoughts on paper, which I did in a "Memorandum on Black Africa" in November, 1951. (See Appendix No. 3)

While always expressing an interest in my views, I have no illusion he ever shared them. On the contrary, he once said to Bill Donovan "Tell Jolis he's always looking for Communists under the bed." When the Cold War could no longer be avoided, it is my suspicion that he was at best a tepid cold warrior.

CHAPTER TWENTY EIGHT

HOME COMING

In discussing the early years of my marriage to Eva, I made only passing reference to her family. Since this was one of the factors that led to the eventual breakup of the marriage, the omission needs to be corrected.

Eva's mother, a French woman from the Auvergne, had died some years before I met her. The family now consisted of the father Frank Ortega, and five children; Eva the eldest, plus two boys, Frank, of draft age, though in poor health; and Louis about 16, a student at New York Military Academy; plus two twin sisters, Lita and Lucette, about ten years old. Also included in the household was the late mother's sister, Tante Antoinette. In theory, Tante Antoinette was supposed to excercise the role of surrogate mother, especially on behalf of the young twin girls; but in practice she didn't. She didn't do much of anything. The father, Frank was a happy-go-lucky, irresponsible fellow who paid little attention to raising his family. Each member was more or less unbalanced, and deficient in one or another essential human quality. They all lived together in noisy Latin disorder in a large apartment on West End Avenue. No one appeared to be in charge.

As a result, Eva, the only "normal one," had taken it upon herself to hold this disparate family together, and she did it with a fierce determination and concentrated effort, that left all else in her life in second place. I was warned of the dangers this presented for my future happiness, but at the outset of our marriage it did not seem to pose a major problem. I was confident it was something I could cope with. To put it differently, infatuation blinded me to reality. Returning from the war however, brought me up sharp.

I had been overseas two years, and had not yet seen my son. During that time, Eva had done a couple of things I found very upsetting, but which at the time I could do nothing about. Although war-time mails were going through, and we exchanged letters regularly, she acted unilaterally without prior discussion, or even informing me until after the fact.

She discarded the name of our firstborn son, which we had agreed upon after much discussion, and substituted another. This, you might say is not so major. No, it isn't. Even the fact that she threw in her family name Ortega, would have been alright if we had discussed it, but we hadn't. And when coupled with the other unilateral action she took, both took on huge importance to me at the time.

Before I entered the Army, we had established our home in a one-bedroom apartment on West 72nd Street, New York. We had furnished it jointly, and accumulated the usual amount of books, pictures, records, and other paraphernalia. This was the home to which I expected to return. But while I was overseas, without any advance hint, and at what moment I never knew, she liquidated our apartment and moved in with her family. This was where she expected me to rejoin her, once out of uniform. So right after my discharge, I had no choice but to move in to her family's West End Avenue apartment, – that is to say, with her father, her two brothers, her two sisters, and an aunt – each one of them, as I have said, more or less off-center. For Eva, this was quite normal. She was not only perfectly happy to have it this way, she had no thought of moving.

I knew then my marriage had been a mistake. I should have paid heed to my early doubts and the warnings of my family and brother. I consulted a lawyer. He told me I had no grounds for divorce, that my case was classic; all the boys coming home from the war were having trouble adjusting; that this would all work itself out. In other words, he was no help.

I presented Eva with an ultimatum. Either we move out of her family's apartment without delay, and find a home of our own, or I would leave her, divorce or no divorce. She resisted, but finally yielded. We bought a house in Syosset, Long Island. She never really enjoyed living out there, and never missed an opportunity to drive into the city to be with her family.

I wrestled for a long time with my doubts about the marriage. Was it going to work? On the one hand I now realized her family would be a permanent problem and that Eva's character and personality were not at all flexible. While she was warm-hearted, demonstrative, and gregarious, she was also very strong-willed. On the other hand, I was very much in love. She was the woman I wanted. And then there was now my son, Paul. I couldn't reconcile myself to the idea of turning my back on him, just walking away. I did not want to accept defeat. Surely, with determination and resolve, it could be made to work. After all, every marriage has to cope with in-laws; it's nothing new. I decided to ride it out. It had to work. And so it did, sort of, for the next 25 years. And Paul was followed by Jack and James and Alan.

By the end of 1945 I was back in the diamond business. My brother, Bernard had carried on under a draft exemption for a defense-related industry. He had been joined by my father and my mother's brother, Leon Couzyn. The business, now known as Diamond Distributors, Inc., had expanded significantly. Two new non-family partners had joined the firm, Paul Klein and Stephen Hoffman. I had a great deal of catching up to do.

1946 saw a new pattern of life develop. Our second son, Jack was born on June 19. I was now a full-fledged suburbanite, commuting daily to Manhattan. Old friendships were resumed, new ones developed.

I discovered that Bill Casey and his family lived in Roslyn, not far from our Syosset home. I had gotten to know Bill during the war, and though we shared many common views, we had never spent much time together. I was anxious to renew the relationship. This blossomed into a lifetime friendship, and our two families remained close ever since.

Then one day, an incident occurred which I will describe as the Alekseev story.

CHAPTER TWENTY NINE

THE ALEKSEEV STORY

Lydia and Ivan Tolstoy whom I had helped escape from the Kremlin's clutches in Paris, were now in the United States. They had taken up temporary residence at Reed Farm, in Connecticut, the establishment of Ivan's aunt, Countess Tolstoy. At Reed Farm, the good Countess had for many years, harbored an assortment of White Russians, recent immigrants, and the occasional defector. One day, Lydia, or Lily, as she now known, phoned to say she had to see Eva and me most urgently; that it was something that could not be discussed over the phone.

We met in Manhattan, and she told us that a major Soviet defector had unexpectedly shown up at Reed Farm; that his defection was not yet public knowledge; that Reed Farm was penetrated by the KGB (MVD), and that it was urgent he be taken away before being recognized.

This is the Alekseev story:

Alex Alekseev was Commercial Counsellor at the Soviet Embassy in Mexico City. In accordance with normal diplomatic rotation, he was due for reassignment in the Soviet Union. On the day of his departure, he was scheduled to present himself with his family at the port city of Vera Cruz, and board a Soviet ship for the return journey to Odessa. Alekseev packed his wife and two small children, plus bag and baggage into his car, and headed out of Mexico City. He had arranged to sell his car to another staff member who would take delivery at dockside.

But Alekseev did not take the eastbound road to Vera Cruz; instead, he drove north toward the U.S. border. It was an impulsive decision. Though he had toyed with the idea for some time, the trouble was he knew no one in the United States. He had only one contact, a Chicago-based businessman with whom he had dealings in Mexico City some years before, who told him if he ever came to the U.S. to look him up, and gave him his card.

Arriving at the Laredo border crossing, Alekseev passed through U.S. Immigration easily. He had a diplomatic passport and his car bore diplomatic plates. He was now free and clear in the United States. Driving north toward San Antonio, he wondered how long it would be before the Soviet Embassy noticed his disappearance. They surely knew it by now, he figured. The drive to Vera Cruz was only two to three hours; he had already been gone over twelve hours.

In San Antonio he stopped for gas, and telephoned his businessman friend in Chicago. He learned the number had been disconnected, and the name was not listed anywhere. Now he was in serious trouble. On the long drive north, he realized how ill considered and ill planned his defection had been. The KGB, by now must have a continent-wide alert out for him.

When night fell, the family checked into a roadside motel and registered under the name of Orlov. Nobody asked for their passports or other ID, what a country! He decided that New York, which he knew slightly from previous official visits, was safer than Washington, so, after a gruelling and desperate journey, he arrived in Manhattan without any fixed idea of where to go or what to do.

He parked his car on the upper West Side, and told the family to wait. Then, walking over to a newsstand, he picked out the two Russian language journals on display. Back in his car, he scanned the two journals to determine which had the more conservative slant; it was the **Novoye Russkoyo Slovo**. Then, noting the editorial office address on the masthead, he drove to the office building, and again told the family to wait in the car. When the editor received him, Alekseev announced that his name was Orlov, that he was a Soviet defector, and he didn't know where to turn.

The editor, whose name I don't recall, but it could have been Roman Gul, sat dumbfounded, but asked him no questions. Instead, he called his old friend Countess Tolstoy, who answered: "send them to me." So the Alekseev family drove to Reed Farm in Connecticut and introduced themselves as Orlov. The Countess took them in and gave them a room, where they bedded down for a hard-earned rest.

Next day, they met Ivan and Lily Tolstoy. Without disclosing his real name, nor where he came from, Alekseev confided to Lily that he was a defector, and that the KGB would surely be looking for him. Lily knew that Reed Fram was not secure. "That is why," she insisted when we met in Manhattan, "we have to get them out of there as soon as possible!"

So that same night, Eva and I drove up to Reed Farm in my old two-tone green Buick station wagon, picked up Alekseev with his wife, two children and baggage, drove them down to New York City, and parked them with Eva's family at West End Avenue.

That was the easy part. But now, what to do with them? The one person who I was sure would steer me in the right direction was Jay Lovestone, the former Communist, now bitter foe, whom I had approached several years earlier to help stem the desertion of allied seamen on the Eastern Seaboard. Jay directed me to a young lawyer called Robert Morris who had served in Naval Intelligence on General MacArthur's staff during the war, and who now had a private law practice in New York. Morris came to visit Alekseev next day, and told him the first thing to do was to hold a press conference and go public. Alekseev froze in horror. "Never!" he said, "then they'll surely get me." Bob Morris was patient. "Its just the reverse," he explained "if you don't go public they'll surely get you. Once you are a public figure its more difficult for them."

In the end a press conference was held. The media ran the story. The FBI and the CIA each had a go at Alekseev, after which they lost interest in him. The most difficult part was getting them off our hands. They stayed at the Ortega's West End Avenue apartment for months, while I struggled to find the man a job. Eva had managed to get the two little girls enrolled in a Spanish language Catholic school in the neighborhood under the name of Aguilar. (Aguilar and Orlov both mean eagle.) They all spoke Spanish from their sojourn in Mexico.

Alekseev was a coal engineer by profession, and not surprisingly, no one was looking for a coal engineer. None of the job interviews I managed to get for him with extreme difficulty, was good enough. He turned each one down with disdain. He was unable even to contemplate the idea of accepting a job below what he considered his rightful standing. Obstinate, ungrateful, and a snob to boot. I had already lost patience and was ready to turn the family out into the street, when a piece of luck got us out of the jam. I found him a job which he finally accepted at the Sikorsky helicopter plant in Connecticut.

Bob Morris went on to become Chief Counsel to the Senate Internal Security Subcommittee, and has remained a good friend ever since.

*

CHAPTER THIRTY

FRIENDS OF FIGHTERS FOR RUSSIAN FREEDOM

One day, a young man came to see me, through what recommendation I don't recall. He was an ex-GI, just out of uniform. Among his duties in occupied Germany had been participation in the program of forced repatriation of Soviet citizens in accordance with the agreement the Western Allies had made with the Soviets. He told horrendous stories of having to force unwilling displaced persons and ex prisoners-of-war at bayonet point on to railroad cars; of attempted suicides; of mothers throwing their babies to bystanders at the rail side so that they could remain in the free world. The experience had so traumatized him, he now wanted to do whatever he could to help these poor unfortunates escape. Could he volunteer his services to the International Rescue Committee?

The young man's name was Frank Barnett, who later earned national recognition as a lecturer and specialist on international affairs, as President of the National Strategy Information Center.

I decided the International Rescue Committee was not the right place for him. The IRC was operating under internationally approved refugee guidelines. This problem required more unconventional treatment. I talked to Bill Casey, and together with Lydia Tolstoy and Sheba Strunsky, we created an organization called Friends of Fighters for Russian Freedom, whose purpose was to save whoever we could from forced repatriation to the Soviet Union. We succeeded in raising enough funds to get started. Frank Barnett was our overseas director. Field offices were was established in Frankfurt, Munich, Hanover and Kaiserslauten. One sure method of avoiding forced repatriation was to prove you were not a Soviet citizen, and in pursuit of this end Frank Barnett displayed boundless ingenuity in the forging of false Polish and Serbian identity papers. Before our funds ran out, which was bound to happen sooner or later, we were able to document several hundred Russians as Poles or Serbs, and assist their emigration to South America, Canada and the United States.

The participation of the United States in the horror of forced repatriation, under the code name "Operation Keelhaul," is a shameful blot on our history.

My good friend, Robert Morris, in his book, *Self Destruct,* (Arlington House, 1979), had this to say, after the Senate Internal Security Subcommittee, of which he was General Counsel, held hearings on this episode in 1958:

"The essence of the story is that the United States, Great Britain and France forcibly returned, against their will, and contrary to the Geneva Convention and all the international accords, except the secret Yalta Agreement, about two million screaming and beseeching men, women, and children to Stalin's security police, who proceeded to punish them in forced labor camps or by execution.

The victims were beaten, bludgeoned, bayoneted, and doped as they were trucked off to their doom. And when Stalin received them, *Pravda* mockingly said, "It is a lesson all Russians must learn well. For it shows you cannot trust the capitalist states in the future."

Who was responsible for this infamous crime? The weakling (Secretary of State) Stettinius? The ailing Franklin Delano Roosevelt? Some advisor as yet unidentified? Or was this another of the contributions that Alger Hiss made to history?

We shall not know the answer until the relevant documents are declassified. It is high time that this be done. Secrecy should protect American security. It should not protect the reputation of men who disgrace the traditions of their country."

*

CHAPTER THIRTY ONE

I AM NOT A ZIONIST, OR AM I?

Once again, the reader may be forgiven for imagining that all I
was involved with in those days was Russians! And once again I
must repeat: "Not so."

In 1946 a major preoccupation and universal topic of conversation
was Palestine, Zionism and the Jews. The British mandate was still
in force; the State of Israel not yet born; shiploads of illegal Jewish
immigrants were being diverted to Cyprus by the British. The King
David Hotel in Jerusalem was blown up by Irgun terrorists, killing I
don't remember how many British soldiers.

American Jews in overwhelming numbers were pro-Zionist. A
few were not. I was one of the few. To me the argument seemed
irrefutable. The creation of an independent sovereign state of Israel
would confront every Jew in the world who decided not to settle
there, with a divided loyalty. It was impossible for all the Jews in the
world to settle in Israel, even if they wished to, and since the diaspora
was almost global, it was certain that sooner or later the national
interests of one country or another would be in conflict with those of
the new state of Israel. The question of divided loyalty was bound to
become a major problem in future years.

The Zionists had a simple answer. "But look at the Holocaust. If
this can happen in one country, who can guarantee it will never
happen again in another? If the Jews are to survive they must have
their own nation state."

But of course there was not then, anymore than there is today any
guarantee that a Jewish State would survive. The American Jewish

Committee, whose views I supported at the time, argued for resettlement and assimilation of the Jews in the free world.

These considerations spilled over into the diamond business. One day I was selling a parcel of industrial stones to a customer at our 40 West 40th Street office. After the usual back and forth over the price, a deal was agreed. As I was making out the sales slip, the customer said: "Yes, but I will only go through with the purchase if you make a contribution to Irgun." I was stunned. "What's that got to do with our deal? I asked. "It's got everything to do with it," answered the man, "You're a Jew aren't you?"

"Yes," I answered, "I'm a Jew, but I am an American. The Irgun are terrorists."

"You think you're an American," said my customer, "But the day will come when they won't want you here anymore. It will be just like Germany. Then what will you do?"

"I'll take my chances." I replied.

By this time our diamond deal wasn't going anywhere. To get it off dead center, I made him a proposal. "I will make a contribution to Irgun," I told him, "if you make an equal contribution to The International Rescue Committee."

"What's that?" he asked. "Never heard of it."

"Its an organization of which I am a director, that helps victims of totalitarianism, both Nazi and Communist. Many of these victims are Jews, but not all."

He looked at me, unconvinced, but finally we shook hands. Mazal – the deal was done.

Forty-eight years later, as I write these lines, the issue of divided loyalty no longer troubles me. The State of Israel is here, and has survived three wars and Saddam Hussein's Scud missiles. It is the only pro-Western free democratic society in a sea of nastiness. It's survival is a priority concern for the entire free world. Let us hope it can survive the badgering of successive U.S. Administrations, who persist in pressuring Israel into what in my opinion is an illusory "peace" with the Palestinians. As for abandoning the Golan Heights, it is madness.

CHAPTER THIRTY TWO

SOVIET DIAMONDS AND THE AMTORG SHUFFLE

Russia, today is one of the largest, if not the largest producer of diamonds in the world. It was not always so.

The first discoveries at Yakutia in Siberia were made in 1953, but major production did not come on stream until 1962. Up until that time, the Soviet Union was obliged to import all the industrial diamonds it needed for deep rock mining, oil drilling, tool-making, tungsten filament-wire-drawing, grinding-wheel dressing, and the host of other operations for which they are essential in modern industry.

One day, in 1947, a New York diamond broker, Sam Brodsky, called at my Diamond Distributors Inc. office at 40 West 40th Street, to inform me that the Soviet Government was in the market for a large quantity of industrial diamonds. He wanted to know if we would be interested in the contract.

"I have the connection," Sam told me. "If you are interested, I can get you the business."

My first impulse was to tell him I was not interested. I had no wish to trade with the Soviets. To me it was as unethical as doing business with Nazi Germany. My father had turned down profitable business opportunities with Germany after Hitler came to power, and rightly so. I saw no reason why I should treat commerce with Stalin any differently, and I was determined not to do so.

I said to Sam, "Yes, I am very interested. What kind of diamonds do they want? How big is the order?"

Sam's eyes lit up at the prospect of a fat commission. "I haven't all the details," he said, "you will have to come downtown with me to **Amtorg,** and I will introduce you." Amtorg was the Soviet trade office in New York.

The next day he escorted me downtown to the Amtorg office in the heart of the Wall Street financial center.

I was received by Victor Bessmertnyi, Amtorg's president, (not to be confused with Aleksandr Bessmertnykh, who later became Soviet foreign minister.) A clean-cut athletic looking blond man in his early forties, he had the unmistakeable bearing of an apparatchik bureaucrat.

He occupied a spacious office on one of the high floors. I could have been sitting in the president's office of any major finance house, except for one detail. On the wall behind his desk, hung...... and here my memory fails me, either a large portrait of Stalin, or two smaller portraits, of Lenin and Stalin. Whichever it was, I could not help smiling inwardly at the incongruity, as I looked through the window at the surrounding temples of finance and commerce, and then back at Stalin's moustached Georgian face.

Sam Brodsky had already prepared the terrain, so there was no need for me to introduce my firm. Victor Bessmertnyi stood up to greet me with a big smile, we shook hands, I handed him my card, and we got right down to business.

I asked him if I could examine the specifications of the proposed purchase, and these were soon brought in by an aide. The details and quantities were instructive. From the sizes and descriptions of the various categories of diamonds listed, I could tell which industries they were intended for. Ball-bearings was one of them. It was a large order, running, as far as I could mentally calculate to well over half a million dollars. This might not sound like much in 1996, but fifty years ago it was not to be sneezed at.

"Yes," I said to Bessmertnyi, "we can furnish this material, but it will take time to assemble. This is not an off-the-shelf proposition."

"How long?" he asked.

"From two to three weeks," I said. "Following reception of your confirming purchase order."

"Very good, I will see this is forwarded to you without delay."

At this point, dear reader, you might be asking yourself, "Why did the Soviets not buy their diamonds from De Beers? After all, they traded with the monopoly in massive fashion some fifteen years later, when they became major producers themselves?" And to that question, I have no satisfactory answer.

As promised, two days later the purchase order arrived, and my partners were delighted at the unexpected and profitable transaction it heralded. But when I explained to them I had no intention of filling it, and gave them the reason why, they stared at me in open-mouthed disbelief. "You're stark raving mad," exclaimed my brother, Bernard, "you have accepted an order from a foreign government, and now you say you will refuse to deliver. How do you propose to do that?

I had it figured out.

Industrial diamonds were a strategic material. During World War II they were on the prohibited list for export to Axis countries. After the war the United States government initiated a program of buying industrial diamonds for the National Stockpile. Man-made diamonds had not yet been developed. In 1947, there was no interdiction against selling diamonds to the Soviet Union. I strongly felt there should be.

I went to see Bill Donovan at his Wall Street law office, Donovan, Leisure, Newton, Lombard & Irvine.

I showed him the Amtorg order, and explained I was not going to fill it. "How can we get industrial diamonds put on the prohibited export list?" I asked Donovan. He was immediately responsive, and called up David Bruce in Washington. Bruce was at that time Assistant Secretary of Commerce. "Go and see David," advised Donovan.

It was three years since I had seen David Bruce, when as heard of OSS London station, he was my commanding officer. He greeted me most warmly, but showed considerable surprise when I explained my business.

"I don't know the answer to this, Bert," he said after looking at the Amtorg order. It seems to me there's nothing to stop you from going ahead and filling the order."

"But that's exactly what I don't want to do," I explained, "I have two to three weeks before being called upon to deliver; surely that allows enough time for diamonds to be put on the prohibited list."

"Hmm," said Bruce. "Look, Bert, you better go and talk to the man who is more familiar with these details than I am." And he buzzed his intercom to inform some official whose name I don't recall, of my purpose. Then with his usual disarming charm, he stood up, grasped my hand and said: "Great to see you Bert. Stay in touch."

I wandered down the corridors of the Department of Commerce until I found the right door. Once again I produced the Amtorg order. And once again I was told. "It's OK, you can go ahead and fill it; there's no interdiction." And once again I implored, "But that is exactly what I don't want to do. Is it so difficult to understand? I want you to tell me I can't."

The way the man looked at me, I could see he thought I was not all there.

"Mr. Jolis," he said, "These are complicated matters. We have an inter-departmental committee that examines these questions, commodity by commodity. The next meeting will be in about a month and a half. The best I can do for you is to bring it up then. Thank you for your trouble."

Utterly frustrated, I returned to New York.

The problem now was how to extricate myself. After vainly searching for an elegant exit, I concluded there was none. Sam Brodsky, the broker, phoned me every day to ask how I was making out with assembling the material. I temporized as long as I could, while Sam got more and more agitated. "It's tough, Sam," I told him, "I'm having real trouble with those specifications."

"But you said they were OK," protested Sam, as he saw his commission fast evaporating."

"I know I did," I answered lamely.

The end came when, with egg on my face, I wrote a letter to Amtorg advising them that their specifications were too stringent and we wouldn't be able to meet them.

"Goddam fool!" exploded my partners.

My brother, Bernard took me aside and said: "You know, Bert, you have to decide. You are either in business or you're in politics. If you try to do both, you'll only get in a mess."

Well, I did do both. In due course, diamonds were put on the prohibited list; though not soon enough to save my face at the time.

*

Years later, after the Soviet Union became a major diamond producer, many opportunities to trade with them came my way. I always refused. On one occasion I was approached by Occidental Petroleum, Armand Hammer's company, to join with them in a joint diamond venture. If anyone had the inside track with the Soviet Government, it was they. It could have been a most profitable venture. I turned it down.

CHAPTER THIRTY THREE

THE MARSHALL PLAN

Shortly after the Amtorg episode in 1947, I received a telephone call from David Bruce. "Can you come on down to Washington," he said. "I'd like to talk to you." He was still Assistant Secretary of Commerce.

Seated in his office the next day, he informed me: "I have been appointed to head the Marshall Plan Mission to France," and I'm in process of recruiting my team. How would you like to come along?"

"I'm flattered you should ask me," I told David Bruce " the only trouble is that I am not an economist, and don't know a thing about government finances, economic planning and so forth."

"Don't worry," he told me, "I've got people for that. You know your way around France and you know the French. That, plus some common sense and basic intelligence will get you through. I'm sure you will be a help. You should count on this taking one to two years out of your life."

It sounded a lot more exciting than the diamond business, so I said: "Sure, I'd be happy to come along."

So, in early June, with our Syosset home rented, I sailed for France on the SS. New Amsterdam; accompanied by Eva and the two boys, four year old Paul, and one year old Jack, and Celina Belmonte, the Colombian nanny. The day after arrival in Paris, I reported at the American Embassy on the Place de la Concorde, and was assigned my place of work.

France was slowly putting itself back together, rebuilding its damaged towns and cities, restoring railroads, utilities and communications; all thanks to the money poured in through the

Marshall Plan. For a while this made Americans wildly popular, and it was just like the Liberation all over again.

But just as it happened after the Liberation, when the euphoria wore off, so did American popularity. By the Fall of 1944 we were hearing French criticism of the vulgarity of the average GI, his sloppy appearance, and his lack of respect for his own officers, his general rowdiness. Then when Von Rundstedt launched his counter-offensive in the Ardennes, and almost broke through to Antwerp, when Patton stopped him at Bastogne, Americans suddenly became popular again.

Now it was the same with "Le Plan Marshall." Daily editorials filled the French press, praising the generosity of the American people, until the moment came some months later, when we heard the first grumblings about "Coca Colonization." One of the pet criticisms of Americans at the time was that they understood nothing about good food and cooking; all they knew was how to eat out of cans. The subject was likely to come up at every dinner party. On one occasion, I was pleased to point out to the dinner guests that the French were putting pate-de-foie-gras and sardines into cans before the Americans even thought of it.

The Communists were riding high in 1947. When a series of strikes almost shut down the country, the Communist Party in the industrial north around Lille, issued their own currency! Speculation was rife as to when or whether they would take over the whole country.

My work at the Embassy included receiving visits from a steady stream of French businessmen with propositions for which they were seeking Marshall Plan aid. The proper channel was for them to go through our opposite numbers in the French government, but they thought they'd have a better chance coming to us directly. It never worked. Some of the propositions were truly extraordinary.

I remember the most notable. It consisted of a scheme to divert the Congo River, so that instead of flowing west into the Atlantic, it would flow north into the Mediterranean. The man brought with him stacks of maps, graphs, drawings, and tables, showing how this could be done. The plan was nothing if not visionary. The diversion would start at the river's northernmost point about two hundred and fifty miles west of Stanleyville (today, Kisingani). Then a series of locks would raise the water level to that of the Tchad plateau. From there it would flow north across the Sahara, detouring the Tibesti mountains, and empty into the Mediterranean between Benghazi and Tripoli, in Libya. The profile was precisely calculated at every step. The scheme would turn vast tracts of Sahara desert into productive agricultural land. And at its terminus, hydro-electric installations would provide enough electric power to all of Southern Europe. He even produced a detailed cost estimate!

For a nation that produced Jules Verne and Ferdinand de Lesseps, this I thought, was true to form. Too bad it had to be shelved! All those maps and charts are no doubt moldering today in some Ministry's archives, waiting to be resurrected some time, if ever.

In the 1980s, 40 years later, my son Alan, then working for the Mobil Corporation, came across a similar project, promoted by a dubious Middle Eastern businessman. The story made it into a UPI dispatch, but has not been heard of since. Could it be the same?

Meeting with French government officials was always a challenge, not confrontational so much as linguistic. David Bruce would lead his team across the river to the Quai d'Orsay, and there we would sit around a huge table in the gilded Foreign Office chamber, face to face with the French team, headed by Hervé Alphand. The meetings were mostly technical, dealing with such arcane matters as inflation, currency supply, gross national product, and so forth. US Treasury Department economists on our team would present the American viewpoint, and the French would answer. It was then that I realized why Anglo-Saxons have always found it difficult dealing with the French. The French are so maddeningly articulate! They simply had the unerring ability to out-talk us on every point.

After such a meeting, I would confide in Bruce: "I don't think we came out so well, David. We bring the money, and they out-talk us. I mean, we hardly got a word in."

"Don't worry" he would answer. "It will all come out all right. The French love to talk, they just have to talk; its the national pastime."

Hervé Alphand later became French Ambassador in Washington, and David Bruce, American Ambassador in Paris.

The underlying principle on which the Marshall Plan worked went something like this, in broad outline:

The United States would make available to the recipient country a given amount of dollars, which could be used for hard currency needs. At the same time, the recipient country would set aside out of it's own budget the local currency equivalent of the dollars, and place them in a special fund known as "Counterpart Funds." These funds were earmarked for approved reconstruction projects. A small portion of the Counterpart Funds were reserved for special use by the US Government. One of these special uses was the development of strategic minerals for Washington's National Stockpile.

The French Franc zone included Morocco. Morocco was a producer of lead. Lead was one of the strategic minerals of interest to Washington. The biggest lead producer in Morocco was a French company in which a minority interest was owned by American stockholders among whom was Margaret Biddle of the Philadelphia Biddle family. Margaret Biddle was a serious player in the Paris social scene. The French lead company was seeking Marshall Plan aid to develop its mining properties.

All this is but a preamble to an evening I spent as a dinner guest at Margaret Biddle's luxurious apartment on the Quai de Conti. It was a seated dinner; place names; four tables each seating five. I was placed at Margaret Biddle's table, which to my astonishment included the Duchess of Windsor. Dinner conversation was easy, since the Duchess did all the talking. The impression I retained was that of a hard woman; sharp featured hard face, harsh voice, brittle laugh. She kept referring to her husband as "The Dook"; not "Teddy" or "Eddie" or "my husband." It was "The Dook wasn't with me on that occasion... " or "The Dook told me......" I felt sorry for the Dook.

Working with David Bruce was a real pleasure. Tall, handsome, and urbane; he was a courteous Virginia gentleman – a real charmer. On one occasion he invited me to join him at lunch with André Malraux, who at that time was beating the drums for General de Gaulle, then in the opposition. I was hoping for some fascinating conversation, but there was none. I tried to steer it more than once into such avenues as: "How do you feel about the Communist threat in France?" or "What about East Europe?" but Malraux wasn't having any. All he wanted to talk about was how much better De Gaulle would run the country. It was rather a dull lunch, and I was disappointed.

Sitting at my desk at the Embassy, I got my first taste of bureaucracy from the inside. Up till now I had only seen it from the outside. The daily staff meeting; the "in" basket; the "out" basket; buck the memo on its journey down the distribution list; the weekly report; sign for this; sign for that; the pecking order. Nothing like this happened in the diamond business; not in ours at any rate.

One day a cable crossed my desk that was anything but routine. It came from the American Embassy in Teheran, addressed to Washington and all American diplomatic posts. It concerned a man who had just turned himself in as a Soviet defector, and who claimed to be "El Campesino." Teheran had no way of verifying whether the man's claim to be "El Campesino" was true or not, and was asking for assistance.

"El Campesino" had been one of the leading Communist military leaders in the Spanish Civil War. The Party apparatus had built him up in a worldwide publicity campaign as a "peasant military genius." He was one of the international stars of Communist folklore on a par with La Passionaria. At the war's end he had fled to Moscow.

I grabbed the cable and ran down the hallway to the office of Norris Chipman, the Embassy's political officer, a good personal friend, and politically very savvy.

"Look," I said to Chipman, "I have a fail-safe way to determine whether this man is or is not "El Campesino""

Chipman did not speak, but his eyes said: "Yes? Go on."

"It is Julian Gorkin," I said. "Give me a few hours and I'll bring you the answer."

I had met Julian Gorkin through my friend Pepe Escuder. He had been a colleague of Andres Nin and one of the leaders of the POUM in Barcelona. He now lived in Paris and was a "regular" among my circle of anti-Communist friends, along with Manes Sperber, well-known author-psychologist and student of Jung.

When I told Gorkin of the contents of the cable, he bristled with excitement. "El Campesino' was the presiding judge at the Communist Party Tribunal that sentenced me to death", he said. "Only Franco's victory saved me from the firing squad. I could identify 'El Campesino' blindfolded in a dark tunnel."

Norris Chipman fired cables to Teheran and Washington, and soon arrangements were made for Julian Gorkin to meet with and confirm the identity of "El Campesino" in a safe house in West Germany.

When El Campesino fled to Moscow at the end of the civil war, he was given a hero's welcome. He was installed in privileged conditions at the Frunze Military Academy, where he gave lectures on his exploits in the Spanish war. But the hero's welcome did not last, as his propaganda value to the Comintern faded. Soon he was a forgotten man. This did not sit well with him. He fretted and fumed, and finally, nine years after arriving as a hero, he decided he'd had enough of the socialist paradise.

The meeting between "El Campesino" and Julian Gorkin in the safe house was dramatic. As Gorkin entered the door, the other stared in disbelief, then froze in horror. He shrank against the wall and attempted to flee the room. He was convinced Gorkin had come to kill him. Why not? After all, he had sentenced Gorkin to death. For two days he refused to talk, until finally Gorkin was able to persuade him it was not his death he was seeking, but his story.

"El Campesino's" defection was big news, and was a propaganda defeat of no small significance for the Kremlin in 1948, particularly among the hundreds of thousands of Spanish refugees still in France at that time.

*

A happy circumstance made it possible for us to move into a splendid apartment upon arrival in Paris. While still in the United States awaiting my travel documents, a Paris-based friend of my father, Mario Pinci, phoned him one day. "Jack," he said, "I have a great opportunity for you. How would you like to have an apartment in Paris?"

"I don't need an apartment in Paris," replied my father.

"But you don't understand," continued Mario Pinci, "apartments are extremely hard to find, and this is an extraordinary opportunity."

Then my father had a genial idea. "Come to think of it," he said, "my son Bert is planning to join the Marshall Plan in Paris. He'll need a place to live. I'll put him on to it."

So it happened that on arrival in Paris we were able to move into 10 Avenue Foch, a prestigious residence in a prestigious location. Ancient plumbing and faulty wiring, to be sure, but a huge living room and dining room, and a magnificent view of the chestnut trees on the broad avenue out front and a glimpse of the Arc de Triomphe to the left. Starting out as a sub-let, then a straight lease, and finally ownership, it has remained in the family ever since.

It was the all-time good life while it lasted; a diplomatic job with no worries, living like a king in the beautiful city of Paris. My marriage which had caused such worries a couple of years earlier, for now at least, seemed relatively placid. Having Eva's family safely on the other side of the Atlantic did a lot to help. The troubles ahead were not yet imminent.

*

On December 1, 1948, our third son, James was born at the American Hospital in Paris. It is a hoary cliché to observe that all newborn babies look like Winston Churchill, they nearly always do. But Jimmy was different. To me he looked more like W.C. Fields. A very handsome W.C. Fields, to be sure, but not Winston Churchill. There are now three boys in the family! James would have the option at age twenty-one to choose French nationality, having been born on French soil. That he did not do so when the time came, hardly surprised us; he was too busy touring the world as a singer and arranger with the Barry Manilow show, and by now infinitely better looking than W.C. Fields.

CHAPTER THIRTY FOUR

DAVID BRUCE

We were frequently in the company of David and Evangeline Bruce. The beautiful Evangeline Bell, who had so stunned me as a young OSS officer when I walked into 10 Grosvenor Street, London, in 1943, to report to my commanding officer, Colonel David Bruce, was now the beautiful Evangeline Bruce.

Our sons, Paul and Jack, would go horse-riding at a riding school in the Bois de Boulogne with the Bruce children, Sasha and David. All four of them also attended the Mc. Jannet Summer Camp at Talloires on Lake Annecy. On one occasion, it happened that David and Evangeline were visiting their children at the same time Eva and I were visiting ours. Unknown to each other, we both landed at the Hotel de l'Abbaye, a beautiful converted 17th Century Benedictine monastery on the shores of the lake.

Dining together that evening on the terrace we talked about everything, and especially what was going on in France. I held forth about "the treason of the intellectuals" – people like Jean-Paul Sartre, Simone de Beauvoir, Louis Aragon, and others who were all following the Communist Party line. I also berated the American liberals who were uncritically glorifying these same people. David listened, but did not say much. But I noticed Evangeline getting rather nervous. I should have stopped there, but I didn't. I went on to say there were serious intellectuals in France who were not in accord with the Communist line like Raymond Aaron, David Rousset, Daniel Benedite, Manes Sperber and Arthur Koestler, and it was too bad that American liberals did not give them the same accolades they gave to the likes of Simone de Beauvoir. I had obviously overstepped the limits, because Evangeline's distress had mounted to the point where she quietly excused herself from the table.

It was no use kicking myself under the table, it was too late. Before attacking American liberals, I should have remembered that Arthur Schlesinger Jr., American liberalism's high priest, was among Evangeline's closest friends. David retained his charming diplomatic good humor. The incident was forgotten. Bruce did not hold strong views on Left and Right, and was certainly not a "liberal" as that term is currently used. He was a non-ideological Virginia Democrat and a social patrician. But as a Truman appointee, he could not fail to reflect some of the New Deal positions. Nonetheless, he was open-minded and gentlemanly enough to listen to my frequently-voiced anti-Communist opinions, and even show interest.

When my Marshall Plan stint was about to terminate, David Bruce told me that there was an opening for chief-of-mission at the Marshall Plan mission in Brussels. Would I like him to put my name forward? I thought about it, but concluded that if I accepted, it would probably lead to further assignments of a similar nature in due course. I didn't quite see myself as a middle-level bureaucrat as a final career. I thanked Bruce and declined.

In the summer of 1949 we sailed back to New York, again on the SS. New Amsterdam. One of our co-passengers was William Saroyan, an amiable and jolly shipboard companion.

*

Some twenty four years later, tragedy befell the Bruce family. Daughter, Sasha, now 29, was found dead at the family home in Virginia. It was ruled a suicide, but circumstantial evidence pointed to murder, by her husband, Marios Michaelides, a Greek businessman. When I learned of this shocking news, I wrote to David and Evangeline in Brussels, where David was serving as United States Representative on the North Atlantic Council.

I received the following reply:

January 21, 1975

My dear Bert:

The sympathy of such an old and valued friend is a deep comfort to Evangeline and me. It was for us a distressing and inexplicable tragedy. I am resigning next month, and intend to return directly to Washington on February 1st, with hope and expectation of spending some time in Europe in late Spring. Never again do I wish to be limited to a total per annum of two or three days in Paris.

I have many things to discuss with you when we meet. You must be highly disturbed over what is happening in Angola.

With love from us both to you and the family,

Evangeline and David.

David Bruce died in 1977 at age 79.

CHAPTER THIRTY FIVE

BACK AGAIN TO DIAMONDS

First, a mini-refresher on the diamond industry. Whoever controls the source of raw material controls the industry. By source I mean the output of rough diamonds from the mines. Since the 1920s, the De Beers Corporation has controlled some 80% of the world's rough diamond production. As a result, fierce competition has raged in the trade to secure a share of the remaining 20%. Those fortunate enough to own or control a portion of the 20% of "independent" production, enjoy a double benefit. Such production is free of the monopoly constraints which De Beers imposes on it's 80%; while at the same time it enjoys the benefit of the pricing umbrella which De Beers is able to establish through its monopoly.

The discovery of a new diamond field is a major event in the diamond world.

In the 1930s a French company called La Compagnie Minière de l'Oubangui Oriental (CMOO,) was mining gold in the colonial territory of French Equatorial Africa. One day, around 1936, a prospector panning in a river bed in the Oubangui Province, found a dark greenish-brown stone in the gold clean-up. He had no idea it was a diamond, in fact he didn't know what it was, but he kept it. In the following days more similar type stones were found in the same river bed. The mine manager, unable to identify them, (no diamonds had ever been produced in French Equatorial Africa,) shipped the stones to Paris along with the monthly gold shipment.

At the Paris head office no one could identify the stones either. Though diamonds were suspected, no one could be sure. However, one of the directors had a friend who, he assured CMOO management, could help them. His name was Mario Pinci, about whom a good deal more will be said later.

Pinci was not a diamond man, he was a pearl trader. But he took the stones to show a friend in Antwerp, a certain Frans Raeymaekers who *was* a diamond man, and who identified these unprepossessing greenish-brown stones as diamonds, and not of bad quality either. This was sensational news. Raeymaekers called his friend Jac Jolis, then in London. Jolis flew to Paris, contacted Pinci, saw the stones for himself and asked for a meeting with the Board of Directors.

The CMOO Board was composed of elderly French "colonials," and "finance" men from La Banque de L'Indochine, the company's major stockholder. CMOO's president, Colonel Eduard Benedic, had spent most of his life in Morocco as an aide-de-camp of Maréchal Lyautey. All of which is to say, none of them had the faintest notion of what was involved in these strange-looking brown stones.

Jolis told them. He did more. He offered to be their diamond consultant on production and marketing strategies. With his credentials in the industry beyond dispute, the Board did not hesitate, the Jolis offer was accepted. CMOO was a publicly-owned corporation and its stock was traded on the Paris Bourse. Jolis bought stock.

Up to this point, there was no diamond *production*. There was only a small quantity of accidental prospecting finds. The company now undertook a systematic prospecting campaign to determine the existence of a commercial deposit.

Jolis waited, and followed the prospecting reports with intense interest. In 1939, his minority stock interest had grown significantly, and he was elected to the Board of Directors. Then World War II broke out. There was still no commercial production.

When the German armies occupied all of France north of the River Loire in 1940, the attitude of it's colonies was ambivalent. While French West Africa threw its support to the Pétain Government in Vichy, French Equatorial Africa rallied to General de Gaulle in London. As a consequence, all communications between the Paris headquarters of CMOO and its mining properties in Equatorial Africa were cut off, and the mines were obliged to carry on under the sole responsibility of the local mine manager.

The prospecting campaign was starting to show positive results, and a small but regular production was beginning. The mine, cut off from its normal source of funds, urgently needed current working capital. Only the proceeds of the diamond production could supply this, but where to sell it?

General de Gaulle's Free French Committee in London had extended it's rule over those colonies which had rallied to De Gaulle's appeal. The Governor General of French Equatorial Africa who sat in the Governor's palace in Brazzaville, now depended for policy directives on the French "Government-in-exile" in Carlton Gardens, London, a stone's throw from Buckingham Palace. De Gaulle, in turn was subject to the dictates of the British Board of Economic Warfare.

As a result, during the entire duration of the war, the diamond production of CMOO, which was increasing steadily, was shipped to London. Here, as you will not be surprised to learn, it was marketed through De Beers. For De Beers, this was perfectly normal, all diamond production was expected as a matter of course, to flow through it's Central Selling Organization.

So normal in fact, did De Beers consider this arrangement, that they fully expected it to remain uninterrupted following the conclusion of the war.

In 1945, when the Paris office of CMOO was able to reestablish normal communication with its African mining properties, the question arose whether or not to continue the marketing arrangements with De Beers. Jac Jolis, still a member of the Board, who in the interim had transferred his activities to New York, stressed the advantages for CMOO to market its production in the United States through the Jolis family company, Diamond Distributors Inc. The Board hesitated and deliberated for many months.

The matter had still not been settled by early 1946. By that time I was out of uniform and back "in the business." General William J. Donovan, also back in civilian life, had resumed his Wall Street law practice. I went to see him. The "diamond story" fascinated him. He agreed to help.

At the request of Jac Jolis, a special meeting of the Board of CMOO was called. Bill Donovan accompanied Jolis to the meeting, and endorsed the latter's previous representations as to the advantages that would accrue to CMOO, by switching to Diamond Distributors Inc. Not least among these were better prices for their diamonds, and hard currency earnings for the procurement of mining equipment. The Board, whose hesitation had been caused by fear of bucking the monopoly, a fear echoed by bureaucrats in the Ministry of Overseas France, was finally persuaded. The presence of the former head of OSS in support of Jac Jolis was the clincher. A marketing agreement with DDI was approved. I was present at the meeting "by invitation."

De Beers, to put it mildly, was not happy. Ernest Oppenheimer, it's chairman, phoned Jac Jolis to voice his displeasure. DDI was among the largest clients at the Central Selling Organization's monthly "sights." An expression of unhappiness by De Beers carries with it the implied threat of a boycott. "Turn your interest over to us," demanded Oppenheimer. A flat refusal by Jolis would have triggered such a boycott. Jolis temporized – he didn't say yes, he didn't say no. In the end, the boycott was applied anyway. DDI was eventually cut off from any further dealings with De Beers. This caused major financial distress for DDI, and obliged us to seek the help of the United States Government. At Washington's request, the U.S. Embassy in London expressed it's concern to the British Board of Trade, as a result of which trading relations were grudgingly resumed, and feelings remained ruffled for years.

In fact, they remained ruffled until the death of my father in 1953, and the death of his former partner, Otto Oppenheimer, which had occurred a year before. Subsequently, I visited Philip Oppenheimer, Otto's son, who now headed De Beers Central Selling Organization, and who later received a knighthood from the British Government. I had known Philip as a teenager in England. We had been friends. I tried to persuade him that the battle over the Oubangui diamonds was now a thing of the past, only of interest to the older generation, now sadly, no longer with us. We should patch it up, I urged. Our French African diamond production was too small to pose any threat to De Beers, and besides it furnished a "safety valve" argument against the mounting clamor of anti-monopoly sentiment in the post-war world. My efforts to convince him succeeded only half way. He was unwilling to agree there was any merit at all in tolerating even the smallest amount of independent diamond production, but on the other hand, he was willing in our case, to let bygones be bygones. Thereafter, we resumed full and friendly trading relations with De Beers, though they were never altogether happy at our continual itch for independence.

But that was by no means the picture when I returned to New York in 1949, following my stint with the Marshall Plan. We were at daggers drawn with De Beers, and my colleagues at DDI figured the best contribution I could make to the family business would be to return to Paris and nurse along our independent African diamond interest at CMOO.

Before doing so, I was summoned to appear before a Grand Jury in New York, in connection with the US Department of Justice "Anti-Trust" action against De Beers. The Justice Department was attempting to show that De Beers was engaged in business activity on American soil through captive sales outlets. Our resistance to pressure against turning over our CMOO interest to De Beers, and the resulting boycott to which we were subjected, was sufficient evidence that at least our firm DDI was not a "captive."

Eventually, a "Consent Decree" was signed under which De Beers agreed not to do business in the United States.

We were only back in our Syosset home for a year, when we sailed once again for France, and resumed residence at Avenue Foch.

This time it was for the long haul – nearly twenty years. Jac Jolis resigned from the CMOO Board and I was elected in his place.

CHAPTER THIRTY SIX

HEART OF DARKNESS

The map of colonial Africa used to be dotted with cities, towns and locations named after the nineteenth century explorers and empire builders who carved up the continent for the European powers. But nowadays, since the end of the colonial era, most of these places have been renamed out of a desire to stamp out the memory of colonialism. Rhodesia became Zimbabwe, Leopoldville became Kinshasa, Stanleyville became Kisingani, Fort Lamy became N'Djamena, just to name a few. But somehow, Brazzaville has remained Brazzaville. Has anyone ever thought to ask why? Perhaps the explanation can be found in a passage from Thomas Pakenham's book, °The Scramble for Africa" (Weidenfield & Nicolson-London,1991):

People found Pierre Savorgnan de Brazza a strange kind of Frenchman. It could be questioned whether he was French at all. He spoke in a sing-song voice with a strong Italian accent. He had been brought up in Rome, the seventh son of an Italian nobleman from Udine, Count Ascanio Savorgnan de Brazza, who had influential connections in France and a cultivated mind, including a taste for romantic novelists such as Sir Walter Scott. From boyhood young Pietro (as he then was) was obsessed with exploration. With the encouragement of his father, his Jesuit schoolmasters in Rome and a family friend who happened to be a French admiral, he joined the French naval school at Brest. He won a commission as an ensign, and came to Africa. In 1871 the "Jeanne d'Arc", one of the South Atlantic fleet, ferried reinforcements to Algeria where tribesmen of

the Kabyles had rebelled against French rule. He was shocked to see
French troops shooting down the insurgents.

At this time, 1875, Brazza was a coltish, awkward, taciturn boy of
twenty-three, with a long aristocratic nose and large brown eyes.
His resourcefulness did him credit and so did his idealism, naive as
it often was. At Lope he was awoken by the cries of a slave begging to
be rescued from a cruel master. Brazza bought the slave for 400
francs; the going rate was a ten-centimes string of beads. Of course
he was then besieged by other slaves begging to be redeemed – no
doubt prompted by their masters. So he hoisted the tricolour flag in
his camp and told the astonished Africans that by touching the flag
they could win their freedom, as France did not recognize slavery.
The magic worked. But Brazza was saddened to find that most of the
slaves wanted to return to the relations who had sold them originally.

Throughout his career, Brazza fought to expose and curb the
brutal treatment of Africans by the concession holders who were
exploiting the natural resources, such as rubber and timber. In 1905,
deathly sick, he was repatriated to France, but he never arrived. At
Dakar he was taken ashore to the Mission hospital, accompanied by
a colleague, Felicien Challaye, a writer for **Le Temps.** Pakenham
quotes Challaye:

Four sailors carried Brazza off the boat at Dakar. By now he was
clearly dying, his body stiff and emaciated, his eyes fixed and glassy,
the bristles white on his shrunken cheeks. Challaye went to the
stretcher and shook his hand for the last time. Many of the mission
wept – and not merely for themselves. Africa, too, had lost a leader:
one of the few imperialists revered by Africans, a man whose name
would symbolize a new kind of chivalrous imperialism – so Challaye
ventured to hope – the only kind compatible with a democracy like
France, a real mission to civilize Africa and set it free.

Is this why Brazzaville remains Brazzaville to this day?

*

In 1950 I took my first trip to French Equatorial Africa. I did not sail up the Congo River like Brazza, I took Air France. A DC4. from Paris to Douala, Cameroun, and a DC3 from Douala to Bangui. With three intermediate stops and an overnight lay-over at Douala, I had plenty of time to ponder over Joseph Conrad's **Heart of Darkness,** which I had read some years before. Consequently, when I stepped off the plane at Bangui, I thought I knew what to expect. As a member of the CMOO Board representing a large minority interest, I needed first-hand contact with the mining operation.

My African experience has covered a span of over twenty-five years between 1950 and 1975. This straddled the whole period of decolonization, starting with the French Colonial Empire and ending with Jean-Bedel Bokassa. I saw the emergence of an African ruling elite, educated in Europe, the USA and the Soviet Union. I saw health standards improve, and for some, living standards as well. I saw rampant corruption, I saw primitive tribalism posturing as nationhood. I saw "African Socialism" destroy a civilizing infrastructure previously put in place by the much maligned white "colonialists."

In 1950, when I first arrived, it was not all that different from what Joseph Conrad described. It was still very much "colonial" Africa, and despite the mostly well intentioned efforts of local French administrators, the Chefs de Region and the Chefs de District, there were still large areas where conditions had not changed since the days of the early explorers.

French Equatorial Africa, with it's capital at Brazzaville, consisted of four provinces; Gabon, Middle Congo, Oubangui, and Tchad. The Governor-General sat in Brazzaville, and there was a Governor for each province. During the 1960s each of the provinces became independent nations, gained membership in the United Nations, and established embassies around the world. Oubangui became known as the Central African Republic.

Bangui, the Provincial capital, was a sleepy little town on the Oubangui River, one thousand miles upstream from Brazzaville. A series of rapids blocked further upstream navigation, and that is why the town was settled.

I was met by the CMOO mine manager, Monsieur André Claude, a Frenchman of commanding presence in his fifties, in white sun-helmet and short-sleeved military-style kahki tunic. He was bald and portly, shaped like a Perrier bottle and full of his own importance. He escorted me to the company guest-house, a tin-roofed open sided bungalow, identical to all the other structures in town. There being no asphalted streets, a thick haze of red dust hung over everything. After an evening meal, served by a young African in white uniform and white gloves, I spent my first night under a mosquito net.

We would leave for the mining center at Berberati, 200 miles to the West, near the Cameroun border in the morning.

Before proceeding out of town next day, we made a perfunctory call on the Governor. His mansion stood on a high bluff overlooking the river. It later became the palace of Emperor Jean-Bedel Bokassa. The Governor, a French civil servant, dressed in an immaculate white uniform with gold epaulettes, received Monsieur Claude as an old friend. The CMOO mining operation after all, was a valuable asset in the local economy. I was introduced as "le nouvel administrateur americain" – the new American director. The governor inquired "how things were going out there at the mines." Claude complained there was a shortage of manpower, and the slow recruiting of labor was holding things up. The Governor promised to see what he could do. Handshakes. The meeting was over.

We climbed into the company car, an old Dodge sedan and started off for Berberati.

Two hundred miles is a four-hour drive on a modern highway. It took us fourteen hours on the single-lane red dirt track that wound through dense forest. Where no bridges existed over small streams, these had to be forded – very tricky when the bottom was invisible. An occasional bridge consisting of loose planks laid across parallel tree-trunks was equally challenging. Two large rivers had to be crossed by ferry. These contraptions consisted of a series of planks laid across three or four dug-out canoes lashed together. A cable slung across the river and linked to the craft by means of a sliding ring prevented it from being carried downstream. Power was provided by the ferryman and his pole. Since the ferry was always on the opposite bank, this added to our leisurely progression. Oh yes, at one point a huge tree-trunk had fallen across the dirt-track, blocking all passage. We had to round up some nearby villagers who hacked away at the trunk with axes and primitive hand-saws for hours before we could get through.

An average bush trip.

But what mesmerized me was the humanity. Every few miles the road passed through a village. These were wide dusty clearings, bare of all vegetation, on which there was scattered a series of grass huts. The villagers would be sitting on the ground, singly or in groups in front of their huts. They sat in silence, totally naked. Not a stick of furniture, no possessions, no animals. The only object I noticed was the occasional black pot over a wood fire.

Between the villages, women walked on the road, carrying enormous loads of what looked to me like firewood. Slung on their backs and held by a band across the forehead these loads were frequently supplemented by one or two babies, one in front and one behind. The weight on the back forced the woman to lean forward as she walked, pushing her forehead against the headband. They plodded silently in single file along the side of the road, all stark naked.

In fact the entire population, young and old, was stark naked except for a minuscule grass G-string fore and aft.

I learned we were at the border of tsetse fly country. There are two strains of tsetse fly, one that attacks humans and the other which leaves humans alone but attacks domestic animals. The French had made strenuous efforts to eradicate the anti-human strain, but pockets of infested areas still remained. On the other hand, the anti-animal strain remained rampant throughout the country.

In the villages I saw numerous cases of advanced elephantiasis, goitre and blindness.

I never saw a domestic animal, I never saw a wheel.

This was my first contact with primitive humanity. I am no anthropologist. The culture shock was unnerving. I kept telling myself that all men are created equal under God, and had to keep repeating it because I had trouble convincing myself these too were human beings.

Oubangui province was the most backward of all the territories in French Equatorial Africa. It was arguably the most backward in all of Africa. Its population had been decimated by centuries of slave trade, during which the healthiest and strongest members were carted off. The genetic consequences for the remaining population were devastating. And though slave traffic to the New World had ended some one hundred and fifty years earlier, the evidence was still visible. Moreover, slavery had not stopped in the direction of Arabia. In fact slave traders from the North were still making incursions, and were a source of concern for the Colonial administration.

I personally encountered "clapper-lipped" women; a horrible form of mutilation, and about the only reason the name Ubangi was known to the outside world.

During the ten years between the date of this first visit and the time the country got it's independence in 1960, I witnessed undoubted improvement in the condition of the people. But the initial experience remains vivid in my mind.

*

The mining operations at Berberati were alluvial diggings in river flats and diverted river courses. At that time there was no mechanical earth-moving equipment, everything was manual, that is to say, picks, shovels and wheelbarrows. First, a river diversion had to be excavated so as to permit the river bed to be worked. Then, overburden had to be stripped so as to expose the underlying diamond-bearing gravel. The gravel was then transported by wheelbarrow to the washing plant. This was a Rube Goldberg affair powered by a wood-fired donkey-engine. Oversize chunks of gravel were removed via a rotating trommel at the top of the structure, then the gravel passed into rotary pans where the lighter elements gravitated to the center and the heavy elements spun out by centrifuge into a sluice which carred them to a battery of hand-operated jigs. Here, once again the heavy elements were further concentrated. The final concentrate was then carried to the mine office and carefully picked over by hand, under close supervision. Each diamond, if there were any, was picked out of the concentrate with a tweezer.

To get a rough idea of the amount of overburden and gravel that had to be processed in order to produce a single diamond of approximately one carat in weight, imagine an average size living room filled solidly from floor to ceiling and packed down tight.

And even when you find that single diamond, it remains to be determined whether it is a gem grade stone or of poor quality, good only for industrial use. The difference in value is big.

CMOO run-of-mine production contained a high proportion of gem grade stones of fine quality.

Watching this process for the first time, and seeing the first diamonds recovered was an immense thrill.

The entire operation was primitive and labor-intensive. I learned this posed a major problem for the management. Shortage of labor was the prime obstacle to increased production.

But what shortage of labor? The villages are full of people sitting around doing nothing. I expressed my bewilderment to Monsieur Claude and got this answer: "Those you see sitting around in the villages," he told me," won't work because they don't need to. In the first place the women do all the work; the men go off hunting when they feel like it. My problem is to create incentives. This is not yet a consumer economy. Cash wages have limited appeal. Sure, they're pleased to have cash; its a status builder, but there is not much they can do with it. We have a company store, but apart from beer, little appeals to them. Fabrics for clothes? They don't wear clothes."

He then told me of the efforts he had made to draw the villagers to the mines, and demonstrate the advantages this could bring them. Cash wages were supplemented by food rations. Manioc, bananas, oil. There was a first-aid post and a company infirmary. All this was only partly successful. Somehow, the labor force could not be increased beyond a certain point.

Then Claude had an idea.

Infant mortality in the villages was horribly high. When a woman went into labor, the local witch-doctor was summoned, and he took over from there. That some healthy babies were born notwithstanding, was in itself surprising. The women did not like losing their babies, nor did their menfolk. It was an evil omen, and it diminished the value of the woman.

Claude had the idea of recruiting a trained French midwife, and he set her up at the company infirmary. Now the problem was, how to convince the mother to come to the infirmary. They were scared. It meant flouting authority and tradition. It took a lot of coaxing. The first woman who dared, delivered a healthy baby. Another followed, and then another. In order to encourage the process, Claude offered a cash bonus to any woman who had her baby in the infirmary. The bonus went to the mother not the father. This worked.

It worked so well, that before long, a delegation of witch-doctors arrived at the mine office, wearing full ceremonial paint and headdress, and carrying spears. They demanded a "palabre" (palaver) with the manager. They accused the manager of undermining their authority, of flouting traditions of the population, of destroying the social fabric. They demanded the instant dismissal of the French midwife.

This was the kind of situation that could easily get out of hand, and Claude had no wish to find himself embroiled in a controversy involving the colonial authorities whose only wish was to see that nothing disturbed the habitual calm.

André Claude was a mining engineer, not a diplomat, but he was not lacking in diplomatic finesse. He palavered with the witch-doctors all day. He flattered them, he rendered homage to their profession, and he affirmed his solemn respect for the traditions and customs of their people. He summoned refreshments, and offered snacks. In the end he offered them a treaty:

The company made a solemn commitment to refrain from interfering with the witch-doctors in the pursuit of their profession, especially concerning such matters as, family disputes, doweries, the price of wives, fortune-telling, the reading of omens, inheritance, and so on. In return, the witch-doctors agreed to stay away from mothers in labor and let the company watch over the birth of the babies.

The treaty was sealed with gifts and more refreshments and the witch-doctors departed satisfied.

Soon there was more work than one midwife could handle, and another had to be brought in from France. The women had their babies at the mine, and the men followed their wives. In time they saw the benefits of working for the company. They started to wear cotton shorts instead of a G string, then came the T shirt, and finally sandals and sneakers. Andre Claude had succeeded in building a larger labor force and diamond production was correspondingly increased.

The diplomatic skills which André Claude displayed on this occasion were a natural gift, surely not acquired at the "École des Mines," the mining school he attended in France. Good as they were, however, they had their limits, as I was able to observe on the following occasion.

*

Just prior to World War II, CMOO had obtained a large exploration concession in Gabon, where diamond finds had been reported by gold prospectors following their discovery in Oubangui. Only after the conclusion of the war however, was the company able to start exploration. I visited there in 1951. The area where diamond occurrences had been reported was densely covered by primeval rain-forest, difficult of access, and unhealthy. Despite these obstacles, André Claude had established a headquarters in the heart of the jungle, and had fanned out his prospectors in all directions, where they had to hack their way through dense undergrowth before setting up their prospecting camp.

Once again the problem of manpower presented itself. The local population, such as it was, consisted of pygmy tribes who shunned the white man and retreated deeper into the forest. Claude imported his labor force from the CMOO pool in neighboring Oubangui. Entire families with children, as well as single men, were transported one thousand miles down the Oubangui and Congo Rivers, and then by truck up to the mine center in the Gabon forest, known as Makongonio.

On the occasion of my first visit with André Claude, an event occurred, which surely must be unique in the history of corporate management.

The executive bungalow where we slept and ate, stood on a hillock which permitted a view over the surrounding forest. At six-thirty one morning, Claude and I stood on the patio admiring the sunrise and enjoying the only few moments of cool fresh air in the day. Morning coffee was over, and our work-day was about to start. We then saw a group of men coming out of the trees and approaching the bungalow. They were followed by more. Soon there were about two hundred men, all carrying machetes, standing in silence, watching us. Claude and I watched back.

Then a spokesman stepped forward. Before he could speak, Claude shouted, "Why aren't you all at work?" Then another spokesman stepped forward, and the two spokesmen in great agitation, started shouting at each other. This went on for some time. Then there were voices from the crowd. The general hubbub grew louder and louder. Finally, with the stentorian voice of a drill sergeant, Claude roared "Enough!" Then everything quietened down and there was silence again.

Claude summoned the interpreter. So far, we had not understood a word they were saying.

The first spokesman stepped forward again, and with the help of the interpreter, this was his story:

They were a deputation of single men. They had decided to go on strike, and remain on strike until the management corrected a grave injustice.

What was the injustice? The married men were exploiting the single men by exacting too high a price for the services of their wives.

I could not believe my ears, but I did manage to capture the scene on my 16mm movie camera. Claude stood impassive, his face betraying nothing, but obviously thinking furiously how to handle this one. At length he spoke:

"If the married men are forcing you single men to pay too much for their women, this is no business of the company; it is a matter in which the company cannot and will not get involved. You are asking us to fix a fair price? You are all mad! You tell us – what is a fair price? If we accept your price, next we will have a deputation of the married men, who will tell us it is a grave injustice and threaten to go on strike. The company does not fix prices for women.

"I refuse to accept your lamentations, and order you to go back to work instantly.

"This is a matter for the District Commissioner, not for me. Go talk to him."

I reflected how happy the District Commissioner was going to be when he heard this.

While the palaver was in progress, I noticed at the edge of the forest, groups of women, standing in clusters. These were the wives. They were giggling in huge merriment, poking each other in the ribs, while their small children ran around their legs.

Nobody moved at Claude's order to resume work, they just stood silently staring at us.

Finally, Claude roared at them: "Back to work! Anyone not on the job in the next ten minutes will forfeit food rations for a week!"

This triggered an explosion of babble and shouting, which gradually subsided into a grumbling mumble, as the men shuffled off back to work, frustrated and unhappy.

With the episode closed, Claude led me on a tour of the prospecting sites. But all day, the scene remained before me. In the history of corporate management and labor relations, is there any precedent for such an incident? What would Harvard Business School have to say about this one? How would the National Labor Relations Board handle it?

CHAPTER THIRTY SEVEN

ALBERT SCHWEITZER AND OTHER MISSIONARIES

In January 1951, I made a second visit to the rain-forests of Gabon. A company prospector, a young Frenchman called René Cavallace met me at Brazzaville airport with a Dodge pickup, and we headed north along what was euphemistically known as "La Route du Gabon," the only north-south axis in this part of the country. In fact, a single-track red dirt, rutted trail that wound endlessly through a dark tunnel of towering trees and hanging lianas. I was again in Heart of Darkness country.

As our vehicle labored painfully in low gear, hour after hour, I happened to glance at the map. To my astonishment, Lambarené seemed not far away. "Hey, Cavallace!" I shouted over the noise of the grinding gears, "Lambarené? Isn't that where Schweitzer has his hospital?"

Cavallace looked at me blankly. "Alors?" – "So?"

"Well I mean, let's go and call on him, I never realized we were so near." I was excited.

"Monsieur Jolis, c'est completement impossible," answered Cavallace. "It is not so near, it is at least 200 KM from here and completely out of our way. We will lose two full days, and they expect us at Makongonio camp tonight."

"I don't care," I said. "I want to call on him even if it takes a week."

Cavallace persisted: "But, Monsieur Jolis, le père Schweitzer is just another missionary. There are others in this area, much closer by. If you want to call on a missionary, we will be passing close to one in about a half-hour. Why not call on him?"

Cavallace held the prevailing French colonial attitude to Schweitzer in those days. The man was not a Catholic, he was a Protestant; and whereas Protestant missionaries were tolerated when they were foreign, it was a different matter when they were French. Besides which, Schweitzer was not really French, wasn't he German? Well... all right... if you insist, an Alsatian. It was hard for these French "colonials" to forget that Alsace was twice annexed by Germany in the last fifty years, and much of it's population was German-speaking.

Wielding Board of Directors authority, I broke down Cavallace's resistance and we continued our painful progress up La Route du Gabon, well past the turn-off we should have taken for our camp. Several hours later, in late afternoon, we reached the south bank of the Ogoué River. There, a half-mile across the water on the far side, lay the low outline of Lambarené village.

No bridge. No ferry. Ferry? What passed for such was a single "pirogue," a dugout canoe, which just happened to be on the far side. Somehow, it always is. No bell. No flag. No signal. Shouts, gesticulations, and flashing truck headlights finally raised the ferryman, and he set out to paddle across for us.

During the one-hour wait, Cavallace informed me that he had recently delivered to Schweitzer a gasoline-driven generator which allowed him for the first time to have electric power in the hospital operating room. It was the only one he posessed, a gift from our exploration company. For the rest they had only oil lamps.

Light was fading as we approached the far side, and to my surprise, there was Albert Schweitzer himself standing on the bank, waiting to receive us. A towering figure in colonial sun-helmet, flowing moustache, sizeable midriff, hands on hips, peering into the gloom to identify these unannounced visitors. At his side stood Schwester Anne-Marie, the imposing matron who had charge of the strapping young Alsatian girls who came out as nurses for two-year tours of duty. Cavallace whispered to me, "It is also rumored she is the Doctor's woman. Of course, only when Frau Schweitzer is not here!"

Schweitzer recognized Cavallace, and greeted him warmly. But looked askance at me. Only when it was explained I was a CMOO company director, did he extend his hand in greeting. "I wanted to be sure," he said, "that you were not from the United Nations!"

Let me point out that Schweitzer had not yet become the global public figure he later became. What had already started though, in French intellectual leftist circles, was an undercurrent of negative whispering about his paternalistic and colonialist attitudes. He was accused of treating the African forest people to whom he ministered, as his personal wards, his adoptive children.

The charge was not entirely undeserved, and Schewitzer resented it. He was convinced it all started with the United Nations, who at the time, were calling loudly for colonial liberation.

Once reassured on my account, he became the genial host and insisted we stay as his guests as long as we wished. After showing us to our quarters, he took us on a tour of his domain, starting with his own private accommodations.

We were ushered into a small room, approximately 15ft x 10ft, stiflingly hot, damp and cluttered. In one corner stood his mosquito-netted cot; against one wall a small church organ; in another corner his writing desk. A fetid stench pervaded everything, and when I looked into the other corner, I understood. It was closed off by chicken-wire, behind which was a live baby antelope.

"Why the antelope?" I asked.

Schweitzer explained:

This was tsetse-fly country. That meant sleeping sickness, fatal to man and his domestic animals. Where there are no domestic animals, there is a chronic lack of protein; but worse, there is no manure. No manure means no fertilizer. How do you grow fresh vegetables for sick, undernourished patients in the equatorial forest without fertilizer?

On the other hand wild animals are immune to the tsetse-fly.

So, Schweitzer improvized an ecological solution, by bringing wild animals into his sleeping quarters. "After three months," he explained, "the animal is used to human proximity. It is then safe to let it out. It will not run off into the forest. Then I bring in another, and another."

So, here in this small steamy room, without benefit of air-conditioning, the great theologian, who had arrived in Africa in

1913, slept, played Bach organ music four hours a day, maintained a worldwide hand-written correspondence, raised young antelopes, and supervised his missionary hospital.

Later, walking around the hospital grounds, I saw many tamed wild-animals grazing peacefully. I also saw busy hands collecting every scrap of droppings and carefully spreading them over the vegetable patches.

This was not a hospital in any recognizable form. It was an African village compound. The ailing, the sick and the dying would come in from the far depths of the forest, accompanied by all members of the family. For shelter, the able-bodied were obliged to build their own thatched huts, using materials scrounged from the forest.

There were no wards, no hospital beds. Schweitzer explained that he once tried beds, but gave it up; the patients climbed out and preferred to sleep underneath them on the floor. The patients lay in their thatched huts, surrounded by the family, each preparing it's own food on an open fire.

Just before dusk, with the evening meal in progress, a thick haze of smoke hung over the crouching figures, and the stench was indescribable.

A central structure contained the European living-quarters where Schweitzer presided at mealtimes. It also contained the operating room, the only place in the whole establishment that was kept sterile.

When not performing surgery, Schweitzer would visit his patients in their huts, accompanied by one of the visiting doctors, of whom there were two or three at all times, and a nurse.

Schweitzer ruled his world with a hand of iron and the voice of God.

Family members accompanying the sick were obliged to perform daily work in the compound, unpaid of course. If the good doctor spied one of these workers leaning on his shovel, the laggard would be jolted from his reverie by a roar, which reverberated around the compound, and which everyone knew for sure, came down from heaven. The man instantly resumed his task.

The Doctor was feared, loved and worshipped. He in return, ministered to the sick, comforted the dying, spoke to them of the Almighty, and treated them as his children.

When the time came for me to leave, Schweitzer accompanied me down to the river bank where the ferryman waited in his dugout canoe. As we walked he mused: "I am getting old. I will not be here much longer. When I am gone, the forest will grow back and everything will be as it was before I came out here. But these forest children will remember me, and their children's children."

He handed me a small engraving depicting the Lamberené hospital, which he personally autographed. It hangs in my office as I write this.

But Schweitzer misjudged his impending death, which only occurred some fourteen years later. In the interim he became the darling of the international intelligentsia. This noble man, became a naive dupe, as did also Albert Einstein, of the Soviet manipulated anti-nuclear movement. The Soviets forgave the good doctor his "colonialist" attitude and his paternalism in exchange for his signing their "ban-the-bomb" petitions.

When he died in 1965, the forest did not grow back and envelope the hospital. On the contrary the "united nations" came instead. There are now beds and wards and equipment and visitors from the world over. But it is no longer Schweitzer's hospital.

I never returned to Lambarené, but I often look at the engraving on my wall. It is dated January 30, 1951, and hangs above a photograph of the doctor, which I took just before stepping into the pirogue after that memorable visit.

*

All missionaries did not move in such lofty spheres. There was the case of the Reverend Everley, an American Baptist, at whose mission we stopped one day on the road between N'Dendé and Mouila.

Young Everley grew up in California, and as a youngster found himself irresistibly drawn to the local travelling circus. He hung around with the circus roustabouts at every opportunity, and stood transfixed at the spectacle of those massive lumbering elephants.

At thirteen he ran away from home and begged the circus boss to give him a job. Any job. It didn't matter as long as he could be near the elephants. So Everley was given the job of cleaning out the elephant stalls, a job nobody else was particularly anxious for. But Everley was in heaven. He stayed in the job for several years. He grew to know the elephants, and to understand them. He even "spoke" to them; they in turn responded.

Everley wanted to go where the elephants came from. He wanted to go to Africa. Someone told him the only chance he would ever have at getting to Africa would be as a missionary.

A missionary! Why, that's crazy. How on earth does one get to be a missionary? Well, to begin with, you have to go to mission school; then you have to be ordained; and then you go wherever they send you. If you're willing to go through all that, you may have a chance of being with your elephants.

So Everley went to Mission School in Kansas. He was duly ordained, and he was sent out to establish a mission in Gabon.

The site he selected was not far from our exploration center at Makongonio, and one day I told the young prospector who was driving me, "Lets drop in on the mission."

Everley's establishment was handsome, and built with loving care. In an open clearing surrounded by the forest, he had built his house, a meeting room and a chapel. His materials were not bamboo poles and thatch, he built with brick! He made the brick himself. Mud-brick if you must, but brick nonetheless. He received us in true American "down home" fashion, introduced us to his Norman Rockwell-looking wife and tow-headed children, and offered us ice-cream! Ice-cream? In the heart of the rain- forest? Hard to believe.

He had diverted a stream and built a small hydro-electric plant which gave him electric light and refrigeration.

As we sat eating the ice-cream, he told us of his early circus days, and what brought him to Gabon. The elephant population in the forest was quite different from the great herds that wandered on the Serengeti savanna in Kenya. Here there were smaller numbers, more scattered and less visible. But Reverend Everley knew them all. He had established a census.

We continued amiable small-talk for some time, until I felt it was time to leave, when suddenly a figure rushed out from the trees and addressed Everley. He was a pygmy, carrying a spear, and naked except for G String fore and aft. He spoke excitedly at great length, gesticulating all the while. The Reverend Everley nodded.

He then turned to us and reported that an unrecorded elephant had been sighted some distance away. The animal was alone. It was absolutely essential that he go to verify. Seizing his rifle, The Reverend Everley bade us a hasty "Sorry, gotta go! Glad you dropped by. Be sure you do it again some time!" And he vanished into the forest behind the disappearing pygmy.

We took our leave of Mrs. Everley and the tow-headed children and rejoined our camp.

*

CHAPTER THIRTY EIGHT

VIEILLE FRANCE OR VICHY

Concerning the members of CMOO's Board of Directors, the least one could say is that not one of them was exactly your average man-in-the-street. Two members representing the Banque de l'Indochine, CMOO's majority stockholder, had been wartime collaborators. One of them, René Bousquet, was later charged as a war criminal. The other, Paul Baudouin, was a former Governor of the Banque de France, who served for nine months as Foreign Minister in the Government of Pierre Laval during the events leading up to, and including the fall of France.

Winston Churchill, in his memoirs, referred to Paul Baudouin as "the silky Monsieur Baudouin." And indeed, silky he was. In his sixties, urbane, always dressed impeccably, and affecting a refined, almost effete manner, he would address me as "Mon cher Bertie," causing me a twinge of doubt as to his sexual orientation. On this score, I was never quite sure, despite his being married to an Indochinese lady of high pedigree, and having fathered a son and a daughter by her.

René Bousquet, on the other hand was quite something else. A handsome Frenchman, thirty-five to forty, he had just been released from jail where he had been held as a collaborator. France was full of such people at the time, most of them pretending that notwithstanding their service with the Pétain government, they were really trying to help the Resistance.

The real story of Bousquet, which I only learned many years later, was much more sinister. He had been Chief of Police in the Pétain government. In that capacity he had ordered the expulsion of

Jews to Germany, and was in particular, responsible for the notorious round-up of Paris Jews at the "Vel d'Hiv", the Velodrome d'Hiver, where thousands were assembled in 1942 for shipment to transit camps and from there to the death camps. Through influence, Bousquet managed to get released from prison, and the case against him was blocked for some forty years. In 1991, now an old man, he was finally brought to trial as a war-criminal. His case filled the French press, even spilling over to the US press. His defense was that by delivering some Jews to the Nazis, he was able to save a great many more, an argument that impressed neither the Court, nor the public. But before the verdict could be declared, and before any sentence was pronounced, René Bousquet was assassinated by a crazed gunman in 1993, an old and broken man.

How is it possible, I asked myself many times, that the case against René Bousquet could have been blocked for some forty years? There is a possible answer.

In 1994, a French investigative reporter, Pierre Paen, published a book – "Une Jeunesse Francaise," in which he describes in detail the wartime activities of Francois Mitterand during the German occupation. Mitterand supported the Vichy government and was part of Marshall Pétain's team. He was even decorated by Pétain. The book states that Mitterand was a close friend of René Bousquet. This has been admitted by Mitterand himself, who has stated in a TV interview in September 1994, that he saw no reason to break off his friendship with René Bousquest until 1986. As World War II approached it's end, Mitterand switched sides and became a "résistant." After the war, he became an influential figure in the French Socialist Party, and would certainly have been in a position to help his friend René Bousquet. Whether this was how René Bousquet got sprung from jail after such a short incarceration, I do not know. But there he was in 1950, facing me across the table at CMOO Board meetings.

Finding myself in the company of these gentlemen, defending the family interest, made me more than a little edgy. Even without knowing his full story, I felt René Bousquet was quite simply not a man I wanted to have dealings with. Paul Baudouin was different.

He was certainly not a Nazi, he was a conservative of the old school, philosophically and politically opposed to socialism in all it's forms. This led him to side with Pétain rather than De Gaulle, who openly admitted the Communists into the Free French Committee in London. It also led him to question some of the fundamental virtues of democracy. I had many relaxed conversations with him on these questions, either at his home, where he was always the gracious host, or at other social meetings.

As a former Governor of the Banque de France, for instance, he voiced serious doubts whether inflation and depreciation of the money could ever be avoided under a democratic system. "It is too easy," he would say, "for politicians to tax and spend, and thus ensure their re-election. It doesn't matter which political party they come from, they all do it. After all, its always other people's money. This is the road to disaster and chaos, which in the end can only be resolved by some strongman, not hampered by the shackles of universal suffrage." I pondered over his words in later years. Many have followed this line of thought, Mussolini and Pinochet, just to name two.

Then there were others. Comte Guy du Boisrouvray was a Belgian aristocrat related to the Belgian royal family. He was also brother-in-law of Antenor Patino, the Bolivian tin magnate. A handsome outdoors-looking fellow, he combined an athletic physique with an upper-class effete bearing, giving rise once again to doubts as to sexual orientation. Around the Boardroom table, he was no heavyweight.

And of course, there was Count Mario Pinci, the man who brought Jac Jolis into CMOO.

Mario's story deserves something of a detour. Once again, not your average man-in-the-street. Standing six-feet tall, slim, with aristocratic bearing, a Roman nose, and dark hair, he looked like an Italian nobleman from central casting. In fact he was not an aristocrat at all, but the son of Giovanni Pinci, a small-time Rome jeweller, who entered his father's business as a young man.

When diamond salesmen and pearl traders called at Giovanni Pinci's jewellery store to sell their wares, young Mario would engage them in conversation and try to learn where these men obtained their supplies. "If only we could go to the source," he would say to his father. The salesmen were certainly not willing to help him in this endeavour, but Mario had an engaging way with him, and little by little he got the information he wanted. In the case of polished diamonds, the source was Antwerp or Amsterdam, but Mario did not feel he had enough expertise to plunge into these sophisticated markets. Pearls were a little different. He had studied pearls and thought he knew enough to take a chance on his own. The Japanese had not yet revolutionized the industry with the introduction of cultured pearls, and real pearls were fetching high prices. Divers in Northern Australia were bringing up exceptionally fine specimens. Mario travelled to Australia and bought pearls for his father's store. He made such good connections, that in time he was able to buy more pearls than his father's business could absorb. Mario was ambitious, he wanted to branch out. So he left his father and moved to Paris, the world's leading pearl market following World War I.

Between the two wars, he established himself as an independent pearl trader, and before long his business prospered. On one of his regular buying trips to Australia he met Gwen, very blonde, very pretty, very Anglo-Saxon. He brought her back to Paris as his bride.

When I first met them after arriving in Paris, Mario and Gwen lived in an elegant townhouse on the Rue de la Faisanderie in Passy, the chic 16ème arrondissement. Mario had become an inveterate social climber, given to cultivating high society big names and the titled gentry. Nobody knew exactly how he became a count. That is to say, nobody except Gwen, who, blunt and down to earth, made no bones about it. "But my dear, what do you think, he bought it of course!"

Comments such as these to third parties did little to help solidify the marriage which, at the time, was showing more than a little wear and tear. Gwen was getting tired of Mario's social posing, and Mario was beginning to have enough of Gwen's outspoken "matter-of-factness."

It was not long before Mario found what he was looking for. The Countess Elizabeth du Luart, daughter of the Duc de la Rochefoucauld, one of the great noble families of France. Her husband, Count du

Luart was a handsome polo-playing "aristo," with a roving eye, and always most affable. The couple had two teenage children, a son and a daughter. Elizabeth du Luart was not beautiful, but she was striking, and carried herself with an imperious bearing and overwhelming self-assurance.

She fell for Mario's charms.

The affair blossomed, and the time came when Mario brought her to live with him at Rue de la Faisanderie. But Mario had not counted on Anglo-Saxon obduracy. Gwen refused to move out! In other circumstances this might have developed into a charming "ménage a trois," so familiar in French comedy. But no, not in this case. When I called at the residence on one occasion, I found Mario and the Countess occupying the two lower floors, and Gwen barricaded on the top floor.

When she heard me talking to Mario in the hallway, she leaned over the upper balustrade and screamed: "Bert, for God's sake, help me! This is the most outrageous situation. Mario has gone stark raving mad. Help me get that bitch out of here!" Mario and Madame du Luart, standing in the lobby, raised their eyebrows to heaven as if to say "really, what a bore she is!" Sadly, there was nothing I could do for poor Gwen.

Of course there was a divorce. There were two divorces. Gwen retired to England, and Elizabeth du Luart became Countess Pinci on October 22, 1958.

Then one day in 1967, the two of them showed up in New York. Mario had been having some financial difficulties and he asked whether we could not see our way to making him a short-term loan of say, $50,000. He added, that Elizabeth would of course, co-sign for the debt. Mario was a valued business colleague, and also a friend. We did not wish to refuse him. Moreover, we judged there was little risk.

Elizabeth's father the Duc de la Rochefoucauld, close to ninety years old, was one of the richest men in France. He owned vast tracts of real estate on the outskirts of Paris which he was in process of cashing in to suburban developers. The Countess Pinci would some day be a very rich lady.

The loan was made for a period of one year, at the end of which we asked for repayment. Mario was full of excuses. Could we please extend it for one more year. The Duc de la Rochefoucauld had recently died and it would take some time for his estate to be sorted out.

At the end of the second year there were more excuses. The Rochefoucauld estate was tied up in family complications, and so Madame had not yet received any part of her inheritance. But Mario assured us this would all be cleared up soon, and the loan would be paid off. So we waited, and waited, and waited. Reassurances were regularly furnished, expressions of good faith repeatedly reaffirmed. Mario, as already stated, was a valued business friend and a man of great charm. Though not a little irked at the extended delay, we were reasonably sure that in the end the debt would be honored.

Mario told us their villa in the South of France was being put up for sale, and as soon as concluded, we would be reimbursed. But several more years went by and nothing happened. Then Mario told us he had some valuable 18th and 19th century paintings. Perhaps one of these would satisfy the debt. How about a Zurbaran? We said: "Maybe. Let's see it and find out how much it is worth." But the Zurbaran never materialized.

Meanwhile, we learned through indirect sources that Countess Pinci had decided she did not wish the debt to be repaid at all. She was simply prepared to renege. "Enfin, Mario, tu n'y pense pas. On ne va pas rembourser ces Juifs." So that was the reason!

When we learned that, our patience exhausted, we decided to sue.

But then we encountered a further roadblock. We discovered that in the interval Mario had managed to get himself appointed diplomatic representative of the Republic of San Marino with the rank of ambassador. He thus benefited from diplomatic immunity and could not be sued. We gave up.

But that is not the end. Mario's diplomatic post lasted for several years, until one day the Republic of San Marino decided not to renew his appointment. He no longer enjoyed diplomatic immunity. We started a legal action, and got a favorable judgement in the French courts in January, 1987.

Pinci died on April 2, 1987, before the judgement could be executed.

So we turned to the co-signer, Countess Pinci, rich widow, heiress to the Rochefoucauld fortune, and specifically named in the judgement. But neither she nor her lawyers deigned to answer our communications. We had every reason to expect they would offer to settle. But no, nothing but haughty silence. We did not exist.

Despite exhaustive search, we found no bank accounts or other assets against which to execute the judgement. So in the end we were obliged to obtain a court order to enter the private residence of Countess Pinci in Paris, and seize antique furniture and works of art. This was done under court supervision, and the effects were sold by auction at the Salle Drouot. The $50,000 loan made twenty years earlier, with accrued interest, now well in excess of $120,000 (no allowance for inflation,) was finally paid off. Neither the Countess nor her lawyers ever manifested themselves, gave any sign that they were aware of these happenings, or expressed the slightest interest in the affair..

Ah, Vieille France!

CHAPTER THIRTY NINE

RAJA RAO

For one thing I shall be ever grateful to Mario Pinci. It was through him that I came to know Raja Rao, Indian novelist, poet and philosopher, with whom I developed a close and lasting friendship over the years.

The circumstances were hardly prosaic.

As already mentioned, the diamond mines in Oubangui suffered from chronic labor shortage. In order to provide manpower for the expanded production we so badly needed, labor recruitment had to be conducted farther and farther afield, with increasingly mediocre results. Mechanization was still beyond reach. Where to find the necessary brawn and muscle?

Someone on the CMOO Board of Directors suggested Indian labor. The British had imported Indian labor into South Africa toward the end of the nineteenth century to help build the railroads. In fact Mahatma Gandhi launched his career as a young lawyer and civil-rights activist, defending their interests. Indians were not strangers to Africa. Throughout East Africa and South Africa there were large Indian populations. The idea was not outlandish.

India at this time, following partition and Hindu-Moslem mutual slaughter, was awash with millions of displaced persons and refugees. Our timing appeared favorable. Mario Pinci suggested we talk to his friend, Raja Rao.

Raja had lived in France for a number of years, arriving at the age of twenty-one in 1933 to attend the University of Montpelier and the Sorbonne. He had married a French school teacher. He was at home in the intellectual and social environment of France, and though thoroughly familiar with European cultural and religious heritage, he remained a devout Hindu and a Brahman scholar of Vedanta.

About forty years old, slightly built, almost bird-like, he posessed a noble visage with high cheek-bones, large nose and a sensitive mien.

Raja thought that a proposition involving the import of Hindu labor into Central Africa, drawing upon the pool of Hindu refugees now swarming in India, would have appeal in his country. He was prepared to bring it to the personal attention of Nehru himself.

So, CMOO arranged for Raja Rao to visit the mining properties where he could observe conditions first-hand. He also visited Abba Pant, Indian High Commissioner for East Africa in Entebbe, Uganda. The company drafted a detailed proposal which Raja took with him to India, where it met with Nehru's personal approval.

But the project never came to fruition. French officials at the Ministère des Colonies in the Rue Oudinot, back in Paris, turned it down. They peered across the borders into East Africa and decided the British were not having all that easy a time with their Indian minorities. They did not think it would serve French interests to duplicate the problem in French zones. The decision was probably right, though at the time, we were disappointed.

The mining properties never got their Hindu labor. But in time, they got Caterpillar tractors, front-end loaders, and Bucyrus-Erie draglines.

I found Raja Rao a fascinating person. Here was the first Indian intellectual, and I had met a number of them, who did not instinctively disdain everything American. On the contrary, Raja was intrigued by the United States. He did not share the prevailing intellectual mindset that America was crude, crass, materialist, and consumer-driven. He was familiar with the writings of Walt Whitman, Emerson and Thoreau, and chuckled when he said: "You have your Brahmins too!"

He was persuaded that America became great, not through greed and material lust, but through spiritual inspiration. When, a few years later I accompanied him to New York, and he stood before the towering skyline, he remarked: "These are your Gothic cathedrals."

Through Raja I was made aware of dimensions of the spirit that had eluded me until then. He introduced me into the mysteries of Vedanta – of how, through meditation one could escape the mundane limitations of "duality" and move into the higher realm of "oneness" – and then, always in deeper meditation, ultimately achieve the awakened soul and emerge into the transcendent absolute of "Nirvana." Listening to Raja talk of these matters during long evenings of conversation held me fascinated. I had no experience of such Oriental concepts, and even less of Hindu philosophy – a serious lacune in my education. Raja talked of the "Upanishads," of the "Bhagavad Gita," of Rama, of Krishna, of Shiva, of rebirth and reincarnation. He spoke of his Master, Guru Natan, and encouraged me to "cross over." Also, reading Herman Hesse's "Siddharta," around this time, gave me a first introduction to the world of the Buddha.

This was an exotic and totally unexpected journey. I was stimulated and deeply interested. Raja had hopes of converting me to Vedanta, and I even considered it. But as I moved closer to the threshold I stepped back. The "oneness" was not for me. I could not see myself sitting at the feet of a guru. I felt then and still do today, more in tune with the Judeo-Christian "duality:" – good and evil – black and white – up and down – yes and no. Nonetheless, it was hard not to be intrigued by Raja's outlook on the world, one aspect of which he expresses in a phrase, here quoted from his collection of short stories, *On the Ganga Ghat*, (Vision Books, New Delhi,) where he writes: "There is no accident in existence. Yet there is the miracle of chance."

Arthur Koestler explores the same mystery in his *Roots of Coincidence,* (Hutchinson, London, 1972)

Despite my rejection of Vedanta, Raja and I remained close and dear friends throughout the years. On occasion he would insist we had been brothers in an earlier incarnation.

Notwithstanding his spiritual and mystical leanings, Raja was no ascetic. On the contrary, he had a surprisingly earthy quality about him. Women played a large role in his life. In what is probably his most important book, *The Serpent and the Rope,* he describes his lifelong love for Susheela who, despite Raja's ardent courtship, became the wife of Rejeshwar Dayal, Indian diplomat and United

Nations representative. Containing haunting passages of sensuous prose, using the English language as none other, this is truly a poignant love story. The book never made clear whether the affair was at any time consummated.

Among other of his books, **Kanthapura, The Cow at the Barricades,** and **The Cat and Shakespeare,** take us into the inner world of Indian village life, while **The Rabbi and the Brahmin** brings us an East-West philosophical dialogue. In all these writings, Raja's use of the English language has a rare lyrical quality, never before encountered, in my experience.

When I met him, Raja had been living for some years in France with Mamie Colin, an attractive widow whose aviator husband had died in a plane crash. A conventional middle-class "bourgeoise" with a teen-age daughter, she ministered to Raja, was wife and mother, and adored him.

Over the years, Raja was a frequent guest at our home. In fact, this was one of the rare cases where it was I who extended the invitation. For me, he was always welcome. He stayed with us at Avenue Foch in Paris. He stayed at Green Meadow Farm. We would have long discussions late into the night. He was aware of my domestic problems and I valued his perceptive insights. Some have criticized him for "using " me materially, but I never shared that view; I enjoyed his company, and his mysticism. If "using" is the proper word, I "used" him also, to give me and my family another dimension.

When my eldest son Paul graduated from Chapel Hill, North Carolina, as graduation present, I sent him to India with Raja. For Paul, this was an enriching experience, and I shared it vicariously through Paul's detailed diary and through long conversations with Raja. There was a journey to visit the Dalai Llama at his dharmasala (sanctuary) in the Himalayan foothills, a trip Paul will never forget.

Then something happened which had a twofold effect. It radically changed Raja's life and introduced the smallest grain of sand into the otherwise limpid relationship he and I had theretofore enjoyed.

At one of his lectures in the United States, a young Texas co-ed called Katherine sat at his feet and gazed at him in awe-struck worship. When he returned to Paris he informed me he had had an affair with her. More than that; he was proposing to continue the affair, leave Mamie Colin, and make Katherine the new woman in his life.

I didn't know Katherine, and I didn't need to know her. I knew Raja, and I knew he was quite unprepared for American womanhood. "Raja," I said to him, "you don't know what you're getting yourself into, my advice to you is don't do it." Raja was unpersuadable. "She loves me," he said, "I cannot walk away from this."

He left Mamie Colin, and married Katherine. The ceremony took place at the Mairie of the 16ème Arrondissement in Paris. In attendance, among others, were Susheela and Rejeshwar Dayal and myself. For me it was an occasion of mixed feelings. I could not avoid the suspicion he was taking his life in the wrong direction. Not surprisingly, Katherine had less than the warmest feeling for me after this.

Katherine had literary aspirations of her own, and Raja's name helped her move in the right circles. As I had feared, even before knowing her, she was not the right woman for him. Divorce came a few years later after the birth of a son, Christopher. Raja lectured at the University of Texas and took up residence in Austin. Later, he married again. This time he was more fortunate. Susan is a nurse and physical therapist, and a devotee of the same Guru as Raja. She is a warm and caring person. I must qualify what I said about American womanhood. Though he and I have seen each other less and less in recent years, it has mattered little. We are able to pick up the thread at any moment. We have retained the same close bond and I continue to hold him in deep affection.

CHAPTER FORTY

GARY COOPER, ARE YOU THERE?

HIGH NOON AT THE PORTE DE VERSAILLES

During the early 1950s, my sons, Paul and Jack were attending the American Community School of Paris, on the city outskirts. Eva was a member of the school's Parent Teacher Association. When the end of school-year came around the ladies would organize a School Day Bazaar and invite a visiting celebrity to address the children. Someone had learned that Gary Cooper was in town. "Wouldn't it be just wonderful," they dreamed, "if we could get him." But how to get Cooper? It seemed impossible. But there must be a way.

There was one person in Paris who knew everyone, and that was Art Buchwald, who the previous November had published his famous column in *The Herald Tribune,* instructing the French on the meaning of Thanksgiving Day. He called it **"Le Jour du Merci Donnant,"** and it made Buchwald instantly famous. One of the parents knew Buchwald, who graciously agreed to set it up with Gary Cooper.

I volunteered to collect these gentlemen and deliver them to the school. My transportation at the time was an old Ford station-wagon that had seen better days. On the day of the event, I picked up Buchwald at his residence, and we proceeded to the Hotel Plaza Athenée where Gary Cooper was staying. Leaving my seedy vehicle among the limos and Rolls Royces at the entrance on the Avenue Montaigne, I went inside and asked for Gary Cooper at the desk.

Pretty soon Cooper came striding through the lobby in unmistakable "High Noon" manner, and the guests gawked in wonder and delight.

Once in the station wagon, and on our way, Gary Cooper let loose a monologue of four-letter obscenities which continued uninterruptedly till we reached the school. "For Christ sakes, Art, what the f— have you got me into? What is this piece of f—ing sh-t? "A bunch of f— school kids for Godsakes? What have you done to me Art, you f—ing son-of-a-bitch?" And on and on in the same vein.

Art Buchwald tried without success to quiet him. "Hey, Coop! Cool it!" "Coop, for Christ sakes, calm down." I drove in silence.

Arriving at the school, Gary Cooper was still swearing. A reception committee of ladies was waiting at the gate. Cooper climbed out and I witnessed an astonishing performance. An instantaneous mood change. Flashing his most seductive smile, exuding effusive charm, he greeted each lady with such genuine warmth, I feared they might swoon.

The event went off beautifully. Gary Cooper talked about how they made Westerns in Hollywood, and had the children in a trance, and Art Buchwald told funny stories. Refreshments, some small talk, and then the good-byes.

"You see?" said Buchwald, as we drove back to Paris, "It wasn't so bad, was it?" "Mmm," mumbled Cooper.

When it comes to organizing the flow of automobile traffic, the French are great believers in the traffic circle. At major intersections, especially where multiple roads converge, they are more likely to have a traffic circle than an underpass, overpass, or traffic lights. The prime example, is the Place de l'Étoile, where at times of rush-hour, a mad torrent of cars, trucks and buses, swirls around the Arc de Triomphe in seemingly uncontrolled and endless chaos. But thanks to "priorité à droite," some minimum order is miraculously preserved. Expatriate Americans affectionately call it the "Bendix Washer."

The Porte de Versailles, which we were about to negotiate is another example, less famous but no less typical. It was end-of-the-day rush-hour and the swirl of trucks and buses was at its densest. The Korean War was raging. Every wall and flat surface on the surrounding buildings was plastered with French Communist Party graffiti, screaming in huge letters: **"U.S. GO HOME!"** and **"GENERAL RIDGWAY – ASSASSIN!"**

Halfway around the circle, my old Ford motor conked out. I mean just that – it went stone cold dead. We sat for a moment in horror, while in less than a second the most unimaginable traffic jam piled up around us.

After futile efforts to start the motor, Gary Cooper and Art Buchwald slowly got out without saying a word and started pushing. And amidst the honking of horns and the shouted expletives of exasperated drivers the Sheriff of "High Noon" – (nobody recognized him) and funnyman Buchwald pushed me in my old Ford to the sidewalk, at which point they told me: "Sorry old fellow, guess that's all we can do for you. Its been nice knowing you." And they jumped into a cab and took off.

There are some moments in life when the humiliation is just too painful to bear.

Of course the U.S. DID NOT GO HOME, and "High Noon" has never stopped playing in Paris movie houses, even to this date, more than forty years later.

CHAPTER FORTY ONE

THE NEW AFRICA – BOKASSA

During the decade of the fifties, decolonization was taking place throughout Africa, and despite the efforts of the British and the French to delay the process – L'Union Francaise for the French, – the East African Federation for the British, ultimate independence was never in serious doubt.

The financial world was nervous at the prospect of political instability to come, and private investment faltered. Bankers were reluctant to commit to long-term plant and equipment renewal. The Banque de l'Indochine, principle stockholder of CMOO was among them. They began to lose interest. As a consequence, the company fell victim to a hostile takeover by an Italian buccaneer called Giorgini, banker, speculator, and real estate developer. The Jolis family interest was buffeted by rough seas. Toward the end of the decade however, we succeeded in acquiring the mining interests of CMOO through outright purchase, and were now in sole control.

It was easy to understand why the bankers and investors saw the coming independence of the colonies with apprehension, there were safer investment opportunities elsewhere. The Banque de l'Indochine later merged with the Suez Canal Company and became known as La Banque Indo-Suez. We had no choice. Needing the diamonds, we invested in Africa.

It is fairly routine in the world of business for a minority stockholder in a publicly held corporation to increase his stake and take control. This is usually done by another public corporation or some sophisticated corporate raider. It is less routine when new ownership and responsibility for management is taken over by a modest-size family business with no track record in large employer-related problems or foreign mining affairs. I found myself thrust into the leading role; it was like leaping a chasm.

In 1960, French Equatorial Africa was divided into four separate independent nations and the Central African Republic became a member of the United Nations. France nevertheless, continued to run the show behind the scenes. Every African minister and every African department-head was backed up by a French official who remained discreetly in the background, but kept his hands on the levers. Appearances were maintained through a nicely crafted piece of mutual hypocricy. All notions of "colonial administration" were abandoned; these French officials were now "gifts" to the new country, and fell into the category of "Foreign Aid." The French Ministry of Colonies now became the Ministère de la Coopération, and the French officials in the former colonies were now known as "coopérants." The system worked reasonably well as long as the African ministers remained docile, and outside influences could be resisted. By the time Bokassa came along, both these prerequisites had been somewhat eroded, but even so the system still prevails to this day.

Jean-Bedel Bokassa, a simple sergeant in the French Army of Indo-China, siezed power on December 31, 1966, in a bloodless coup, when he ousted the country's first president, his cousin David Dacko. In short order, he succeeded in projecting an image of world-class bogeyman, and ended his career accepted into the Pantheon of "The World's Great Tyrants." This was no mean achievement in a field already crowded by the likes of Lenin, Stalin, Hitler, Ceaucescu, Kim il Sung, Pol Pot, and yes, even Idi Amin.

But did he deserve such honor? My contention is that he did not. He didn't really belong in that league. He was a minor player, a creation of the media, the French media at first, and the rest of the world's media later.

After all, what were the crimes against humanity he was charged with?

1. It was reported he ate human flesh, and kept human body parts in his refrigerator at the Presidential Palace. Now, to the best of my knowledge there has never been any independent confirmation of this charge, despite the photographs which appeared in ***Paris Match*** showing unidentifiable objects in an open refrigerator which were said to be body parts. I personally doubt he kept body parts in his ice-box. Why do I doubt it? Simply because cannibals have no need of ice-boxes. The eating of human flesh is a solemn ritual, performed on rare occasions, it is not a daily diet.

Having said that, I would not guarantee Bokassa never ate human flesh. There were times I was not sure myself what I was eating, when enjoying the ceremonial hospitality of some village chief. I once had the temerity and bad manners to ask, and was rewarded by an icy stare and the answer: "monkey."

Though cannibalism is rare today in the Central African Republic, it is not unknown. The French never succeeded in stamping it out altogether.

Come to think of it, since we are now being asked by the "politically correct" to believe all cultures have an equal value, what, you may well ask, is wrong with cannibalism? Only the beastly Eurocentric colonialists wanted to stamp it out.

2. He cut off the ears of prisoners in the Bangui jail. Well, yes he did. A few. But the poor man was sorely provoked. Bangui had been plagued by a rash of hold-ups, robberies, and break-ins. The Europeans and the diplomatic corps were becoming nervous in their homes. Bokassa was most anxious to demonstrate his ability to maintain law-and-order. He was going to show the international community just how he meant to go about it. The police rounded up the robbers on the next occasion, and Bokassa cut their ears off in the Bangui jail. He did not order someone else to do it, he did it himself, slashing away with a machete. Not all the ears, mind you, just a few. Law and order were immediately restored. When the European community expressed their outrage, Bokassa was utterly baffled. "What do these people want?" he exclaimed, "Is there no way to satisfy them?" No one was killed – a few ears were missing.

3. He massacred 100 school-children. Well, yes, he did, though the number 100 is open to question. Moreover, they were not exactly children; they were sixteen to eighteen year old high-school toughs who went on a politically-inspired riot because they refused to wear the prescribed school uniform. The scuttlebut had it that the riot was instigated by the Libyans. At 16 or 18 years old, an African is an adult, not a child. No excuse for a massacre, to be sure. Just making the point.

Anything else? Well, yes. A minister here, or a minister there, getting a bit too uppity at a cabinet meeting, might never reach home that night and be found in a ditch the next day.

All of this, granted, is savage, gruesome behaviour, and an abomination. But where does it rank in to-day's scale of monstrosity? There were no gas-ovens, no Gulag, no genocide, no politically-induced mass starvation, no ethnic cleansing. Bokassa's crimes against humanity were small potatoes in comparison. A monster – yes. But not a world-class monster. He was a small monster. Why then did the media so demonize the man? I have a theory, which admittedly I cannot prove, but here it is.

Bokassa was not a "lefty." He was not an African intellectual. He was neither a product of European or American universities, nor a devotee of African-style socialism. He did not fit the left-wing media image of the "progressive" African leader. Had it been otherwise, the media would no doubt have treated his savagery as but minor peccadillos as they did for those pseudo-Marxist African leaders they approved of, most of whom were no gentler than Bokassa.

A good example of what I mean is the case of President Francisco Macias of Equatorial Guinea. This man committed murder, torture, rape and mutilation against his people on a scale never dreamed of by Bokassa. Yet the media rarely, if ever, mentioned such unpleasantness. You see, he had Russian, Chinese and Cuban advisors helping him run his country.

Also, it must be admitted, Bokassa's extravagances and gaudy showmanship made him an easy target.

Bokassa wanted to make an impact on the world stage, and he succeeded. Given the unlikelihood of his starting point, this was no mean achievement. He was essentially a tribal chief, endowed with an overwhelming ego, and a keen grasp of the essentials of power. When addressing his people he did so with demagogic mastery. He could whip them into hysterical frenzy in cadenced stages. In person-to-person contact he could be charming and menacing almost simultaneously. In a flash, a sunny disposition could switch to violence with unpredictable suddenness. Cracking jokes at the expense of some terrified interlocutor was a favorite sport. He was childishly vain. He listened to his witch-doctors, and believed in the omens.

This is the man with whom I found myself obliged to have dealings over a period of some ten years. It was a ten-year roller-coaster of tension, drama, light comedy, and improvization, marked often with success and no less often with frustration. The stakes involved, both physical and material, were a matter of simple survival. Our mining operations and buying offices were spread over hundreds of miles of equatorial forest and bush country. Some forty European and American technicians, many with wives, some with children, lived and worked under the most difficult conditions of climate and comfort. The maintenance of health and morale were a continuing concern; excitement and challenge were constant; nervous and emotional wear-and-tear inescapable.

About Bokassa, one thing was always predictable – the unpredictable. He and I started off, as do all roller-coaster rides, at the top.

At the outset, Bokassa appointed me "Official Diamond Advisor to the Government," a post he himself invented. It provided obvious advantages.

While I was still enjoying this "honor", Bokassa, in 1969, invented a new mining tax of crushing proportions, made it retroactive five years and demanded instant payment. It ran to many millions of dollars. While trying to negotiate my way out of this imbroglio, he seized the mines and expelled all the expatriate staff.

Then Bokassa restituted the mines. It had all been a most unfortunate mistake. He granted us a ten-year tax holiday by way of compensation, and reinstated me as "Diamond Advisor."

Four years later, he accused me of raising a private army and plotting his overthrow.

Once again he seized the mines and held all expatriate staff, including my son Paul, hostage for ten weeks. This too was eventually explained as an unfortunate misunderstanding.

On the occasion of his coronation as Emperor in 1977, Bokassa awarded me his country's highest decoration, which I still have in my desk drawer, along with my World War II "Marksman Insignia." He wrote a personal letter to President Jimmy Carter, thanking him for the U.S. Government's Coronation gift, and asked me to deliver it personally, rather than send it through Embassy channels. I duly executed the charge and received a courteous acknowledgement from Carter's foreign affairs advisor, Zbigniew Brzezinski.

Interspersed with these ups and downs, were incidents where company employees would be siezed and held on trumped up charges of one kind or another, requiring my immediate intervention, sometimes jumping a plane urgently from Paris or New York.

American investment in this country apart from ours, was almost nonexistent, so we were of some interest to the American Embassy. Were they any help? It was hardly noticeable. All nice people, high on sympathy, low on help. Among a succession of friendly Ambassadors, I especially remember Al Lukens, who lost his wife and two children in the tragic crash of an Air France Constellation over the Sahara. Also Tony Quainton, an exceedingly pleasant fellow, who would have wanted to do more, I'm sure, but couldn't. Bill Swing, another friendly soul, gave encouragement. He is now Ambassador to Haiti, trying to leverage Aristide back into his slot as I write.

Why did we persist in submitting to such horrors? Why didn't we pull up stakes and leave? Was it all worth it? What was the bottom line? Hard to tell. There were times it was very profitable, and we were willing to accept the negatives. But, to mix a metaphor, when the roller-coaster hits the deep trough, you can't pull up stakes, there was no way to get out. The only time to get out is when things are going well, which is what we eventually did.

The quality of the times has been beautifully captured by my son Jack, writing under the pseudonym, P.N. Gwynn in his wicked satire, *Firmly by the Tail.* (G.P. Putnam Sons, 1976)

As a companion piece, I wish my son Paul would write the story of his ten weeks detention as a Bokassa hostage, or his expedition to

Ouanda-Djalle in the far north near the Sudan border to build an airstrip which never was used.

So much for the overview.

1

2

Jac and Rosette Jolis, 1910.

3

Bert Jolis

London, 1918.

4

In liberated France,1944.

5

Major General William J. "Wild Bill" Donovan, 1946.

The inscription reads *"To Bert Jolis with great appreciation for his gallant service in the O.S.S. from his friend Bill Donovan."*

6

George Orwell (1935?).
Photo Corbis – Bettmann

7

David and Evangeline Bruce, 1964.
Photo by Cecil Beaton

8

Doctor Albert Schweitzer at his hospital in Lambarene, Gabon, 1951.
Photo by Albert Jolis

President-for-life,
Jean Bedel
Bokassa, 1975.

10

Emperor Bokassa I, on his throne, December 1, 1977.

11

Bert and Mona Jolis, 1986.

12

Vladimir Bukovsky and Armando Valladares.
The Cuba Tribunal, Paris, April 1986.

14

Albert Jolis and
Vladimir Bukovsky.
The Cuba Tribunal,
Paris, April, 1986.
Photo by Daniel
Franck, Paris

15

Albert Jolis, Martin Colman, the
Hon. Jeane Kirkpatrick, Armando
Valladares, at the Washington DC,
première of "Nobody Listened",
May, 1988.

16

17

From left to right: Armando Valladares, Vaclav Havel, President of Czechoslovakia, and Vladimir Bukovsky at the Prague Conference, July 4, 1990, organized by Resistence International, attended by the pro-democracy leaders from the Soviet Union.

Photo: Anne-Laure Baron-Siou, Paris

18

Albert Jolis with Jean-Francois Revel at the Prague Conference, July 4, 1990.
Photo: Anne-Laure Baron-Siou, Paris

19

Albert Jolis with Vaclav Havel at the Prague Conference, July 4, 1990.
Photo: Anne-Laure Baron-Siou, Paris

21

President Ronald Reagan and William J. Casey, May, 1984.
Photo UPI/Bettmann

To Bert Jolis
With appreciation and best wishes, Ronald Reagan

President Ronald Reagan Greets Bert Jolis at the White House on April 18, 1985. The occasion marked the visit by a delegation of World War II resistence leaders, brought to Washington by Resistence International to voice their support for Ronald Reagan's tough anti-communist foreign policy.

22

CHAPTER FORTY TWO

GISCARD D'ESTAING – L'AFFAIRE DES DIAMANTS

In October 1979, a political scandal erupted in France that swirled around the head of Valéry Giscard d'Estaing, then President of France, seriously embarrassed his government, and helped defeat him in the Presidential elections of 1981. The left-wing humorous and satirical daily, *Le Canard Enchainé,* in a series of sensational disclosures, reported that Giscard d'Estaing, when Minister of Finance, had repeatedly accepted gifts of diamonds from Bokassa when visiting his country on big-game hunting trips between 1973 and 1976. Giscard, it was alleged, failed to declare these gifts to Customs when returning to France, as the law required, nor did he disclose them in any other manner.

Giscard did not deny the charges, and only offered mealy-mouthed devious explanations. "L'Affaire des Diamants" assumed major proportions. The entire French press took it up. The Socialist opposition in parliament demanded an investigation. It became a political albatross around Giscard's neck. *The New York Times* covered it. The French called it "Le Watergate Francais."

It happened that we found ourselves involved in the middle of this brouhaha. "How, in heaven's name,?" you may well ask. It was the culmination of a fairly long story.

Among the economic nostrums extensively peddled in the former colonies when they gained their independence, was the notion that great benefit could be derived from transforming their raw materials into finished products. The Central African Republic was no exception. "Why can't we polish our own diamonds into finished gems instead of exporting the rough stones to the cutting centers of

New York, Antwerp and Israel?" was the leitmotiv. "The exporting of raw materials is a relic of colonialism," it was said. "Besides, look at the added value we could earn." These ideas were encouraged by foreign-aid bureaucrats and others with little knowledge of what practicalities were involved.

The reasons for not undertaking such a program were compelling. It would take years to train local workers to the level of skill needed to compete in the international marketplace. In Europe, sons and grandsons of diamond-cutters undergo long training as apprentices before they are trusted on their own. Who would underwrite such an effort with raw African boys having little or no formal education? Furthermore, a large proportion of the diamonds produced were of industrial grade, unsuitable for gem cutting. If the top qualities were to be creamed off for gem cutting, the remaining run-of-mine would be correspondingly depreciated in value. Where was the trade off? Finally, diamond cutting is not labor-intensive; employment opportunity would be limited.

If such arguments made sound sense to us, they failed to impress the Central African Government. Starting with President Dacko, before Bokassa seized power, all wanted a diamond cutting factory for both profit and national pride.

We wrestled at length with the problem; we didn't want get involved in such a doubtful project. In the end though, we capitulated. Being deeply implanted in the country, we had much at stake. If we didn't undertake the job, someone else would, and the quid-pro-quo they would extract from the government would be at our expense. Figuring it partly as insurance, partly public relations, we finally, if reluctantly agreed. We would undertake the project as a fifty-fifty joint venture with the government. But wait a moment; fifty-fifty did you say? Well, yes. We would put up 100% of the money and bear 100% of the risk; the government would own a 50% interest and agree to let us do it!

Then we encountered an extraordinary piece of good luck. There was a German Foreign-Aid mission in town looking for economic development projects to underwrite. They had failed to unearth a single project that made sense to them. We remembered there was a small diamond cutting industry at Idar-Oberstein in the Rhineland. We also remembered that we had good friends there, Ph. Hahn Sohne, an old-established family diamond cutting enterprise. We suggested to the German mission that they might consider underwriting the training program, and bring in for that purpose German instructors. They were delighted to discover such an interesting project after almost going home empty handed. They agreed.

I then proceeded to Idar-Oberstein and put the matter before our friends, Fraulein Hildegarde Hahn, the elderly unmarried sister of the defunct founder, and her young nephew Dieter. I tried to sugar-coat the picture, but was not too successful. The simple facts were that we were looking for their help in training a labor force for a new diamond cutting factory in the heart of Black Africa. They were utterly aghast. "This is pure madness," they protested, "It will never work, and if it does, it only means competition for us." I couldn't but help agree with them.

But when I explained that the German Government had expressed an interest in the project, they began to see possibilities. There followed a series of meetings at the Foreign Aid Ministry in Bonn: the Bundesministerium Fur Wirtschaftliche Zusammenarbeit und Entwicklung. Some objections were raised, since this was an American enterprise. But in the end an agreement was hammered out. The German Government would underwrite a five-year training program for a diamond cutting factory in Bangui, and Fraulein Hahn and her nephew Dieter would supply the instructor-technicians from their family-owned factory. We would have responsibility for overall management. Would five years be enough? Who knows? At least, it was a start.

Specialized machinery was shipped in, the German instructors arrived, and the program got under way. The young trainees were not given diamonds to work on at the outset; they were given wooden blocks cut into various geometric patterns to illustrate diamond facets. The first material they were given to cut on the wheel was stone. When it came to starting on real diamonds, they were given the poorest quality stones. It would be a long time before a trainee would be entrusted with even a half-way decent diamond.

We were now in for a surprise. The young African trainees showed unexpected aptitude. They developed fast. Their quality of work steadily improved. We cautiously revised our timetable. The five-year program which at first we thought far too short, now seemed attainable. We were even able to forecast a moment when the operation could start commercial production. In anticipation of such an event, we started construction of a spanking new building to house the enterprise.

A delighted Bokassa inaugurated the new Cutting Factory Building in 1966 before the entire diplomatic community of Bangui. The first fully polished diamonds of good quality were shown to the assembled diplomats, newsmen and public. This was the first such diamond cutting factory in the whole of Black Africa. A commemorative postage stamp was issued. The *National Geographic Magazine* published a full-page colored photo along with a story in their August 1966 issue.

With the onset of regular commercial production, The Comptoir National du Diamant, as the enterprise was called, became one of the few tourist attractions in the capital. All visiting dignitaries were taken on guided visits by officials of the Presidential Palace. The Jolis name was in high repute. This was one of our peak points in the Central African Republic.

Whenever a foreign dignitary was received on an official visit, Bokassa would mark the event by a gift of diamonds. These usually consisted of, say fifteen to twenty stones varying between a quarter to half carat each, pressed into a wax disc in a flat plastic gift box. The stones would be disposed in different formats; a circle, a heart, a cross, and so forth. Each time a gift was planned, the Presidential Palace would issue a purchase order to the Comptoir National, stipulating the intended recipient and the approximate value. (Anywhere between $5,000 and $12,000.) In due course, all gifts thus ordered were paid for by the Presidency.

Valéry Giscard d'Estaing enjoyed big-game hunting. He also enjoyed, according to Bangui's international gossip mill, young

African girls. Bokassa was pleased to provide both. Of course Giscard, whom Bokassa addressed as "Mon cher Parent," received a gift of diamonds on each of his visits. In this respect he was treated like every other V.I.P.

Under French law, the only government official exempt from the obligation to declare gifts from foreign heads of state is the President himself. Giscard was Minister of Finance at the time, so there is no doubt he was breaking the law. But the matter was never likely to see the light of day, unless somebody leaked it. So, who leaked?

It is now several years later. Valéry Giscard d'Estaing was elected President of France in 1976. Bokassa has ratcheted up his excessive extravagances to the increasing exasperation of the French authorities. First he declared himself President for Life, then, feeling he was not doing himself justice, he declared himself Emperor, and staged his outrageous coronation ceremony. The French Government was losing patience. When it was rumored he was dickering with Khadaffi of Libya, the French decided they had had enough. On September 20, 1979 Bokassa was overthrown in a French-orchestrated coup. He fled to France. But before his arrival, an order went out from the Elysees, no doubt endorsed by Giscard d'Estaing, not to let Bokassa disembark when his plane landed in Paris. He was kept waiting on the plane at a military airfield outside Paris for many hours, while desperate messages he managed to get hand-delivered to his friend Giscard went unanswered. The plane finally refuelled and took off with Bokassa aboard, bound for the Ivory Coast.

Meanwhile, in Bangui, French paratroopers, newsmen, and the general public were ransacking his palace, his offices, and his personal records.

On October 10, 1979 **Le Canard Enchainé** published its first revelation of Giscard's failure to report Bokassa's gifts of diamonds. Who leaked?

There are two suppositions. One is that it was Bokassa himself, as an act of revenge for Giscard's betrayal. The other is that the incriminating information was recovered in Bangui by political opponents of Giscard. The Socialists were especially anxious to discredit him and his government. The source has never been established.

Overnight, I found myself besieged by the French press, as was also our manager of the Comptoir National in Bangui, Mr. Gevreykian. *Le Canard Enchaîné, Le Monde, Le Point,* were all on the phone. Though my political sympathies lay with Giscard, there is no doubt he handled the matter most unskilfully. First he denied everything. Then when he could no longer ignore the evidence, he made a financial contribution to the French Red Cross, which gave rise to a controversy as to whether the amount corresponded to the value of the diamonds. The Socialist Party had a rare good time exploiting Giscard's embarrassment.

I had no desire, as a foreigner, to become involved in the French electoral process, and tried hard to stay out of it. I was not altogether successful. *Le Point* interviewed me extensively, and in its October 22, 1979 issue, published a full page story in which I was quoted to the effect that reports as to the value of the diamonds given to Giscard had been greatly exaggerated. To the best of my knowledge, I said, no gift ever exceeded $10,000 to $12,000. The media were tossing around numbers in the hundreds of thousands. Moreover, I added, this was the way Bokassa received all visiting VIPS.

This of course in no way attenuated Giscard d'Estaing's political stumble.

Was it "Le Watergate francais? Insofar as it contributed to Giscard d'Estaing losing the Presidential Election, yes it was. And while it might be tempting to stretch the analogy, and also call it "L'Affaire de L'Eau-blanche" or "Le Whitewater francais," this would be taking it too far. As of this writing it is too early to tell.

CHAPTER FORTY THREE

JOLIS, DON'T YOU LIKE OUR AFRICAN WOMEN?

When Bokassa inaugurated the new diamond-cutting factory in 1965, he was so pleased with it that, on the eve of the event, he offered me an official state dinner at the roof-top restaurant of the Safari Hotel. All the members of the government were invited with their ladies, along with the diplomatic corps and leading members of the European community. As guest of honor, I was at the head-table, Bokassa on my right, and the American Ambassador on my left.

The local Afro-Carribean combo provided *de rigueur* non-stop music, and dancing was expected.

The standard procedure at these functions is that the VIP ladies invite the VIP gentlemen to dance. Soon, an enormous, and I mean truly enormous African lady stood before me and flashed an inviting smile. I instantly accepted, got down to the floor and waded in, hardly able to get my arm around her. She was surprisingly light-footed. As we moved around the floor I made several attempts at conversation, but my efforts were signally fruitless. She maintained a grim silence, but danced with gusto. The music went on, and on, and on. It never stopped. Finally, deciding I had to do something, I risked all, mumbled profuse thanks, gave her a big smile, and navigated back to my seat. Bokassa was beaming.

He leaned over to me and whispered, "Jolis, how do you like our African women?"

"Monsieur le Président, je les trouve magnifiques. Je les admire enormément." Anything less enthusiastic would have been foolhardy.

"Eh bien, mon cher Jolis, I will have a surprise for you – you will see."

Oh Lord, what now, I wondered. That night, fast asleep in my hotel room I was awakened by an insistent knocking at the door. A glance at my clock – it is 4 am. I staggered to the door, and there in the doorway standing demurely side by side were two really beautiful African girls, and believe me, I mean really beautiful. Before I could say anything, they smiled flirtatiously, and whispered "Bonsoir Monsieur, nous venons vous rendre visite, compliments de la Présidence." I was not too bleary-eyed to note that these were two real bimbos, such as I had never encountered in Bangui so far.

Sonofabitch Bokassa! What the hell do I do now? If I send them away, I'll be in trouble. If I invite them in I could be in worse trouble. Though AIDS was as yet unknown, there were plenty of other horrors around. Besides, I was half asleep, and it looked to me like a set-up. Impossible situation.

I fished for some CFA Francs, gave each girl a handful of bills, mumbled profuse thanks to the Présidence and a thousand excuses, bade them good-night, and hoped for the best. The girls went away, only too happy.

Next day, I encountered Bokassa at the official opening of the diamond factory. All the guests, the diplomatic corps, le tout Bangui, were sitting in the tribune before the building, under flags and bunting. Bokassa greeted me with a loud guffaw, and shouted so as none could fail to hear: "Alors Jolis! So you don't like our African women. I always suspected you were a racist!"

When a head of state shouts such accusations against you in a public arena, what is the appropriate reply? "Sorry, Mr. President, I really love your women, but honestly I was too tired. " I didn't think that would quite fit the situation, and didn't even try; better keep quiet. The only consoling thought was that I was making invaluable contribution to the Bangui gossip mill.

There is another anecdote, similar yet different.

The Minister for National Economy of the Central African Republic made a visit to the United States for the purpose of seeking American private investment. He asked if I could help him meet the right people. With an assist from banker friends and the Donovan

Law Office, I was able to arrange several meetings in the Wall Street offices of some prestigious finance houses.

As the Minister expounded on the phenomenal opportunities awaiting development in his country, the assembled bankers and investors listened politely, but made no noticeable signs of rushing to invest. The Minister was unfazed. He thanked me profusely for my help and returned to his country convinced there would be a stampede of investors not far behind.

Next time I visited Bangui, he met me at the airport, and though no investors had yet shown up, he repeated his profuse thanks and said he would like to reciprocate the favor I had done for him with a small gesture.

That evening at the Rock Hotel, while washing up preparatory to joining friends for dinner, the front desk rang to say the Minister for National Economy was in the lobby and would like to see me. He greeted me with an effusive embrace, and adopting a conspiratorial air, he led me out of the lobby into the street. Taking me by the arm, he guided me to his vehicle, a small old model Citroen utility van, parked outside. At the rear of the van he flung back the canvas flap and exclaimed: "Voila, mon cher ami, c' est un cadeau pour toi!"

Standing in the tailgate was a little African girl about 12 years old, in a print dress, with her hair tightly braided in spikes sticking out all over her head. She gave me a frightened wide-eyed stare, and then looked down. "She's for you!" exulted the Minister. "She's yours. Take her!" I stood dumfounded. Refusing to accept a gift is a mortal offense. This was a government minister too! I wondered how my competitors in the diamond trade would react to this situation. One or two, I suspected, would have no scruples.

I plunged in. "Mr. Minister," I began, "Your generosity is breathtaking. How can I thank you enough? You really shouldn't have. I mean, this is really too much. " He stood before me with a huge self-satisfied grin on his happy face. "But, Mr. Minister," I continued, "You must excuse me. I am already late for an important dinner appointment." And I looked anxiously at my watch. "It is simply materially impossible for me to take her now. May I ask your indulgence to allow me to be in touch with you tomorrow? And once again, my deepest and most heartfelt thanks."

With that I hurried away, and hoped for the best. As I rounded the corner on my way to dinner, I glanced back. The little girl was still standing motionless in the van's tailgate and the minister stood alongside gazing out into the distance at nothing in particular. I thought of my partners in New York; they hadn't the faintest idea of what was involved when trying to secure a supply of diamonds outside of De Beers' monopoly.

The next day, I conveniently omitted to contact the minister regarding his gift, while painfully aware that this too would go down as another black mark against my reserve of goodwill with the government.

CHAPTER FORTY FOUR

THE SEIZURE OF OUR MINES

This happened not once, but twice, and to understand the atmosphere in which these events occurred, it might help to take a quick look at the geology of diamonds and the political fallout it produced in a country just emerged from colonialism.

Diamonds are produced in the bowels of the earth, when intense heat and pressure on pure carbon in molten magma cause crystalization. The stones are thrust to the earth's surface in volcanic pipes known as Kimberlites, named from the town of Kimberley, South Africa, where the first such pipe was discovered. In some parts of the world these pipes still exist, but in most cases, and throughout central Africa, they have been eroded in the course of geological ages, and the diamonds carried off by ice and water into stream beds and river valleys. Such deposits are known as alluvial, and the diamonds are found in the alluvial gravels which lie under varying depths of overburden.

Where the overburden is relatively shallow, say, ten to twelve feet in depth, mining can be done manually by pick and shovel methods. When it is deeper, mechanized earth-moving equipment is necessary. In colonial times there was scarcely any mechanized equipment, it was all manual labor. At the same time, under Colonial law, no African was permitted to have a diamond in his possession, on pain of jail or worse.

After independence, the Africans, understanding perfectly well how to mine, and no longer constrained by the colonial veto, invaded the mining concessions and started mining for themselves. The concession companies were unable to protect their mining rights.

The government legitimized the artisan miners and provided them with a marketing outlet by authorizing and licensing European diamond firms to open buying offices. The mining companies retreated to deeper ground under new concession agreements. Thus two systems of mining evolved, side by side. We reorganized the old CMOO operation, naming it CENTRAMINES, and also opened buying offices in our own name Diamond Distributors, Inc.

A further development occurred; the emergence of a class of Moslem middlemen from West Africa, Senegalese, Nigerians, Mauritanians, who would buy directly from the artisan diggers and resell to the buying offices. Competition between the buying offices was intense. Prices paid for diamonds frequently exceeded prevailing market levels, motivated by an unspoken undercurrent aimed at forcing the weaker competitor out of the race. At the same time there was a clamor from foreign dealers in the USA, Europe and Israel requesting new buying-office licences from the government.

We were the leaders, longest established in the country, and with most at stake. In order to provide and maintain an orderly and stable environment in this volatile market, I conceived an idea and proposed it to Bokassa and the other foreign firms. The idea was that if the Government would agree to freeze the number of licenced buying offices at its present level – they numbered five at the time – the latter would form a Consortium and agree to grant to the government a twenty-five percent share in their off-shore marketing profits. To ensure fair and accurate financial reporting, the Consortium would agree to an independent audit by an internationally recognized firm of Auditors. Bokassa agreed. The Office National du Diamant would be created as a government department to oversee the operation. There were five buying offices, including one operated by an Israeli government-owned company, Pituach, and another by Maurice Templesman, Jackie O's future boyfriend. Templesman agreed over lunch in New York. I had to fly to Jerusalem to get Israeli Government agreement.

In mid-1966 the Consortium and the Office National du Diamant were launched, and functioned successfully for three years, returning substantial profits to the Central African government.

Should all this smack of "restraint of trade" to some purists, let me add that competition between the buying offices was at all times fierce and relentless.

But three years was a long time for Bokassa. In 1969 he decided to go into business for himself. He hooked up with a Lebanese diamond dealer in Antwerp and issued himself a buying office licence. He created a new company to operate the licence, calling it CENTRADIAM with his Minister of Foreign Affairs as president, and himself a director. This was a clear violation of our Consortium Agreement. We registered our objection and pointed out the violation. We attempted to negotiate a compromise. We invited Bokassa's buying office into the Consortium. All was of no avail.

There was no escaping the conclusion that the Consortium Agreement was now null and void, so we discontinued returning 25% of its profits to the government. But, not on your life! Bokassa figured everything should continue unchanged, and demanded immediate payment of what he considered his share of Consortium profits.

And he did not stop there. He summarily ordered mining taxes increased by some 1000% effective retroactively five years, and demanded immediate payment.

Such was the background to the first mines seizure. Here is how it unfolded.

*

In October 1969, my eldest son Paul, having completed jump school at Fort Benning, GA, was commissioned a second lieutenant in the Green Berets. His mother and I attended the ceremony, and afterwards, took him to dinner at a local restaurant. He looked good in his Green Beret uniform; Papa was most proud. He was due to ship out to Vietnam any day.

That night, in our motel in Columbus, GA, I was awakened at four in the morning by a phone call from Bangui. Bangui! At four in the morning, for Godsakes! It was Fred Oelbaum, our resident manager to say that Bokassa had issued an order for us to pay what he considered his share of the Consortium profits within eight days, or have all our personnel expelled and our operations closed down.

Next day, October 19, 1969, I phoned my brother in New York, and asked him to send the following urgent telex message to Herman J. Cohen at the State Department in Washington:

FOR URGENT DELIVERY TO MISS MARIANNE COOKE OR MR. COHEN

On Saturday morning, October 19, Robert Johnson (our employee) was called to the Presidency and informed by President Bokassa that DDI has eight days in which to pay up what he says are the amounts due as of this date. He did not specify what amounts were due, but referred to an amount of 160,000,000 CFA as representing the revenue he received from the Consortium in 1968. Bokassa added that until the payment was made our offices would be ordered closed.

He added that if payment was not made within eight days, all employees of DDI would be expelled from the C.A.R. A decree to this effect is to be published Monday.

A full report was broadcast over Radio Bangui, Saturday and Sunday.

At the close of the interview which lasted fifteen minutes, Johnson was escorted back to our offices by the Chief of the Gendarmerie, Lieut. Colonel Lingoupou, who proceeded to lock the offices, place seals on all doors, and post gendarmes outside. Nothing was allowed to be removed and all access is henceforth denied, including files, records and substantial quantities of merchandise and cash located in safes.

Ambassador Lewis, duly informed, says he is awaiting instructions from Washington.

Please remind Miss Cooke that:

1. All sums due under Consortium Agreements are fully paid up to March 31, 1969, at which time Bokassa violated them when he created Centradiam, a private company with Kombot-Naguemon, his Minister of Foreign Affairs as president, and himself as a director.

2. A lengthy correspondence has ensued in which we have attempted to seek agreement – even accepting his ultimatum that Centradiam be accepted into the Consortium.

3.. After we agreed to accept Centradiam, this firm refused, and Bokassa put no pressure on them to join, as he did on us to accept them. Instead he maintains a position which is legally untenable that there is no violation of the agreement and that the Consortium may continue to function validly while his own company, Centradiam operates independently on the outside.

4. We urgently ask that Ambassador Lewis be instructed to intervene on the grounds that rights and property of an American firm are being unjustly and arbitrarily jeopardized in a discriminatory manner and that our personnel, including several American citizens are threatened with expulsion without any justifiable motivation.

5. There is an arbitration clause in our agreement which we have invoked. The blockade of our offices and the threat of expulsion should be lifted immediately.

6. More effective than intervention in Bangui, but not as a substitute, we would appreciate it if representations could be made to the C.A.R. Ambassador in Washington.

LAST MINUTE

As of this morning, we have been informed from Bangui that the mines have been closed down too. This gravely aggravates the problem, and clearly demonstrates the discriminatory nature of the action.

The foregoing is being sent to confirm our telephone conversation of today's date.

Signed: Bernard Jolis
Diamond Distributors

*

My first impulse was to jump on the first plane to Bangui, but quickly realized there was no point, unless I was prepared to hand Bokassa a check. Arriving empty-handed, I would either be held hostage or expelled with the others. I further realized that United States leverage in the Central African Republic was limited. On the other hand, surely the French had more clout. Our employees were mostly French, a few Belgians and a couple of Americans. In no time I was on a plane to Paris.

Those were no idle threats of Bokassa's. Within forty-eight hours some thirty-five expatriate employees of our mining operations, including families, were summarily expelled. They all arrived on an Air France plane, late at night at Orly airfield, under the glare of TV lights. I met them in my Paris office next day, where they straggled in, tired, bewildered and angry. Their arrival in Paris created a sensation. It was a front page story that caused considerable public indignation. This made it easier for me to enlist help from the French authorities, who did not look kindly at Bokassa's expulsion of French nationals. Diplomatic notes and protests started flowing. In Washington, we continued our efforts at the State Department and also briefed the International Monetary Fund and the World Bank.

But Bokassa took his own sweet good time to come around.

Weeks turned into months. At one point in Paris, a man came to my office – a mysterious fellow, who told me he was fully familiar with our problem, and thought he might be able to help. It did not take long for me to figure out he had something to do with the SDEC (French Intelligence.) By his manner, though he was never explicit, I concluded he was probably not a full-time operative, but more likely a "barbouze," one of those contract irregulars; "action boys." He certainly had the manner of a mercenary. About thirty-five years old, solidly built, tough and intelligent, he told me he and his friends were planning to get rid of Bokassa, and that plans were already advanced. I asked him how he proposed to do this. He smiled and drew his finger across his throat. I raised an eyebrow and told him to leave me out! He told me just to be patient. All would come out well in due time. He called on me several more times, always telling me "Any day now." Why he bothered to contact me in the first place, I never knew, nor did I ever hear from him again. Was he trying to entrap me into a conspiracy? He gave me his name, which I no longer recall, and a phone number where I could contact him. I never did.

Then, one day, in a surprise move, approximately one year after the seizure of the mines, Bokassa issued a press release. He declared this to be the moment of reconciliation and announced his desire to see the mines reopen. I was invited to Bangui to commence negotiations with a government commission he appointed for the purpose. We were seeking compensation for financial losses suffered. They were seeking new investment. The chances of either taking place were less than encouraging. The talks dragged on intermittently for months. Finally a formula was agreed. The government would grant us a new mining concession, the terms of which included an agreed amount of new private investment, and in lieu of compensation we would be granted a ten-year tax holiday.

We were neither in a position nor of a mind to make any new substantial investment, but a mining concession carrying with it a ten-year tax holiday was a significant and negotiable asset. The only problem was "How good is Bokassa's signature?" The record did not speak well.

The new agreement was signed in February 1972. Bokassa pinned a new decoration on my lapel, "L'Ordre de Bokassa," and again named me his personal Counsellor. I was painfully aware of the odor of sick comedy pervading all this; a further reminder, if any were needed, of how few places there were in the world where diamonds occurred outside of the control of De Beers.

*

This time we did not go it alone. We invited a partner to join with us, the Canadian mining company COMINCO, a subsidiary of Canadian Pacific. We contributed the concession and expatriate personnel; they contributed capital and management. The new company was called Société Centrafricaine d'Exploitation Diamantifere (SCED). A new camp was built at Bouli, near the Mamberé River. In addition to repair shops and warehouses, it contained housing for the African workers, expatriate housing for the Europeans, an infirmary, a school, a chapel.

Along with it's normal mining activity in the deep ground, the company operated a program of technical aid to the individual local artisan miners who worked the shallow ground in the vicinity. In undertaking this program, we took a calculated risk. It was popular with the government and earned us real political brownie points. But it was not popular with the Moslem middlemen – Les Collecteurs – as they were called, since their role risked being eliminated.

My two eldest sons, Paul and Jack, both back from Vietnam, played an active role in this venture. Jack ran one of the technical aid centers at a location which became known as Jackville, a name today duly recorded on the maps.

SCED operated successfully for four and a half years. Diamond production flowed; everyone was happy. The roller coaster was once again cruising along the upper-level straightaway. The barometer read "set fair." But we all know roller coasters. The average length of time Bokassa could be expected to honor his own signature was limited.

Under C.A.R mining law, mining companies are authorized to employ mine guards. These men patrol the concession area to prevent unlawful trespass, especially clandestine digging by artisan miners. The existence of mine guards had been a well established and recognized feature of the mining industry for years. SCED employed mine guards.

In November 1975, I was in Bangui on one of my routine inspection trips, when I received a personal message that President Bokassa wished to see me. His emissary told me the interview would take place next day at the Presidential retreat at Bobangi. This was a fortified military camp situated some fifty miles west of the capital, linked by the only blacktop road in the country. I drove out there with certain foreboding, accompanied by Fred Oelbaum, our resident manager. Military guards posted at the outside gates, kept us waiting an inordinate time, then finally admitted us into the camp area. After more waiting around we were at last ushered into the meeting room.

It was a cavernous hall about the size of a basketball court. Down the center was a forty foot polished mahogany and ebony conference table, around which was assembled the entire government, fifteen ministers on one side, fifteen on the other. Bokassa sat at the head of the table. I was invited to sit at the foot. The table was bare, no papers, no glasses. My sense of anxiety increased further. Fred Oelbaum sat next to me, visibly ill at ease. As all eyes were turned to me, I caught a unanimous stare of hostility. Bokassa rapped the table with his carved ivory cane, and opened the session.

"Jolis" he began, "My informants tell me you are raising a private army against me. What have you got to say?"

I was utterly stunned. I could have expected any thing but that.

"Mr. President" I answered, "I'm sorry to say, you have been misinformed. There is no such thing as a private army. I cannot imagine anyone making such an allegation."

"Jolis, you are contradicting me. Are you telling me I am lying?

A supportive murmur went around the table, and the hostile glares intensified. It was getting very tense. I did not like it at all.

"No, Mr. President, I am not saying you lie, I say you have been misinformed."

"Jolis, I have it on good authority there are armed men on your concession."

"Mr. President, these are our mine guards. We employ them under written authority of your Mines Department, and they are deputized by your Police Department to carry arms. They have only one function, to protect the concession area from trespass by illegal diggers who pay no taxes and in no way benefit the country."

Bokassa banged the table again with the carved ivory cane, and continued:

" I have further bad reports about you, Jolis. I am told you are using private planes to import arms and export diamonds fraudulently."

What on earth is going on here? I asked myself. The next step will be I'll be carted off to the notorious N'Garaba prison and locked up in solitary, and where inmates get their ears chopped off by Bokassa himself.

"Mr. President," I answered, "Such information is totally false, and whoever is feeding it to you has no other purpose than to make trouble between you and me. Yes, we do use private planes, we use them between our camp and Bangui, never on any occasion have we used one to cross a frontier. The flight logs are there. The import of arms and fraudulent export of diamonds is mischevious nonsense. I am indignant at such allegations."

There was a pause. Then all the ministers started talking among themselves, until Bokassa silenced them with a bang of the ivory cane. He glared at me.

"All right Jolis, you may go. The session is terminated. But remember, I am watching you."

One more bang with the cane, and everyone rose. The usual handshakes and effusive "good-byes" were conspicuously absent. Fred Oelbaum and I walked out in silence. The whole affair took less than fifteen minutes.

There was no doubt we were in trouble. "Here we go again!" I said to Fred, as we drove back to Bangui. "This must be the work of Les Collecteurs." Our aid program put us in direct contact with the artisan miners, and the Moslem middlemen resented that. Indeed, Paul and Jack, my sons had for some time reported local incidents and mishaps instigated by the "collecteurs."

Nothing more was heard about this incident for several weeks. Then, without any advance notice, on December 18, 1976, Bokassa issued a decree stating that the ten-year Tax Treaty, known as Regime "C" of the Investment Code, signed with SCED in February 1972, was cancelled, effective immediately. This was only was only the beginning.

*

I was in New York when the decree was published. What possible recourse did I have in such a situation? Though, on paper and in theory, there is an independent judiciary in the C.A.R. no one in his right mind would dream of trying to use the courts to get satisfaction against a Bokassa decree. So once again, I sought assistance from our State Department.

I sent a communication on January 6, 1976, to Tom Buchanan, Director for Central African Affairs at the State Department, under the heading: **"An Unprovoked and Unilateral Act of Discrimination Against an American Interest.** (see Appendix No. 2)

Exactly what steps the State Department took in response to my plea for help, I never knew. What I found out soon enough though, is that whatever they were, they produced precisely the opposite results from what we wanted.

On January 15, 1976, I returned to Bangui. On arrival, I called on Ambassador William Swing and informed him I would seek an audience with Bokassa to try and resolve our problem. It took a week before the audience was granted. This time it was at the Presidential Palace in Bangui. Once again, the entire government was assembled around a long conference table. Once again, unanimous stares of hostility from the ministers. Bokassa, always with his carved ivory cane, banged the table to open the session. This one must surely have earned a Guinness record for brevity.

"Jolis, you have politicized this affair. What was a private matter between you and me, you have now raised to the level of an international incident. You have cast a slur on our sovereignty. I do not accept it. You may go. This interview is terminated." The ivory cane slammed down.

I returned to our office, shaken, and found my son Paul, who had just flown in from the mines. I told him what had just transpired. "Look Paul," I said, "He's going to lower the boom any minute. This problem will never be solved from the inside, it can only be tackled from the outside. I'm going to take the first plane out of here and I want you to come with me. I'm not even sure he'll let us leave."

Paul did not feel comfortable about leaving his colleagues at the mine. "Dad, I can't come with you, I've got to get back to Bouli."

"Paul, I know you feel a sense of solidarity with our people at the mine. I understand perfectly. I feel it too. The responsibility for the lives of these people is mine, and you may be sure I feel it intensely. But don't you see, if you go back, Bokassa will hold you hostage, and that will give him even greater leverage over us than he already has. Please get on the plane with me, don't give him that satisfaction."

"No, Dad, I can't. I can't just walk out on those guys."

"They may arrest you," I said.

"I'm not afraid," he answered.

Paul, a Green Beret veteran of Vietnam, had as yet no wife or children, and because I admired his courage and loyalty to his colleagues, I did not put more pressure on him to come with me. Nonetheless, I was filled with foreboding.

So Paul went back to the mines (Jack was on vacation at the time.) On January 26, I boarded the plane for Paris, with heavy heart. Surprisingly, the police let me through.

Three days later, on January 29, Bokassa dispatched his army to surround the mine camp at Bouli. It was a full military operation. All access and egress was blocked by armed soldiers. No persons, no supplies, no mail were permitted to cross the military line. Fourteen French nationals, four Canadians, three Belgians, and two Americans were held prisoner for ten weeks. The group included six wives and four minor children. The danger to these people from a trigger-happy CAR soldier, not to speak of the psychological strain and tension they endured while incarcerated, can hardly be overstated. One man suffered a nervous breakdown. Their only contact with the outside, which was by shortwave radio to our office in Bangui, was cut off.

No charges were levelled against us, no claim, no ultimatum. Our other activities in the country, that is to say, our local head office in Bangui, our four buying offices in the provinces, and the diamond cutting factory, were unaffected. If Bokassa was sending a message, it certainly wasn't getting through to us. More likely he was paying off a political or financial debt – probably both – to the "Collecteurs," the Moslem traders, who resented our activities among the artisan miners

Our local manager Fred Oelbaum expended heroic efforts through every available contact to find a solution to the impasse. I have no doubt that the strain and stress of these days, compounded by the fears and anxiety for the health and well-being of our mine personnel, contributed to the heart attack which caused his tragic death three months later.

For me it was the most stressful and prolonged personal agony I can remember. Unremitting efforts in Washington, personal appeals, to the State Department, to A.I.D., to members of Congress, the World Bank, all elicited much sympathy, but little effective help. In a recurring nightmare, I envisioned drunken soldiers, seeking to curry favor with Bokassa, breaking into the Bouli camp, slaughtering men, women and children. The bloodbaths that had occurred in 1965 and 1966 in Stanleyville, Belgian Congo, (today, Kisingani, Zaire,) were all too vivid in my mind.

An indication of my thinking at the time is that I actually entertained the possibility of some sort of private para-military intervention, to save our people. My sons, Paul and Jack had a Swiss friend they had met on their holidays on the Greek island of Hydra. This man, a self-styled "captain" Alexis Bolens was a mercenary who had recently served with Rolf Steiner in Biafra. When Jack suggested to me that it might be worth contacting him, I surprised myself by agreeing. "Yes," he told Jack, "something could be arranged." It would involve three armed helicopters at a cost of $1 million each, that would come from "somewhere in Nigeria." To illustrate my sense of desperation after these anxiety-frought weeks, I did not reject the scheme out of hand, or even at all. Fortunately, the situation was resolved before these discussions proceeded any further.

William Rogers, Bill Casey's law partner at the time, had met Bokassa when he was Nixon's Secretary of State. With Bill's help he agreed to send Bokassa a personal telegram, reminding him how he recalled with pleasure their earlier meeting and expressing the hope that the "Jolis matter" could be amicably resolved as soon as possible.

Which of these efforts did the trick, or whether it took a combination of all of them, we never knew. But on March 28, 1976, Bokassa withdrew the troops encircling our Bouli camp. The expatriate personnel was summoned to Bangui. Next day, before the entire foreign diplomatic corps, duly assembled at his order, Bokassa paraded our employees and publicly berated them for all manner of "crimes," such as Insurrection, Anti-Government Behaviour, Racism, Colonialist Attitudes, and the likes. Then he released them. After which, in his mind, the affair was ended.

I strongly suspect the assembled diplomats, witnessing this grotesque performance, must have snickered in their beards: "The trouble with Jolis is, he didn't give Bokassa a large enough "cadeau" (payoff.) He could have avoided all this with a little more traditional "tribute." They were right of course, except that bribery of foreign officials is illegal under American law.

The next day, Paul boarded the regular Air Afrique plane for Paris. Strapped in his seat, doors closed, about to taxi over to the runway, the takeoff was suddenly aborted. A police colonel came aboard and summarily ordered Paul to disembark. He was not allowed to leave until the next scheduled departure following day. For what reason? For no special reason. Bokassa's malicious chicanery knew no limits.

Paul made it out, but Fred Oelbaum was not so lucky. On May 27, 1976, I heard the sad news that my close associate of 20 years had died in Bangui of a heart attack.

Stunned with grief and boiling with outrage, my natural impulse was to quit the country there and then, storm off and slam the door. But that was not the smart thing to do. My company still had much at stake in the Central African Republic, both in assets and personnel, all tempting hostage bait. It would take time to disengage. But from that moment on, I started planning and implementing an orderly withdrawal. As long as the benefits outweighed the risks, the game had been worthwhile, but it was clear that from now on the balance had tipped irreversibly the other way. But this moment, in the trough of the roller coaster was not the right time; better to wait for the next peak before quitting. And the next peak came sooner than expected, some twenty months later, when Bokassa crowned himself Emperor.

*

CHAPTER FORTY FIVE

THE CORONATION

Alice in Wonderland, Thousand and One Nights, Grotesque Fairyland, Theater of the Absurd, Hieronymus Bosch madness. Words and images fail to convey the enormity of the monstrous performance staged by Bokassa when he transformed the Central African Republic into an Empire and crowned himself Emperor Bokassa 1st. in December, 1977.

The ceremony took place in Bangui's red brick colonial-era Cathedral to which he and his consort were driven in a cinderalla-style gilded coach, drawn by six white horses. For weeks already, delighted throngs had lined the streets of Bangui, watching this fairytale vision trot by on stately practice runs.

Inside the cathedral, the invited guests, sweltering in the stifling heat, sat crammed into crowded pews; diplomats, socialites, European monarchists, foreign personalities, all by invitation only. And of course, the press. The women wore flowery garden-party dresses and big hats, which blocked the view of the altar, and the men suffered under the TV lights in their boiled shirts and cutaway morning coats.

Bokassa, a laurel wreath on his brow, and imitating Napoleon Bonaparte in every detail, took the crown from the hands of the officiating bishop and placed it on his own head. Then, he took a smaller crown from the bishop and placed it on the head of his wife, Catherine.

Both crowns were studded with diamonds furnished by my Bangui cutting factory, and, I'm pleased to say, paid for. Bokassa had personally selected the stones three months earlier, at a minor ceremony, broadcast on local radio.

A choral group of Central African ladies, dressed in white satin ankle-length gowns, stood in the gallery and sang extracts from Handel's Messiah.

When the ceremony was over, the guests filed out into the blazing midday sun, to be greeted by an assemblage of tribal pygmies who had journeyed in from the rain-forest for the occasion. Naked but for loincloths, brandishing spears and bows, they danced around the Cathedral door in ritual frenzy to the rhythm of their tom-tom drums. The top-hatted gentlemen and their flower-gowned ladies picked their way gingerly through this scene.

I had brought my brother Bernard from New York to share in this spectacle, and as we filed out of the cathedral, with the strains of Handel's Messiah mixing in our ears with the pygmy shouts and the tom-toms, I remember thinking, "Hollywood could never match this, not even Fellini."

The international media voiced their indignation and outrage at the extravagance, but the ordinary folk of this central African backwater loved it. The fact is, had there been no coronation, the Africans would have been no better off. The French taxpayer, to be sure, had reason to be annoyed. Most of the cost was borne by him.

My company, Diamond Distributors, Inc., was faced with a special dilemma on this occasion. Anyone who had an interest in the country was expected to make a gift to the Emperor. The competition to earn imperial kudos was intense. We had absolutely no desire to compete. On the other hand, as already mentioned, we had not yet disengaged, and could therefore not afford to be seen as cheapskates.

What kind of a gift would fit this constraint?

My son Jack proved to be the deus-ex-machina. Sitting one day in our New York office, some months before the event, sorting a parcel of industrial diamonds, he fell upon a large black stone which caught his eye. It was a piece of Boart, the lowest grade in the entire range, suitable only for crushing into diamond powder. Jet black, like a piece of coal, it had a unique characteristic. If turned in a certain manner, it took on the shape of the African Continent. It weight about 70 carats. At $2.00 per carat, it was worth $140.00.

Jack had the brilliant idea of inserting a very small polished diamond into the black stone, as close as possible to where Bangui was located, and mounting the whole thing in a gold ring. Of course it could not be just a simple gold mounting. It had to be an elaborate object, likely to appeal to Bokassa's taste. This we proceeded to do.

The result was a piece of massive vulgarity, too awful to contemplate. But we had now gone so far, there was no turning back. We set the piece in a fancy velvet-lined case, in the inside cover of which we inscribed in gold lettering, in French. "To His Majesty, Bokassa 1st, From the Private Collection of Diamond Distributors." In some trepidation, I took this object with me to the Coronation. It had cost us less than $1,000.

On arrival, I requested an audience with the Emperor, and was told to present myself at Berengo, Bokassa's fortified camp outside Bangui. He was in session with his Cabinet. As I waited in the ante-room, my trepidation escalated. What if he recognized this piece of junk for what it was? I was thoroughly unnerved.

He received me in his private office outside the Cabinet Room, and as I presented the gift, I explained to Bokassa it was unique, that there was no other piece like it in the world. There was never a truer statement!

As Bokassa opened the jewel case, his eyes glistened. He placed the monstrosity on his finger, came around from behind his desk and kissed me four times; twice on each cheek.

Then he took me by the hand into the Cabinet Room where all his ministers sat waiting, and stopping beside of each chair, he asked them to admire the gift. Every Cabinet member, you may be sure, did so with alacrity.

It was an unqualified success. As a result, our subsequent exit from the Central African Empire was accomplished with surprising ease.

Bokassa wore his ring throughout the Coronation, and continuously thereafter. I heard subsequent reports that when he was exiled to the Ivory Coast after being ousted in a French-staged coup, two years later, he was still wearing it. My fears had been groundless – he loved the thing. As I said to my partners when it was all over, "I hope he never tries to sell it."

CHAPTER FORTY SIX

GREEN MEADOW FARM – THE BUCOLIC LOOP

Two momentous events occurred in 1953, Dwight Eisenhower caved in and accepted a less-than-honorable truce in Korea; the first no-win war for America since the British burned Washington, DC during the War of 1812 – worse was to follow, of course – we couldn't yet dream how bad. And secondly, an event of even greater importance, our fourth son Alan made his entry into the world.

When North Korea invaded South Korea in 1950, and Harry Truman, profiting from the Soviet delegate's absence from New York, obtained the U.N. Security Council's approval for a U.S. – led military response, few in Europe doubted this was the prelude to World War III.

With U.S. forces almost driven into the sea at Pusan, nervous Europeans feared Stalin would seize the moment and make a second grab for West Berlin. The French Communist Party leapt into high gear and mounted a virulent anti-American campaign. The walls of Paris were plastered with posters screaming U.S. GO HOME! – A BAS LES USA!

Americans living in Paris began to succumb to a siege mentality. Our children, travelling to the American School on the city outskirts were subjected daily to this barrage of hostility. "Why do we have to live here?" they asked. "Why can't we go and live in America?"

"Sorry kids, Dad has to work here. This is where we stay for the time being."

Nonetheless, I was not at all convinced World War III was not just around the corner. We had sold our house at Jericho, Long Island. If war forced us to return to the U.S., where would we land up? It was then that the idea began forming in my mind to get a small place in the country. I had never really liked suburban Long Island, and dreamed of idyllic pastoral surroundings.

Among the drolleries exchanged by upper-class Englishmen, scanning the *Times* in the reading rooms of their London clubs, when passing an idle morning, is one that goes like this:

"Every man makes two fundamental mistakes in his life. He buys a farm to reduce his taxes, and he buys a green suit."

Well, I already had a green suit, and reducing taxes wasn't uppermost in my mind at that point, but I did buy the farm; a dairy farm on three hundred acres of rolling Dutchess County farmland about nine miles from Vassar College, Poughkeepsie. A hundred-year-old white clapboard farmhouse with pillared front porch and a smokehouse out back. It was a wild idea. The ideal place, I thought, for the children to pass their summers and get to feel American again. Little did I dream what I was getting into.

To say the place was derelict, might be a bit harsh. But it was surely on the way to becoming so. The previous owner had operated the farm for some thirty years, but had died the year before. The dairy herd had been sold off. The barn was in disrepair; milking equipment non-existent; the main house needed everything; the fields badly needed fertilizer. I must have been mad.

Eva had always wanted a girl; that's how we ended up with four boys! I always had reservations about raising a family with our marriage on such unsure foundation. But Eva wanted a large family, and I gave in to her demands, feeling she needed this as compensation for having given up her theater career.

With Eva's fourth pregnancy and the Korean War both in advanced stages, and World War III just around the corner, we decided it would be safer to have the baby in the USA. So, in her ninth month, and counting the days, we found ourselves in New York as Memorial Day was approaching. Eva still had about twelve days to go before term. We were anxious to get out of the city and visit Green Meadow Farm, which we had acquired in April, and it was now late May. After due consultation with her gynaecologist who was due to perform the obstetrics at New York Hospital, we were told there would be little risk in stealing the weekend.

So, we had a placid two days puttering around the neglected empty farmhouse, getting ideas on how to fix it up. Then, late Sunday afternoon, Eva started her first pains. She wanted to lie down, figuring it was a false alarm; they would go away.

"No!" I shouted. "Lets get out of here – quick!" It would be at least a two-hour drive back to New York Hospital, foolish optimist that I was.

Sunday afternoon, Memorial Day weekend, the Taconic Parkway southbound, was an unbroken snake, bumper to bumper, weaving its slow way back to the city. This was going to take hours! Frantic efforts to pass, hand on the horn, headlights flashing, earned me angry shouts, near misses and little progress. The labor pains were now starting to come more frequently. "Where, for Godsakes are the Cops?" I pulled over to the side and told Eva to lie down on the back seat. "There's never a cop when you need one!" The trouble with hoary clichés is, they are always true.

In desperation, I crossed over the median on to the North-bound lane and floored the gas pedal headed south against the oncoming traffic. With headlights on high-beam, I was soon doing 98 MPH. Not a car in sight for a full ten minutes. But my luck didn't last. First one car, then another, then two or three in tandem. Each time I pulled over to let them through. Each time I was showered with screams and curses. Still, not a cop in sight.

Eva's labor was now pretty advanced. Things were getting horribly close. At last, to my eternal relief, I saw a highway patrol car pulled across the road with a New York State trooper standing there in his handsome "Smokey the Bear" hat. He watched me approach with obvious interest. "O.K. mister, where's the fire? Let me see your licence."

"Officer! My wife's in advanced labor. I've got to get down to New York Hospital fast. Can you help me?"

The cop looked in the back seat, saw Eva writhing and said: "Forget it mister. You'll never get there. Follow me I'll take you to the nearest hospital."

He jumped into his car and swung off south, lights flashing and full siren, with me close behind, always against the oncoming traffic. I was so hugely relieved, it was almost fun. We were on the Saw Mill River when he pulled off the Parkway into the side streets of Yonkers. The ride now became scary and dangerous. Traffic lights everywhere. The State trooper sped through the red with blaring siren, and me behind, praying the stalled cars on either side would recognize me as part of the show, and let me through.

At last we arrived at the emergency entrance of Yonkers General Hospital. The State trooper had radioed ahead. An emergency team met us out front, with whatever was needed. Eva was hurriedly wheeled off, and Alan Geoffrey Peter was born about a half hour later.

Whew! One is not born a family man; one becomes a family man. It is one of those situations that creeps up on you. I now had four sons? It takes a little time to sink in. I couldn't help feeling a hint of Old Testament about all this; I'm a patriarch!

*

When Soviet armed might extinguished the brief flame of freedom in Hungary in 1953, thousands of refugees streamed into Austria across the Danube, and especially the bridge at Andau. The International Rescue Committee responded to the limits of its resources. As a member of the IRC Board of Directors, and with the help of Sheba Goodman, a co-founder of IRC, we organized an "Americans In Europe Committee of the IRC" to raise funds in support of the rescue and resettlement program for Hungarian refugees. We were successful in making a significant contribution to the effort. My Paris office served as headquarters.

As chairman of this committee, not a few "special cases" came my way. One concerned a certain Imre Buckert, a Hungarian professor of agronomy and a specialist in the cultivation of the camomile plant from which camomile tea is produced. He wanted to get to the United States in the worst way, and asked if could I help steer him into the right channels so he could pursue the speciality in which he was an expert. I made inquiries at the U.S. Dept. of Agriculture and learned that there was hardly any camomile grown in the United States, with the exception of a very small quantity in Michigan. Most camomile tea was imported. Imre Buckert did not qualify for preferential treatment as a camomile expert.

I was sorry I couldn't help him. He was a decent man. With a wife and a teenage son, he needed work. He couldn't live on Rescue Committee handouts, which in any case were limited. France offered precious few openings. Then I had an idea. Perhaps, he and his wife, while waiting for their immigration papers for the U.S., could work in our Avenue Foch apartment as cook and houseman. It would be a temporary arrangement, and if the French authorities came around for their work papers, which of course the Buckerts didn't have, well, we'd see about that when the time came.

Before making them the proposition, I hesitated. I couldn't help remembering the successful play which ran for years on the Paris stage during the 1930s and was subsequently made into an equally successful film. Called **Tovarich,** it was the story of a refugee couple from Tsarist Russia, a Grand Duke and Duchess, who, having fled the Bolshevik Revolution, accepted domestic employment in the Paris home of a French "butter-and-egg" magnate. Though the satire was light-hearted, the political message came through with acute irony, especially on one occasion when the guest-of-honor at a dinner party was a Soviet Commissar on a mission from Moscow, and the Grand Duke had to whisper into the apparatchik's ear, which fork to use.

Though the present situation was not exactly comparable, there was enough of a parallel to give me pause. "This man is a PhD. He's an intellectual." I said to myself. " I'm going to feel extremely uncomfortable having him as a butler in my house." Any such scruples proved totally unnecessary however. Buckert and his wife accepted with alacrity; they were more than grateful, and everything worked out beautifully. They stayed with us for about a year. Though disappointed that he could not pursue his camomile speciality in the United States, he was just as anxious as ever to make a new life there. His request for an immigration visa as a political refugee was being processed, and might be granted any day. The only problem was that Buckert hadn't the faintest idea what he would do when he got to the United States. True, the International. Rescue Committee would tide him over for the first few months, but what then?

One day I asked him if he knew anything about dairy farming. No, he didn't. I told him about Green Meadow Farm. "Would you like to learn about dairy farming?" I asked him. "Yes of course," he answered. "I'm an agriculturalist. It doesn't have to be camomile. Any kind of farming is my sphere."

"Hmm," I thought. You've never done it though. You're an intellectual, a theoretician, not a farmer.

"Look," I told him. "If I could arrange for you to learn the basics of dairy farming, herd management, crop rotation, and so on, would you be interested in operating my farm in New York State?" He jumped at it with enthusiasm.

In due time Buckert's immigration papers arrived, and with wife and teenage son the family embarked for the USA. The right place to go to learn about farming, of course, is the Cornell University School of Agriculture, at Ithaca New York, the best in the country, probably the best in the world, but that was not what I had in mind – far too ambitious. Instead, I persuaded a neighboring farmer in Dutchess County to take on Buckert for six months as a "student," at my expense.

At the end of six months Buckert knew the basics. How to operate the milking machines, when to plant corn, when to grow hay, how to handle silage, how to maintain the farm equipment.

We started off at Green Meadow with a small herd, twelve Holstein cows. Buckert threw himself into the job with furious energy. He and his family lived in the farmhouse annex. Slowly the operation took shape and Buckert was intensely proud. He had established a first foothold in America.

Then one day he approached me with a somber look. "Mr. Jolis," he began. "My son, who is now eighteen, has just received his draft notice. Could you possibly put him on the farm payroll so he can apply for a draft deferment."

"What?" I exclaimed, dismayed at what I was hearing. "Buckert, you don't really mean that do you?"

He shifted around on his feet and looked miserable. " Its not me," he said, "Its his mother."

"I can't believe what you're asking," I went on, "let me speak to his mother."

Mrs. Buckert was a plump medium height woman, whose friendly smile masked a steely determination. "I don't want my son to be in the army," she announced.

I said to her: "Mrs. Buckert, the best thing that could ever happen to your son is for him to do his military service. The Korean War is over, there is no fighting anywhere, It will make an American out of him. I am astonished that you should ask such a thing. You should be proud to have him serve." Her husband listened, deeply unhappy.

"I am not prepared to put your boy on the farm payroll now, so he can avoid the draft," I told them, "But I will willingly do so if and when he comes out of the service."

Mrs. Buckert glared at me with ill-disguised hostility.

Next day Buckert spoke to me. "My wife is very angry," he told me, I know I am dishonored in your eyes. This has put a poison in our relationship. I don't know how I can carry on managing your farm, into which I have put my heart and soul. I think it would be better if we leave."

The poor man was consumed with shame. I did not wish to make it worse by further moralizing. He stayed on at the job until I could find a replacement.

*

He turned out to be Jim Morrison, a six-foot-four World War II veteran who looked like a cross between Gary Cooper and John Wayne. A graduate of Cornell University School of Agriculture, he was a true professional. Under his management, the farm blossomed, and for the next twenty-five years Green Meadow Farm was a summer focus of joy, challenge and nostalgia for every member of our family.

Mowing, ploughing, seeding, haymaking, milking, barn cleaning, calving, manure spreading, and with thirty cows being miked twice daily, Jim Morrison was El Supremo. Hands always on the levers, directing, organizing, and ever ready with muscle and good cheer, Jim Morrison was assisted by a wiry little man called Charlie Twiss who looked and spoke like a character in a Dickens novel, and acted like Sancho Panza.

The birth of a calf was a big event – a subject of intense interest to the children, of whom there was always a goodly number around. I always remember eldest son, Paul, age twelve, delivering a sex-education primer to a group of wide-eyed six, eight and ten year olds, after they had just witnessed mama cow licking the afterbirth off her newborn calf lying in the straw. "You see, you bring the bull up behind the cow, then the bull puts his zizi in there where the merde comes out, and if you wait long enough the calf will come out in the same place." He got it almost right.

"Wow!" squealed the kids. "That's cool!"

When you buy a carton of milk at the supermarket, you think the price is too high; it should be cheaper. When you deliver twenty drums of milk daily to the Dairylea Co-op, you have no trouble convincing yourself the price you receive is too low. Its something called supply-side economics. The fact that our milk cost about the equivalent of Dom Perignon was something we preferred not to talk about.

As for me, riding my tractor under a blazing sun, with the mowing sidebar cutting swaths of hay, as bees fly around my head, and the occasional pheasant rises out of the grass just ahead with a startling flap of wings, escape was total. No thoughts of Cold War, of creeping Communism, of ministers from black Africa, or the politics of diamond mining. Just concentration on the job at hand. This is going to be beautiful hay. Can we get the field finished before lunchbreak? There's another to be mowed this afternoon. I'd rather do this than lie on a beach. That's right, escape; blissful but brief. Of course, if I had to do it for a living, it would be something else.

Did I say no thoughts of creeping Communism? Well, yes I did, but the fact was, such thoughts were never far out of mind, as my dear good friend Max Yergan who lived in Westchester County about forty miles to the south, never tired of reminding me.

CHAPTER FORTY SEVEN

MAX YERGAN – SHOULD HAVE BEEN OUR MAN IN AFRICA

The Soviet drive to establish hegemony in the Third World started long before the expression "Third World" came into existence. It began almost immediately after the Bolshevik revolution in 1917, when Lenin decided to plough and seed the fertile fields of anti-colonialism. By the end of World War II, his successors were able to harvest a fine crop. Communist parties, and Communist front organizations were in full flower in all the emerging new independent states of Africa and Asia.

By 1950, the danger to the West was self-evident, but as in every other aspect of the Cold War, the West was never aggressively engaged. It reacted defensively, timidly and without conviction. With two notable exceptions, namely, our Greek-Turkish Aid Program and the Berlin Airlift, our policy of Containment was a leaky sieve. One country after another fell under Soviet influence. By the time the Third World became an acknowledged concept, and evolved into the "Non-Aligned Movement," this group of nations, far from being non-aligned, functioned blatantly as instruments of Soviet policy. In only two instances was the West successful in thwarting Soviet objectives in Africa, and these were, the former Belgian Congo, and Egypt.

The family's diamond interests in Africa were not limited to the Oubangui territory which later became the Central African Republic. We were also involved at different times in the Belgian Congo, Ivory

Coast, Gabon, Liberia and Guinea. My travels in these countries gave me ample opportunity to observe the effects of Communist penetration, and I voiced my concerns to David Bruce with whom I had remained in friendly contact since leaving the Marshall Plan.

David was sympathetic. He suggested I talk to Allen Dulles, which I did in August 1951. At that time he had not yet been nominated Director of CIA, but was nonetheless a key figure in the intelligence establishment. Allen Dulles asked me to put my thoughts on paper, and in November 1951, I submitted to him a *Memorandum on Black Africa* (See appendix No. 3.) In it, I emphasized the dangerous level to which Soviet influence in Africa had already risen, and the urgent need for a Western counter-response. Should the African continent fall totally under Soviet influence, I pointed out, the consequences, both strategic, and in terms of access to raw materials, were incalculable.

As one small, but critical step in the process of conserving Western influence in Africa, I recommended that a proposal prepared by Dr. Max Yergan, be adopted.

Max Yergan proposed the creation of a non-profit organization in the United States, to be known as **The Institute of International African Affairs.** The object of the institute was to be no more and no less, to counteract Soviet influence in Africa. This would be done by providing support to anti-Communist African leaders, through publications, conferences, seminars, university grants, support for students, for church groups, youth organizations etc. Help would be especially directed to creating or reinforcing the organizational infrastructure of all groups opposing Communist influence.

In a word, the proposed organization would do for the West in Africa what, some years later, the **Institute of Pacific Relations** did for the Soviet Union in Asia. This latter organization, for those too young to remember, was largely responsible for influencing United States withdrawal of support for Chiang Kai-shek, thus ensuring final Communist control of China. Key figures in this organization were Alger Hiss, Owen Lattimore and Frederick Vanderbilt Field.

The following passage is quoted from Yergan's proposal:

The most important recent victory for Communism in Africa has been its capture of the African National Congress, the organization now leading the passive resistance campaign against the Malan Government in South Africa. The known Communist leaders of the African National Congress are John Marks of Capetown, David Bopape of Johannesburg, and Moses Kotane also of Johannesburg. These men have all been to Europe, and in the case of Bopape and Kotane, also to Russia. From knowing them personally, I can report they are highly capable, ruthless and hardworking leaders, who are largely responsible for organizing and carrying out the campaign against Apartheid in South Africa.

There is an anti-Communist secondary leadership in the African National Congress, which is gradually being pushed aside and will soon be eliminated. Time is of the essence. The anti-Communists should be helped immediately and directly to regain control of their movement, otherwise the Communists will once again be able to claim before the world that only they can lead the underprivileged and repressed "colonial" peoples to emancipation. This is of vital importance for India and Asia.

I am personally in touch with anti-Communists within the African National Congress, men like Dr. Abxuma and Mr. L.D. Nowana in Johannesburg. These men are responsible Negro leaders. They are fighting a losing battle within their own organization. They deserve help.

The two other organizations representing colored populations who are fighting the Malan Government in South Africa are also under Communist leadership. The Indian National Congress of South Africa has been captured. Gandhi's son has resigned in protest, and has refused all further cooperation with it. The president of this organization is Dr. Dadoo, a well-known Communist who has joined with the Communist leaders of the ANC to coordinate their campaign of "defiance."

It is highly dangerous for the security of the United States that Communism should have succeeded in gaining a position of such leadership and prestige in an area which promises to be probably

explosive and at the very least, unsettled for some time to come.
Success in South Africa means added influence and power in other
parts of Africa.

Max Yergan's proposal along with my memorandum were duly
delivered to Allen Dulles, following which Dulles invited me to
Washington for further discussion. But before looking into what
then happened, let us take a look at Max Yergan. Who was this man,
who possessed such insights into African affairs?

Max was a black American, born in 1892, grandson of a slave.
When I met him, he was a courteous gentleman in his early sixties,
with a twinkle in his eye and the urbane bearing of a church minister.
He is no longer alive, alas, but my friendship with him was one of the
more enriching experiences of my life. As a youngster, Max was
indeed destined for the church, but destiny ruled otherwise. Without
totally abandoning a religious calling, he preferred more direct social
action, and joined instead The Young Men's Christian Association.

This was the time of World War I. The Germans possessed
important Colonies in East Africa, notably Tanganyka. A British
expeditionary force was engaged in challenging the Germans for
control of the Colony. Militarily speaking, it was a desultory affair.
The Germans lost the war on the Western Front, not in Africa.
British soldiers had no experience of Africa. Most of them had
scarcely seen a black man. The trouble began when the Tommies
were on leave in Dar-es-Salaam and Mombasa. Their riotous
behaviour led to clashes with the local population and public
indignation was aroused. The British became alarmed at the political
danger.

The Government at Whitehall appealed to Washington for help.
Surely, it was thought, America has experience in dealing with black-
white race relations; they can help us. America was not yet in the
war. This was 1916. Washington was not anxious to grasp this nettle,
so they found a bureaucratic alibi; they decided it had to be non-
governmental; they turned the matter over to the Y.M.C.A.

The Y.M.C.A. had just the man. They dispatched young Max
Yergan to Dar-es-Salaam, where for the next two years he was
attached to British Headquarters, as a civilian consultant in charge of

race-relations. Just how many barroom brawls Max was able to calm down, we don't know, but what we do know is that the experience opened up a vista which changed his life.

At the war's end, Max Yergan returned to the United States. Building on his first African assignment, the Y.M.C.A. sent him for two years to South Africa. Then he became their roving consultant on African affairs. He was on a first name basis with most of the rising African leaders. He became a figure in the nascent Negro "movement" in the United States. It was inevitable that sooner or later, Max would come to the attention of Paul Robeson, it's then reigning and undisputed shining star. The Civil Rights Movement which blossomed in the 1960's had not yet emerged.

The Kremlin had always harbored high hopes and big plans for the American black movement, and the American Communist Party, small though it was, directed a large fraction of it's energies into the effort. Paul Robeson, though his adoring public were for the most part unaware of it, was a dedicated Communist. He sent his children to be educated in Moscow. Max Yergan was not a Communist. He was neither a Marxist nor a revolutionary; he was an "innocent." He was drawn into Paul Robeson's orbit by the latter's magnetism and seeming dedication to the same altruistic ideals which he held himself. Together, Robeson and Yergan formed the Council on African Affairs, and Max became an unwitting accomplice in the leading Communist Front operating among black Americans. At a meeting of the Council on African Affairs held in April 1944, the opening address was delivered by Paul Robeson, and the main address by Max Yergan. They were the co-stars. For all intents and purposes Max had become a classic "fellow-traveller."

As just mentioned, Max Yergan was an "innocent." It took a little time, but gradually, Max began to realize what had happened. He saw that he had been used. He saw how the Council on African Affairs had become an instrument of Communist propaganda. And above all, he saw how his friend Paul Robeson was the conscious driving force in this Kremlin-directed enterprise.

Whittaker Chambers' in his book *Witness*, has described how difficult it is to break out of the clutches of the Party, and though

Yergan was not a Party member, he was obliged to marshal the same courage and resolve.

His disillusionment had already started in 1947, and for a while he tried to counteract Communist influence over the Council from within. It was a losing battle however, and he realized there was no alternative to making an open break. This took place in 1948, when, under Paul Robeson's leadership, the Council openly declared support for Soviet foreign policy and attacked the USA. Max Yergan resigned, and took a majority group of supporters with him.

But this action alone did not satisfy Max. He was determined to draw public attention to the efforts of Moscow to subvert the American Negro movement. The opportunity came in April, 1949, when Paul Robeson attended the Kremlin-organized World Peace Conference in Paris. Max Yergan wrote a long letter to the *New York Herald Tribune* which it published on April 23, 1949. In it, Yergan publicly attacked Robeson as a Communist, and accused him of subverting the Council on African Affairs in the interests of the Soviet Union. (See Appendix 4.)

This public locking of horns with a mega-star of Paul Robeson's importance, created enormous shock-waves. After all, this was "Ole Man River" himself. The liberal media went into paroxysms of indignation. Yergan was vilified, smeared and defamed. The nicest thing they could say about him was he was an "Uncle Tom."

All this is recounted in some detail because of what happened in November, 1951, after I submitted my memorandum on Africa along with Max Yergan's proposal to Allen Dulles. As already mentioned, Dulles expressed interest, and after a number of meetings in Washington with his aides, they decided I should seek support from the Ford Foundation, which I then proceeded to do.

I knew Milton Katz from O.S.S. days. He was then at the Ford Foundation. He and the other members of that body expressed great interest, and after a series of meetings at their California headquarters in Pasadena, a working group was set up to work out details.

Some Ford staff member then suggested there might be a security problem. The whispering and inuendo started. Hadn't Max Yergan been a Communist? Well, yes, you could say that, though he was never a Party member. In any case, he has publicly broken with them and has made no secret of his abhorrence of Communism. Look at his public attack against Robeson. Well, yes, but you know... It would be better if we got FBI and CIA clearance.

What followed was months and months of prevarication, of evasion, of bureaucratic washing of hands; all nameless, all faceless. Nothing was ever final. There was never a clear negative report asserting that Yergan was a security risk. On the other hand there was never a clear statement that he wasn't. The project dragged on for many more months in limbo, and despite my frantic efforts to save it, finally died.

Paul Robeson's friends in the Party had done their job well. By means of classic Party tactics, they had spread the word that no one could be sure Yergan had really broken with the Party. There was reason to suspect, they hinted, that he might still be a sympathiser, or even a secret Party member The Ford Foundation was unquestionably liberal, as were a goodly proportion of government bureaucrats. Liberals are always ready to believe the worst of anti-communists, while forever seeking to justify and making excuses for fellow-travellers. From here, it was just a small jump in the mind of conspiracy-minded liberals to imagine that Yergan's alleged break with Communism was intended as "cover" for his new role as a mole in the ranks of the imperialist camp. The Communists, who were loudest in their condemnation of McCarthyism, were now applying it in reverse to poor Max Yergan.

Alice-Leone Moats, author of numerous best-sellers, put the right spin on it, when she wrote in a column appearing the Philadelphia *Evening Bulletin* of May 27, 1953:

"In all the high-flown talk about 'witch-hunting' and 'smearing,' no mention seems to have been made of the hundreds of anti-Communists of long standing who are ineligible for government jobs because their dossiers were compiled or doctored by the pro-Communists. This is particularly true of the State Department...

Someone must break the news to Secretary (Foster) Dulles that cleaning the Reds out of the State Department is only the first step in the right direction; the second is to erase the smears put in the files by the most accomplished smear-artists of our time. This means revising all dossiers, pruning them of false or slanted reports. It also means destroying the anonymous letters they contain."

Max Yergan's proposal for an *Institute of International African Affairs* never materialized. Today, in 1995, the Soviet Union no longer exists, but the African National Congress certainly does. It is now undisputed ruler of South Africa, and still a Communist-controlled organization. Nelson Mandela, darling of the leftists, adored Third World Elder Statesman and friend of Fidel Castro, by appearing to have "mellowed," would have us believe the ANC is no longer a Communist threat. Should we believe him? Other organizations purporting to deal with Africa, and with names similar to those proposed by Max Yergan, have appeared on the scene, but their aims and philosophy are far different. They are leftist in nature and more inclined to show tolerance for black racism than anything else.

*

Just one final personal anecdote. Max was fairly light-skinned and did not have pronounced negroid features. When travelling to and from British Africa, he was in the habit of stopping off in London for a few days and always stayed at the St. James Hotel in the West End. On one occasion the doorman greeted him with: " Welcome back Doctor Yergan I say! You did pick up a nice tan." Yergan chuckled, and replied: "Son, that tan is over 100,000 years old."

CHAPTER FORTY EIGHT

IN PORTUGAL WE ARE COLOR-BLIND

I always felt Portugal got a raw deal during the anti-colonialist campaigns of the 1950's and 1960's. Why did I feel that way? Because as far as I was able to see, Portugal, among all the Colonial powers, was the least racist in its attitude to the African people, and Portugal never got any credit for this. I saw it in Lisbon and in Angola.

Angola is a diamond producing country, and diamonds were traditionally mined by a government-owned monopoly tied in with the De Beers organization. This company had exclusive prospecting and mining rights over the entire country. No outsiders were ever allowed in. The policy was modified in 1968, when President Caetano took over from dictator Salazar. Then, for the first time ever, the government entertained bids for prospecting rights from outsiders. To be exact, they did not throw the door wide open, but limited the offer to a specific strip of land parallel to the coast, where no prospecting had been done before, but where diamonds were thought to exist.

We (DDI) were first off the mark and put in a bid for the entire strip. This was the onset of my Portuguese adventure. Negotiations had to be conducted at the Ministry of Colonies in Lisbon. It was a long process, and in the course of numerous visits, sometimes running into weeks at a time, I developed a sentimental attachment for Portugal. I think it was their Fado music. I patronized the cafés in the Alfama district and found those songs, disparaged by the upper classes as too plebeian, hauntingly beautiful. They had a sad mysterious quality. How different from fiery, explosive Spanish Flamenco.

I took time off, and visited Sagres at the most southwesterly tip of the European Continent. Here, in the fifteenth century, the pitifully small ships of the early explorers made a final port of call, to receive the blessing of the Church before setting sail for the coast of Africa. I stood atop the tower of the Sagres fortress and watched the Atlantic waves breaking on the rocks below, and could not help reflecting that now, five hundred years later, it was because of the courage and vision of these early adventurers that I am able to explore for diamonds on the African Continent.

With the help of my Portuguese lawyer, Vasco Taborda, a concession agreement was finally signed and sealed, around 1969. The next step was to proceed to Angola to set up our exploration operation. I asked Vasco Taborda to recommend a lawyer in Luanda who could help with the myriad administrative details this was going to entail. "Sure," he said, "I have a classmate from the University of Coimbra Law School, where we both graduated the same year." Armed with this gentleman's name and address, I called on him as soon as I got to Luanda. I was received by a tall elegant African, an Angolan, immaculately dressed, who courteously asked me in faultless English whether I preferred to conduct our business in English or French. Taborda never mentioned to me that his classmate was an African. It obviously did not matter to him.

In due course, our exploration got underway. In charge of our team was a French geologist whom we had brought in from our Bangui operation, Jean Michel. I well remember my first field trip. Jean Michel met me at Luanda airport and we drove about two hundred miles south to the prospecting camp. On the way, we passed through rich coffee plantations and I noticed something which struck me as extraordinary. I saw Portuguese peasants working alongside their African counterparts sharing the same field work side by side. These Portuguese whites lived among the Africans. Their villages differed from the African-style villages in that their adobe huts were painted in bright colors. Such a scene would have been unthinkable in a British or French colony.

As we continued our journey to the camp, I noticed that our jeep driver was a white man. I put it to Michel: "Why on earth have you got a white man driving this jeep?" I asked him, "Surely an Angolan could do it just as well."

"Monsieur Jolis, you don't understand," he answered, "The Portuguese authorities have decreed that wages for whites and blacks should be identical. So, for the same price, I prefer a white man."

"Affirmative action," as a national policy, even in the United States, was still not much more than a gleam in a few eyes at that time, though it was being advocated. But in the African Colonies, it was unheard of. I couldn't help reflecting, "Oh you poor Portuguese, so well-intentioned, but you will get no credit."

Some time later, I was back in the United States. Portugal was under relentless attack at the United Nations for it's colonialist policy. A particularly strong vote of condemnation had just been passed, in which the United States concurred. I felt the Portuguese were getting a raw deal.

Arthur Schlesinger Jr. was an advisor to President Lyndon Johnson at the time, having been originally appointed by President Kennedy. He occupied an office in the White House. I knew Arthur from OSS days and phoned him, saying I would like to see him. He cleared it with security, and I was escorted to his office. I told him I thought the United States should modify its attitude toward Portugal, and not lead the pack snapping at its heels. I pointed out that Portugal's record in racial matters was more enlightened than anyone's, including our own. Arthur was not receptive.

"Bert," he said, "the white man has no place in Africa, and the sooner he gets out of that continent, the better."

I couldn't believe my ears. This from America's leading liberal intellectual.

"Arthur!" I exclaimed, "That's a racist statement, you're not serious of course."

"Yes Bert, I am."

I didn't believe he was serious, and of course he wasn't. This was obviously a figure of speech, intended to needle me. But it was clear, my effort on behalf of Portugal was getting short shrift. There was nothing more to be said, so after a few more pleasantries, I left.

*

This encounter brought to mind an earlier incident that took place during the Eisenhower administration, where racial concepts got thrown upside down, and as I left the White House I inwardly chuckled.

I was on a visit to Liberia during the 1950s. Accompanied by our chief geologist, Mahlon Miller, we were looking into reported diamond occurrences. After a visit to President Truman, we made a courtesy call on the American ambassador. The Ambassador, whose name I no longer recall, invited us to meet with him at his residence at the end of the day. There, he offered us drinks as we sat on the lawn overlooking Monrovia, in the cool of the evening. The Ambassador was black. A successful Chicago businessman and a Republican, he had contributed to the Eisenhower campaign, and had been duly rewarded.

I remember thinking at the time that sending a black ambassador to a black country showed an unexpected degree of sensitivity on the part of the Administration. It turned out I was quite wrong.

I asked the Ambassador whether the Liberians appreciated the gesture.

"Hell, no! " exclaimed the Ambassador with feeling. "The message I am getting from the Liberians, and not always that politely, is: What's the matter with us? Ain't we good enough for a white man?" He laughed good-naturelly as he said this. He was a sophisticated and intelligent man. We enjoyed our visit.

Of course, the Liberians were right to resent this patronizing attitude. If the Administration was so keen to send a message to the world on our enlightened racial posture, they should have sent a black ambassador to Moscow, Paris, or London.

*

Our exploration in Angola continued for several years, and some interesting diamond discoveries were made. We also explored a copper deposit in association the French Government's Bureau de Recherches Géologiques et Minières (BRGM.)

In 1975, Portugal granted independence to their colonies, and Angola was now governed under a tri-partite arrangement known as the Alvor Agreement, which included the Marxist MPLA, the anti-Communist UNITA, and the FNLA, Holden Roberto's middle-of-the road group. But this did not last. Very soon Soviet and Cuban intervention, which had long been planned underground, now came into the open. Russian and Cuban troops in civilian clothes were being ferried in by air.

I remember being in Bangui around this time. One day I was at the Bangui airport to meet an arriving passenger. Bangui was a refuelling stop on the way to Angola. There was an unmarked plane on the tarmac, refuelling, I think a Soviet Ilyushin. Inside the airport lounge the passengers waited to re-embark. There they were, a hundred or more, all young men with shaved heads and identical badly cut civilian clothes, eighteen to twenty years old, all sitting bolt upright and staring ahead, not saying a word. Russians? For sure. Had they been Cubans, there would have been blacks among them.

There came a time in Angola, when the fighting in our exploration area proved too dangerous for our people. When I saw one of our prospectors mount a machine gun on his jeep, "just in case," I figured it was time to pull out. The end came when the road between Luanda and the airport was cut by machine gun fire. That was my last visit. Michel met me at the airport, and as we started driving into town, he stopped at a checkpoint and waited. After a short while came the burst of firing, and when it stopped we proceeded.

This is crazy, I thought. We've got no business here.

"Mon cher Michel," I told him, "Ça y est! This is it!. Get your people out of here before anyone gets killed. Et faites vite!"

Too bad. Angola was a rich and beautiful country. The Soviets knew what they wanted, and were well on their way to getting it.

CHAPTER FORTY NINE

ALL QUIET ON THE HOME FRONT?

When I embarked on this task, I knew the time would come when I would have to deal with the breakup of my marriage. If I have put it off as long as possible, it is because of my inability to overcome an inner reluctance to expose to public gaze such private and intimate matters. I have invented countless excuses and alibis. "Nobody is interested in reading about other peoples' marital problems." That, at any rate, is what I have been telling myself. But of course, this is not true. Other peoples' marital problems are just about what everyone loves to talk and read about. In the end, I realised I am trapped by my own self-imposed stipulation: "Try to keep it honest" I said at the outset. To pass over in silence such an important event in my life would hardly be honest.

To begin with, let me say, one does not walk out of a thirty-year marriage on a sudden impulse. The break only comes after years of accumulated disappointments, deceptions and frustrations reach such a point that they can no longer be patched up.

Following our difficulties, which occurred when I returned from the war, married life seemed headed for calmer waters after we moved to Paris. On the surface, domestic harmony reigned, and whatever small differences arose between us were quickly disposed of, leaving few scars, if any. I was determined to make the marriage work, and for a period of ten years or more it had every outward appearance of doing so.

But under the surface, personality differences were at work. Sooner or later these were bound to emerge into the open, and they did. Eva was an unabashed extrovert, gregarious, effusive and loquacious.

This was part of her charm. She was happiest when surrounded by people. Though I am by nature, less indiscriminately gregarious, and prefer to pick my friends selectively, I had no problem at the outset, and willingly adjusted to her style. If this had been the limit of our differences, there would never have been a breakup. But, along with her extroversion went an unmistakable streak of dominance. It was expressed in an attitude of competition and assertiveness with me that touched upon all matters great and small. It included a habit of making unilateral decisions on family questions without prior consultation with, or even informing me. Some of these were of major importance, others, minor irritations. It even showed up in her regular practice of cutting me off in the midst of conversation with friends or strangers, and preempting the discussion with total disregard for polite discourse.

Eva had the ability to exude enormous human warmth among all the people she was with, and she did this with an all-encompassing lack of discrimination. It was usually quite genuine, and people loved her for it. On occasion though, it bordered on the theatrical. I was an "equal opportunity recipient", and never felt I benefited from any preferential consideration in the spreading of this largesse.

Above all, was her habit of filling our home with people without my having been consulted or even informed in advance. Drop-in guests or social visits, I could understand. That didn't bother me. No, these were dinner guests and house guests. And when I say house-guests I don't mean an occasional overnight stay. Sometimes they stayed for weeks and months. And this did not happen just once in a while, it was continuous. Returning home from my office, I never knew what I would find. When I objected, Eva would say:

"You are the boss in your office. You don't consult me about what you do there. Just let me run the house the way I want,"

In normal circumstances I would have been only too happy to let her do just that, but I did not think this went so far as to require me to live in Grand Central Station.

These incidents led to friction and frequent clashes, and whereas any single incident might have been overcome and soon forgotten, their repeated recurrence had the cumulative effect of erecting a wall between us and making reconciliation harder and harder.

There is no point in providing a detailed list of such offending incidents, but a couple of examples illustrate how they covered the gamut from French Farce to Grand Guignol.

One morning, I emerged from my bedroom at 8AM in my pyjamas and staggered into the breakfast room for coffee, still half asleep, to be confronted by ten ladies of all ages and sizes, seated around the breakfast table in animated conversation. They stared at me, some in horror, some in amusement, and some in pity. Eva had omitted to inform me she had organized a breakfast meeting of the Parent Teachers' Association of the American School in Paris. After a totally ineffectual "Good morning ladies," I beat an ignominious retreat.

All right, this was French Farce. The Grand Guignol was not so funny.

Eva had a girlfriend called Lolita Gomez. She was a professional Spanish dancer, and the sister of Julian Gorkin, the man who identified El Campesino, remember? When Lolita was not on tour with her dance company, she lived in New York. But, along with so many other people, she was the happy beneficiary of Eva's open invitation to "come and stay with us" whenever she felt like it. And she felt like it quite often. She also had a boy-friend whose name I never got to know, to whom the open invitation was automatically extended. Not that anyone ever mentioned it. It was just taken for granted.

These were the summers which the whole family spent at Green Meadow Farm. Alan, aged 7 or 8, was attending a French school in Paris at the time. French school terms opened earlier at the end of summer than American schools. So, as Labor Day approached, I accompanied Alan back to Paris, leaving Eva and the other children at the Farm. Arriving at our Avenue Foch apartment, we were informed by the maid that Lolita's boyfriend had arrived alone some days before, and showed no signs of leaving any time soon. He was holed up in a small bedroom at the back of the apartment. No cause for surprise here, it was the kind of thing that happened all the time.

But wait. On the third day, the maid came to tell me that the
boyfriend had not emerged from his room for three days, and she
was worried he might be sick. I walked back and knocked on the
door. No answer. I walked in. The boyfriend was not sick, he was
dead.

Here begin three days of ghoulish surrealism. First the police
"pour faire le constat."

" Who is this man?

I don't know.

What do you mean, you don't know? He's dead in your apartment
and you don't know?

He's the boyfriend of Lolita Gomez.

Who is Lolita Gomez?

She's a friend of my wife. She's also the sister of Julian Gorkin.

Where is she now?

Don't know – off dancing in Spain I think?

Where is your wife?

She's in America.

Have you contacted Julian Gorkin. Does he know where his sister
is?

Yes I phoned Gorkin. He doesn't want to have anything to do
with it. Moreover, he does not know where his sister is, probably in
Mexico City, but he would prefer to have nothing to do with her
either.

Why is this man in your apartment?

Good question.

The police scribble away at their report. I am invited to make an
appearance at the Commisariat "pour m'expliquer."

Call the Pompes Funèbres to take the body away. Sorry, cannot
remove a body before the Coroner has established cause of death.
All right, call the Coroner. Coroners don't show up at the drop of a
hat. One has to make an appointment. These things take time.

The corpse lies stretched out in the small bedroom for three days.
The maid rushes past the closed door in silent horror, clutching Alan
to her side lest he be exposed to the gruesome sight. It is all straight
out of a Fellini film.

Such were the vicissitudes of happy home life, Eva style. For Eva, the turbulent environment was perfectly normal, and she had no sympathy for my lack of appreciation for it. She was convinced there was obviously something wrong with me. She chided me for being unsocial. "You were never really made for marriage," she exclaimed on more than one occasion.

*

How did I cope with all this? I could of course, on the occasion of the next "incident" have simply said: "That's enough! This is no way to live, lets call it quits," and walk out. I was seriously tempted to do so more than once. But I did not take this course. If I refrained, it was because of the children. It was a calculated decision to stick with it until the boys were of age. The fact that my business kept me away from home much of the time, helped relieve the pressure. I even on occasion contrived to stay away longer than necessary, and sometimes simply invented a trip. This of course, was no solution, but it helped over the bumps.

Having said this, I must admit life was not intolerable every minute of the time. Indeed, there were many happy moments, even if most of them occurred away from home. There was the annual skiing holiday in the Alps at Christmas. This was truly the high point of the year. Val d'Isere, Courchevel, Zermatt, Zurs, Cervinia, Courmayeur, we skied them all. The boys developed real talent and soon left Papa far behind. There were also ritual visits to the Normandy landing beaches, the battlefield of Waterloo, and the endless wonders of France's Gothic cathedrals.

One day, around 1967, my old OSS friend John Shaheen phoned from New York to say he was coming to Paris and would be bringing his friend Richard Nixon with him. This was during the Johnson administration. Nixon, who had lost the Governor's race in California to Pat Brown a few years earlier, was emerging from the political wilderness, and was preparing to make what was to prove his successful bid for the Presidency. Shaheen, rightly or wrongly, thought I might be able to give Nixon a better perspective on the Communist threat in Europe and Africa than he could get from the American Embassy. Could I arrange lunch?

I made a lunch reservation at the Restaurant Ledoyen on the Champs Elysees, and four of us sat down. Richard Nixon, Bebe Rebozo, John Shaheen and myself. The conversation was lively and focused. Nixon was no neophyte when it came to the Communist threat. He understood all the finer points of Communist subversion by way of front organizations, fellow travellers, and "useful idiots" generally. He asked all the right questions as to their activities in France and the rest of Europe. We talked of Africa, and the ideological war we were losing on that Continent.

While we were lunching, Eva was entertaining Pat Nixon at the Ritz hotel. At one point, Nixon turned to me and asked whether I knew anyone who could show his daughters around some of the night spots in Paris. They were particularly anxious to see some of the discos, which, they'd heard, were so much better than those back home. This was not surprising. Whenever the French copy American pop culture, they go one better. Le Drug Store in Paris is like no other drugstore you ever saw. And Le Fast Food is not only eatable, it is delicious. The Nixon girls had heard about the Paris discos.

"Sure," I said to Nixon, "I'm sure my son Paul would be happy to organize the evening. He is a third year law student at the Northwestern University, currently in Paris on a summer job in the law offices of my friend Jules Sauerwein."

"Fine!" said Nixon.

I called Paul: "How would you like to squire Julie and Tricia Nixon around the discos tonight? Can you mobilize a friend and make it a foursome?"

"Wow, er, er, yeah, you bet!" he managed to blurt before falling off his seat.

That evening, as Paul was getting dressed to go out, Nixon called. There had been a change of plans. They were now scheduled for a 7.45 AM departure for Yugoslavia in the morning, and the night jaunt was unfortunately off. So Paul missed squiring Julie and Tricia around the Paris discos.

Eva's fierce and overriding preoccupation with her family was ceaseless, and another cause for stress in our relations. Everyone has family, and most married couples have to suffer their in-laws. With a modicum of give-and-take on both sides, normal civilized relations can be maintained even when there's no great love involved. I was prepared to play my part, not only socially, but financially as well. Among many other contributions, I helped put brother Louis through medical school at Emory, and bought the West End Avenue apartment for them when the rental became a co-op. But for Eva there was no give-and-take. It was all take.

Brother Louis was on drugs. I don't know what he was taking, but when he was high he had a habit of beating up on his half-blind sister Lita, or beating up his wife Toni. On one occasion, I got a desperate cry for help from Toni. She was battered and bruised and afraid for her life. "Get me out of here!" she pleaded. "I cannot stay in my apartment any longer." I put her up along with her young daughter Claudia in a room at the Lexington Hotel on Lexington Avenue for three days, while Louis calmed down.

This occurred while I was on a business visit in New York. Eva was in Paris. Similarly, on another visit to New York, I received a desperate phone call from the West End Avenue apartment. Louis was beating up Lita. I rushed up there and arrived at the same time as the police who came in response to my call. Louis was duly admonished and threatened with legal action, should this ever happen again.

Not surprisingly, Louis threatened me with physical violence, not once but on repeated occasions. One day, I was sitting in my office at DDI when Louis came on the phone. He told me he would be waiting for me when I left the office at the end of the day. "I'll be outside your office building," he told me " I'll be carrying a knife, its a beauty, and I'll be waiting for you." I found it hard to take this seriously, but as the day wore on, I began to wonder. The man is high, I told myself. He's capable of anything. When I walked out of the office that night, I was anything but reassured. Stepping into the street, I looked both ways. Louis was not there. Scary? Yes, you could say that.

When I recounted this to Eva by phone the following day, she had only one comment:

"Poor Louis!"

I had known for a long time that in Eva's universe I was fifth wheel on the wagon, but this surely drove the point home in case I had any lingering doubts. This marriage is finished, I said to myself. "She's not married to me, she's married to her family."

Even so, before making the final break, I gave it one more chance. The boys were out of college and starting their careers. Alan had just graduated from Brown. The time had come.

Before leaving for a trip to Africa, I sat down with Eva in our Avenue Foch apartment and tried to convince her that to save our marriage it was now or never. I begged her to understand how necessary it was to have an island of peace and calm in our home, and if she would only make the effort, we could make a new beginning. She said she would try.

"All right," I said, "then here is the first step. Don't bring your Aunt Antoinette over to stay with us this year." This old lady came over from New York and spent four months with us year in and year out, in addition to whatever other "house guests" happened to be in residence. There was no special need for her to stay with us every year. Eva just thought it was a nice idea. Tante Antoinette had other relatives in Paris she could have stayed with, but no, Eva wanted to have her around.

Normally, she would have been arriving around the time I was now about to leave for Africa. I wanted to make a test out of it. "Just cancel her," I said. "Have her stay with the other relatives."

"We'll see," said Eva.

When I returned from Africa, some three weeks later, I found Tante Antoinette well ensconced in our apartment as always. Nothing had changed.

I packed my bags and moved back to New York. It was 1969, the end of my marriage, and the beginning of a long drawn-out and painful process of disengagement.

For ten years Eva refused to consider any thought of divorce, or even separation. "Over my dead body," she would say to her friends.

She never failed to proclaim both in public and to me in private, her "undying love," while at the same time she did her best to poison me in the eyes of my friends. With one or two, she succeeded; with most, she failed.

CHAPTER FIFTY

LEZO THE BASQUE – "POTATO JOE"

Among the freeload boarders who descended on our Avenue Foch apartment, not all were unappealing. Some were likeable, even picturesque. That was the case of Lezo, the Basque Nationalist freedom-fighter. He was a seaman. During the Spanish civil war he ran the Franco blockade of the Republican coast in order to feed the starving people of the Asturias. He would load his battered coastal tramp steamer with potatoes from Ireland, and sail it into the North Atlantic coastal waters around Bilbao. Then, under cover of darkness, he would make for land and unload his cargo. He would escape back again into open waters in similar manner." Franco's men never caught him. He became famous, and was more than once written up in the British press, who dubbed him "Potato Joe."

Lezo was huge, almost like the Boris Karloff Frankenstein (minus the bolt in the neck.) His head was totally square, with a big protuberant forehead. His hair was cut short. He had big ears, big shoulders, big boxer's hands, and a barrel chest.

Lezo met Raja in our apartment – these were two guests I was happy to have around. Both men took to each other, and became fast friends. They made an exotic pair, Lezo, the gentle giant, and Raja, the fragile Brahmin, as they went off together to visit Lourdes.

Devoutly Catholic and fiercely anti-Communist, Lezo was waging a two-front war, one against General Franco for Basque independence, and the other to prevent a Communist takeover of the independence movement. He militated to get the United Nations to grant a homeland for the Basque people. First he tried to get them to designate some island in the Pacific, where the worldwide diaspora of Basques could congregate, using the 1948 establishment of the Israel homeland as an example. Meeting with no success at the UN, he altered his plan, and tried to get the Mexican government to designate one of their off-shore islands.

In order to attract public attention to his plan, he decided to sail solo across the Atlantic to Mexico, in a tiny one-man 12 foot sloop, with no radio. He built this flimsy craft himself at Saint Jean de Luz, the little French Basque port close to the Spanish frontier. I saw the vessel, still uncompleted, on one occasion.

But he never made the trip. Lezo fell in love with a diminutive bird-like and timorous French woman. She was scared the trip would kill him, and he yielded to her entreaties and gave it up.

Some years later, I was no longer living in Paris, and my separation proceedings had started. I learned that Lezo visited the Avenue Foch apartment. He was now huffing and puffing, out of breath and uncomfortable in a too tight suit. He looked like a broken down Jean Gabin, a small-time hood, an over-the-hill prize fighter. But the truth is, he was none of these. He was an idealist and a romantic. That night, they tell me, he broke down and wept as he talked of his heartbreak that his beloved Basque independence movement, the ETA, had been taken over by the Communists.

CHAPTER FIFTY ONE

A VISIT TO MARGARET THATCHER

Ronald Reagan's presidential campaign was floundering under the management of John Sears. In February 1980 Reagan fired Sears and appointed Bill Casey as his campaign manager. From that moment on, the Reagan campaign picked up steam.

I was in Paris at the time. The European media, mostly British and French, were echoing the line of the U.S. media to the effect that Ronald Reagan did not have presidential caliber, that he had no knowledge of international affairs, that he was nothing more than a trigger-happy cowboy and a grade-B movie actor. These views were then reproduced again in the U.S. media as "European opinion."

I cabled Bill Casey to say how valuable it would be if he could arrange for Reagan to make a quick visit to Europe to correct the false impression.

Bill cabled back saying it was a good idea but Reagan's schedule was booked solid and there was no opening. On the other hand he himself would be prepared to come over, and bring with him Richard Allen, who was slated to become Reagan's national security advisor. They could only spare three days. Could I arrange a couple of events, say one in London and one in Paris?

After consulting with Robert Tyrell, editor of *American Spectator*, I called on my friend Melvin Lasky, editor of *Encounter*, in London. With his help and that of Stephen Haseler, we organized an off-the-record dinner on July 3rd, 1980 at which Bill Casey and Richard Allen delivered the Reagan message.

It was attended by: Brian Beedham and Norman Mac Crae of the *Economist*; Peregrine Worsthorne-*Sunday Telegraph*; Robert Moss-

Daily Telegraph; Rhees Moggs and Bernard Levin-*London Times;*
Ronald Butt-*Sunday Times;* Robin Day-*B.B.C.;* Ferdinand Mount-
Daily Mail and *Spectator;* Melvin Lasky-*Encounter;* and Colin
Welch.

In Paris, the dinner was organized by Patrick Wajsman, editor of
Politique Internationale. In attendance were: Jean Francois Revel
and Olivier Todd of *Express;* Louis Pauwels and Jean D'Ormesson-
Figaro Magazine; Eduard Sablier and Patrick Poivre D'Arvor-*Radio
Television Francaise;* Andre Clement and Almaric-*Le Monde;*
Claude Francois-*France Soir;* Philippe de Baleine-*Paris Match;*
Philippe Theyson-*Quotidien de Paris.* Also Jean-Jacques Servan-
Schreiber and Raymond Aaron. By fortuitous good fortune, the Paris
dinner was also attended by Jeane Kirkpatrick and General Vernon
Walters who also spoke. The Reagan pitch was made con gusto.

In the days following these two events, there was a noticeable
change of attitude in the French and British press toward Ronald
Reagan. References to a trigger-happy cowboy and grade-B movie
actor faded.

While we were in London, Richard Allen arranged for us to call
on Margaret Thatcher at No. 10 Downing Street. An 11 am
appointment had been scheduled, and we were to meet outside the
hotel at 10.45 so as to jump into a taxi and get there on time. At the
appointed hour, Richard Allen and I stood outside Brown's Hotel
waiting for Bill Casey to join us. But Bill failed to appear. Where on
earth is Bill Casey? Nowhere to be found. He was not in the lobby.
He was not in his room. Had he forgotten the appointment?
Catastrophe! I walked along the sidewalk a short distance. A few
doors down from Brown's Hotel there is a bookshop. There was Bill
inside, peering at the titles on the shelves, several books under his
arm, totally absorbed. He was a lifelong collector of books, and an
avid omnivorous reader. At his home in Roslyn, Long Island, he had
collected over 10,000 titles. Despite the anxious moment, we were
not late.

Downing Street is a narrow semi-private road that leads off at
right angles from Whitehall. A Bobby is permanently stationed there
to check on entering vehicles. No. 10 has an undistinguished doorway

similar to all the others in the row of four-story Victorian houses. On entering, one has the impression of a well-appointed townhouse, and on being ushered into what appeared to be a private sitting room-drawing room, all chintz-covered sofas and dark polished furniture, it was hard to believe we were at the nerve center of the British realm. There was not a sound.

Margaret Thatcher entered and greeted us with charm and grace. "How nice of you to drop in'" she said. "Do tell me, how is dear Ron, and how is the campaign going?" She wanted to know all about it, and was given a full briefing by Casey and Allen. The butler brought in a larger silver tray and Margaret Thatcher then poured tea for each of us. She behaved as if she had nothing else on her mind and had all day to spend with us. There were no interruptions, no telephones, no secretaries rushing in to slip her an urgent message. It was like a tea-time visit at the country vicarage.

After about forty-five minutes, out of a concern for the crises which surely must be piling up outside and which, we were convinced, required the Prime Minister's urgent attention, we thanked her for her gracious hospitality and took our leave.

CHAPTER FIFTY TWO

THE MINISTRY OF TRUTH – A WORD ON THE OCTOBER SURPRISE

My visit to London and Paris with William Casey and Richard Allen in July 1980, was to have repercussions some ten years later when a Congressional Task Force, prompted by a Democratic controlled House of Representatives, investigated allegations that Bill Casey was involved in a conspiracy to delay the release of American hostages held by Iran, in order to influence the Presidential election which sent Ronald Reagan to the White House. The date we were in Paris raised a serious question in the minds of the investigators. The charges were eventually proven unfounded and without credibility, but for some time the matter, known as The October Surprise was a "cause celebre."

In the Spring of 1992, I published some comments on this affair in *Democracy Bulletin,* the newsletter of The American Foundation for Resistance International, the organization I founded with Vladimir Bukovsky. Here they are:

What is history? Fact or fiction? Truth or disinformation?

Some sixty years ago during the nineteen thirties, English schoolboys were entertained by a witty satire on the teaching of history called "1066 And All That." It posited the axiom that "History is not what you learn, it is what you remember."

Elsewhere it has been generally established that history is written by the victor. The victor on the battlefield was able to get his story out first and imposed it on the vanquished before the latter could get up off the ground. But that was in the days when victory meant victory at arms. Twentieth century totalitarians changed all that.

The re-writing of history was a major component of the Communist excercise of power. It was a continuous process, and took place while events were still happening. History was constantly revised in accordance with the current prevailing orthodoxy. Leon Trotsky and Bukharin were expunged from the encyclopedia. They became non-persons. George Orwell satirized the practice beautifully when describing the "Ministry of Truth" in his epic "1984."

Contrary to the popular belief that "we won the Cold War," for 74 years the Western democracies strove mightily to prevent the collapse of Soviet Communism, and they succeeded. Even at the height of the Cold War, there was never any intention of destroying Communism. The most the West could bring itself to do by way of countering Soviet aggression, was the policy of Containment, a leaky vessel at best. It never once threatened the existence of the Communist power base.

When Ronald Reagan decided to turn the tide, and started rolling back Soviet Communism, he triggered a chain reaction, which in an extraordinarily short time, led to the collapse of the empire. Of course other forces contributed; the bankruptcy of the economic system, the communications explosion, and not least, the sacrifice and courage of the dissidents. But had it not been for Reagan, the agony would have lasted longer, and had Reagan arrived sooner, that much sooner would the empire have collapsed.

For this Reagan will never be forgiven by the losers. And who are the losers? Why, those who preached for years against "provoking" the Russians; who chided us as "warmongers;" those who parroted the "convergence" theory, meaning they were becoming more like us while we were becoming more like them.

Now at the end of the twentieth century instead of the victors writing the history, it is the losers attempting to re-write the history! The Reagan years must be delegitimized. Reagan's triumph must be expunged from the encyclopedia. He must become an Orwellian non-person!

We live in an age of conspiracy paranoia. It abounds on all sides. It has become a national industry, in which the world of entertainment, the media, Hollywood, and the political jungle of Washington, DC combine to produce a heady mix for the titillation of a public bored with sit-coms and soaps. It is a world peopled by members of the left-liberal establishment, consumed by demonic fantasies in which evil conservatives plot to take over the world. Dr. Strangelove was an early archtype. Oliver Stone is a current Hollywood practioner.

During those glorious days of Watergate, when Richard Nixon was being ground in the dust, how they exulted! What a wonderful feeling it was! And ever since, they have been thirsting for a replay. The Iran Contra affair was heaven sent. It was all the more delicious in that the key villain was none other than the left-wing's favorite bogey-man, Bill Casey. But alas, ultimate joy eluded them. They were denied the final scene of the morality play where the monster-demon writhes in agony under the sword of that latter-day Saint George, Lawrence Walsh. There was no bloody kill, they never got Bill, what a cruel disappointment.

There is a basic rule of human nature which says that people will always believe what they want to believe. A lot of people want to believe, and therefore do believe, that during the presidential election campaign of 1980, Bill Casey organized a conspiracy to delay the release of the hostages until after the election, so as to prevent Jimmy Carter from doing it first, that is to say, springing an October Surprise.

Foremost among these true believers is one Gary Sick, former staff member of the National Security Council under Jimmy Carter, whose book October Surprise, *contains the main arguments. Number two on the true believers' list is the* New York Times, *which gave Gary Sick it's op-ed page early in 1991 to launch his book on the eve of publication, and then gave him more op-ed exposure on January 16, 1992 under the heading "Should Congress Investigate the October Surprise?" Then close behind, come PBS* Frontline *and Ted Koppel's* Nightline, *both of which, while straining to pretend objectivity, could scarcely conceal their conviction that Bill Casey did it.*

Now, as every good conspiracy advocate knows, if you want your theory to fly, you have to assemble enough circumstantial evidence, enough unsubstantiated allegations, enough innuendo and unproven assertions, so that when they are all woven together into a well-written yarn, people will pause and say:" Hmm! Well, yes, what do you know? Sure, it might have happened. Unlikely, but possible." That is all it takes. From then on it is plain sailing. The theory takes on a life of its own. The media, the columnists, the talk-show hosts, all have a field-day. And when the Anita Hill-Clarence Thomas fandango, the Smith-Kennedy rape adagio, and the Mike Tyson danse macabre have run out of steam, along comes October Surprise to enliven our evenings.

So, yes of course, it is a media event.

Unfortunately for him, Gary Sick's conspiracy yarn falls short of the high standards required to make this a winner. His cast of characters is a sorry lot. They are an assortment of sleazy, unreliable flaky imposters, con artists, on-the-make malodorous middlemen, fake intelligence agents, and arms traders, the likes of which would be hard to invent.

The guts of the story goes like this. Between July 27 and 29, 1980, William Casey is supposed to have attended meetings at the Ritz Hotel in Madrid with a high-level Iranian close to the Ayatollah, a man called Mehdi Karrubi. During these meetings it is further alleged that Casey proposed that if Iran were to delay the release of the hostages until after the U.S. election, Casey would see to it that arms which Iran desperately needed would be supplied by the United States.

These meetings were supposedly arranged by Cyrus and Jamshid Hashemi, two Iranian arms dealers who at the same time were dealing with the Carter administration for the same purpose. Both these men were indicted in 1984 for illegal arms shipments to Iran, and became fugitives from justice. In a subsequent plea-bargain, the charges were dropped in exchange for their cooperation in a U.S. Customs sting operation.

Cyrus Hashemi died in 1986. All that is known about the alleged meetings in Madrid comes from his brother, Jamshid Hashemi. There is absolutely no evidence other than Hashemi's assertion, that Casey was present at these meetings or that such meetings ever took place. Mehdi Karrubi, the high-level Iranian whom Casey was supposed to have met there has denied ever being in Madrid.

In his book, Gary Sick writes that five other sources have independently confirmed that these meetings took place, and that Jamshid's account of what was said there is substantially correct. Since, even if the meetings did take place as alleged, not one of these other persons was present, and each of them got his information second or third hand, it is hard to place much store in their so-called corroboration. Let us look at the quality of these independent sources.

First, we have Ari Ben Menashe, an Israeli, who has been extensively exposed in the Wall Street Journal, the New Republic, and Newsweek as a total fraud. In a Wall Street Journal article on November 27, 1991, Steven Emerson writes, "Thorough investigations by journalists from around the world, have shown Mr. Ben Menashe to be an abject liar." Newsweeks' national security correspondent, John Barry said on CNN on November 8, "Mr. Ben Menashe is a fabricator. I don't think myself he knows the difference between truth and fantasy..."

Then comes Heinrich Rupp, a former Nazi pilot, convicted of bank fraud and sentenced to 41 years in jail. He is a friend of Richard Brenneke who was originally considered to be a reliable source for October Surprise but was blown out of the water at an early stage as a monstrous faker. Heinrich Rupp's only connection with October Surprise, is that he claims that on October, 18, 1980, hew flew a plane to Paris carrying George Bush, William Casey, Richard Allen and Donald Gregg. This information was likewise blown out of the water when it was discovered that the plane he said he piloted was actually parked in California at the time.

These are the men, mind you, whom Gary Sick relies upon to confirm "the substantial accuracy" of what Jamshid Hashemi alleges was said by the participants at the Madrid meetings, although none of them claim to have been present at these meetings.

Thirdly comes Admiral Ahmad Madani, former Iranian minister of defense. He was a close personal friend and business collaborator of the Hashemis, hardly an independent, unbiased source.

Fourth, Arif Durrani, a Pakistani arms dealer, who by his own admission said he was not personally involved in any way with the Madrid meetings, but got his information from a member of Iran's Revolutionary Guard.

Finally, Richard Babayan, an Iranian wheeler-dealer, who is currently serving a jail sentence in the United States for securities fraud. This gentleman said he had obtained his information from an Iranian intelligence official who said he had just come from Madrid where he attended meetings between Casey and Karrubi. Gary Sick writes in his notes: "Babayan made this comment to a visitor who asked not to be identified."

Now, it just happens that through totally unrelated circumstances, I myself had a brief encounter with Babayan on one occasion. All I can say, and believe me I am being charitable, I would not trust him as far as I can throw a piano!

These are the five independent sources whom Gary Sick relies upon to corroborate the accuracy of what he says transpired at meetings in Madrid, where Casey is supposed to have first proposed a deal to delay the release of the hostages.

Now, let us look at the alleged meetings in Paris which were supposed to have taken place from October 15 to 20, where the deal was allegedly finalized in the presence of George Bush, William Casey and Donald Gregg. Once again, Gary Sick's sources of information are the same lying imposters, Richard Brenneke, Heinrich Rupp and Ari Ben Menashe. To this discredited trio, Gary Sick now adds another name, an Iranian arms dealer called Hushang Lavi.

This man was an accomplice of Cyrus Hashemi; he participated with Cyrus in the U.S. Customs sting operation by which the latter plea-bargained his way out of an 18 count indictment for illegal arms dealing. According to Gary Sick, Lavi declared that Cyrus Hashemi attended the October 1980 meetings in Paris with William Casey. But Sick goes on to say that "Lavi never made any claim to knowledge about actual deliberations at the meetings, except what he was told by Cyrus Hashemi." So what kind of corroboration is this?

Furthermore, something new has come along since the publication of Gary Sick's book. The F.B.I. has recently released tapes of telephone surveillance they were conducting on Cyrus Hashemi at the time, from which it transpires that on October 14, Hashemi flew to New York and remained there through October 21, i.e. the dates the alleged meetings in Paris were supposed to be taking place. So all this adds up to precisely zero.

But Gary Sick is an indefatigable conspiratorialist. He attempts to bolster all this fiction by quoting two sources which, he says, had ties to French Intelligence. These ties, by Sick's own admission, were pretty slender. One of these men is unnamed. His information is third hand, coming from an article in the German magazine Der Spiegel *in which the unnamed informant is claimed to have read a French intelligence report about the Paris meetings. The second source is identified. He is a French arms dealer called Ignatiew who, some years later talked to an unnamed person in the French government who confirmed that some important meetings with Iranians did take place in Paris during October, 1980, but he goes on to say that their purpose was* **to obtain the earliest possible release of the U.S. hostages – no mention of any delay.**

This fairy tale would not be worth wasting our time on were it not for the decision of the House Democrats to squander obscene amounts of taxpayers' money on a fruitless butterfly chase.

Take for instance, the meeting at L'Enfant Plaza Hotel in Washington in late September or early October, 1980, at which Richard Allen, Robert McFarlane, and Laurence Silberman met with a person who claimed to be Iranian and who proposed a deal to delay the release of the hostages in exchange for arms. Apparently such a meeting did take place and the offer was rejected out of hand. Now, let us ask ourselves this. If, as is alleged, Bill Casey had already established the groundwork for the hostage deal at the Madrid meeting in July, why would another proposal of the same nature now come along three months later?

So what can one say in the end about the whole tortuous fantasy woven with such loving care by Gary Sick, PBS Frontline, *and* ABC Nightline, with *the blessing of the* New York Times?

Well, there are a few things one can say.

First, there is no doubt that the hostage issue was the dominant factor during the 1980 presidential election campaign. There is also little doubt that the place was crawling with promoters and middlemen of all stripes, mostly shady, all anxious to play a role in helping promote the hostage release for personal profit.

There is also no doubt that the Israelis, who traditionally favored Iran against what they considered the greater danger, namely Iraq, wanted to facilitate the flow of arms to Iran.

There is no doubt, and the F.B.I. confirms it, that the Hashemi brothers, Cyrus and Jamshid, were engaged in discussions with the Carter administration in mid-October for the release of the hostages. There is also no doubt that the Carter administration considered an arms deal for hostages.

F.B.I. phonetaps on Cyrus Hashemi further confirm that in a conversation with his cousin in Teheran (speaker of the Párliament,) the latter told him that the Ayatollah got very angry at the thought that accepting the Carter administration's terms for a hostage release might help reelect him, and that consequently he, the Ayatollah himself might deliberately delay the release.

All the rest is speculation. For instance: It is reasonable to imagine that the middlemen engaged in promoting a hostage deal with the Carter administration would want to establish relations with the Reagan team as well. This was after all, no less than ordinary business insurance.

It is not unreasonable to imagine that the Reagan team, knowing they would in all probability be the next administration might wish to explore these contacts.

None of this gives us any basis to assume, nor does it imply there was any plot to delay the hostage release.

But if you suffer from conspiracy paranoia, there are no limits to where your imagination may carry you.

Even Gary Sick in the introduction to his book, seeks a little protection for his reputation when he writes: "This book is not a lawyer's brief to be carried into court. There is not enough evidence at this point to launch a prosecution of any individual, much less to be assured of a conviction beyond a shadow if doubt."

But this is not enough to exonerate Gary Sick of seeking to re-write history, which is exactly what he has tried to do.

One of the best comments on this affair is provided in Richard Ryan's review of Gary Sick's book which appeared in National Review. **Ryan writes:**

Reading October Surprise, one senses a slow drift from the forums of empiricism to miasmic regions of speculative metaphysics. It is easy to understand the theory's quasi-religious hold on the Left, which after all would like nothing better than to believe that Ronald Reagan somehow stole the election. The theory does nothing less, in the eyes of many of its proponents, than delegitimize the last decade of conservative successes, mystically erasing history and substituting self-righteous indignation.

George Orwell, how right you were!

CHAPTER FIFTY THREE

RADICAL SCENE CHANGE

In 1970, my life took a 180 degree change of direction. Mona was now the woman in my life, and though it took ten years before Eva agreed to a divorce, and even then it was a messy one, Mona remained steadfast throughout. We were married in 1980.

Daughter of Romania's leading historian, her father, the late Constantin Giurescu had been a member of parliament, twice minister, and a former provincial governor during the reign of King Carol. The Communists condemned him to five years of concentration camp and stripped the family of all its property. After years of fruitless attempts to flee the country, Mona finally succeeded in escaping the clutches of Ceaucescu, and made her way to the United States where she was accorded political asylum.

That two people, each at a critical turning point in their lives, and starting from such unlikely points of departure, should not only happen to meet, but find such mutual attraction and love, as to embark on a new life together – the second time for each – will be explained by some as a matter of pure chance. "One chance in a million," they would say, and add: "But these things do happen." There are others, on the other hand, who believe there is a destiny here, that such things are pre-ordained. Whatever the explanation, it is undeniable that it ushered in for both of us the happiest years of our lives.

Among her many talents and qualities which are legion, Mona is also a "femme d'interieure." She made a home for me, where we enjoy a quiet intimacy in a serene environment. I am no longer fifth wheel on the wagon. It is now twenty-six years since fate brought us together, and though there is a great deal more to be said about this new life, I must demur. It is too close, too immediate, and I am living it every day.

*

Other radical changes were to take place, both in my business and political activity.

Over the previous twenty years, Diamond Distributors Inc. (DDI) had grown and expanded its activities in many directions. The maintenance of good relations with the De Beers organization as an important source of supply, while at the same time pursuing a policy of developing "non-De Beers" sources of rough diamonds, required fine diplomacy and a careful balancing act. We had mining, exploration and buying programs in far-flung places, among which were Central African Republic, Gabon, Sierra Leone, Guinea, Ivory Coast, Angola, South Africa and Venezuela. With our head office in New York, we also maintained sales offices in London, Paris, Antwerp, and Tel Aviv, and in addition to our American staff we employed nationals of each of these countries. For a small family business we covered a lot of territory. Edward Jay Epstein describes our industry role in his excellent account, *The Rise and Fall of Diamonds.* (Simon & Shuster, 1982)

A combined consequence of the Vietnam war and the O.P.E.C. Arab oil embargo was that America entered a period of mounting inflation. As inflation grew, so people would buy gold and diamonds as a hedge. "Diamonds for investment" became a popular sales gimmick for less scrupulous merchants. We discouraged it. But along with inflation came higher and higher interest rates. There came a time when banks' prime rate rose to 21.5%. DDI, relying heavily on bank financing to cover its large inventory, found itself in a position where, despite booming sales, all its profit margin was being siphoned off to the banks. This could not go on. In order to free itself of the banks more equity capital was needed, and a wide-ranging search was undertaken. But to no avail. We decided to wind the business down. We had no choice. The DDI team was closely knit, some of its members having spent a lifetime with the firm. It was a heart-wrenching process for me personally. In all, it took two or three years. With inventory liquidated, branches closed down, and the banks paid off, the day came when there was no more DDI. A very sad day for all of us!

CHAPTER FIFTY FOUR

WILLIAM J. CASEY

Bill's name has appeared repeatedly in these pages, and yet so far, we haven't really talked about him. That is what happens to good friends; they get taken for granted.

In his later years, the public controversies that swirled around Bill's head became so shrill, that we tended to forget the man, and focused only on the issues. Enormously gifted, a scholar, man of action, successful venture-capitalist, loyal friend and dedicated public servant – there is no question, these were his qualities. To those who shared his views, he was the Supreme Cold Warrior, the man who more than any other, influenced Ronald Reagan in restoring America's power and rolling back the Evil Empire. To liberals and leftists however, and a major part of the media establishment, he was the devil incarnate; the man to be brought down and discredited at any cost.

These were reasons enough for the strong bond of friendship that existed between us; a friendship that began in OSS during World War II, when we discovered we were kindred anti-Communists at a time when there were not many around. But there was the human side of this too.

It was quite accidental that after the war we found ourselves neighbors on Long Island. Over the years, our families grew close. After we acquired Green Meadow Farm, young Bernadette, Bill's only daughter, would spend part of her summers with us in Dutchess County. On other occasions, the Caseys would join us in Paris, and together, we would visit France's magnificent gothic cathedrals.

Then there were skiing holidays in the Austrian Alps, and while Bill was no athlete, he bravely put on skis and wobbled around the slopes with the rest of us.

Sitting around the table at mealtimes, the Casey and Jolis families discussed and argued about the topics of the day in joyful cacophony. Everybody had opinions and was not shy of voicing them. Usually, there was general agreement – especially on such topics as Korea, Vietnam, the student protest movement, the flower children and the hippie generation – all our youngsters were good solid right-wingers. Ony on one subject was there dissension, and that was the topic of abortion. The Caseys, as devout Catholics, were rigorously pro-life; the Jolises were mostly pro-choice, though Jack sided with the Caseys. As the tone and heat of argument mounted and the voices got shriller, Bill would get angry. I then had to kick my crowd under the table to get them to shut up. That put a quietus on things for a while, and after a few moments silence, we moved into something less divisive.

Bill Casey's gangling slouch, his rumpled appearance, and sometimes incomprehensible speech, are legendary; but just as it was in the case of George Orwell, the listener was always richly rewarded, by struggling to understand his words, no matter how great the effort.

On one occasion, a delegation of "Veterans of OSS," of which Bill Casey was president at the time, attended a gathering in the South of France as guests of the French Resistance Veterans group, known as L'Amicale Action. Bill was scheduled to make a speech. He didn't speak French, but thought it would be a good idea, as a courtesy, to read out a speech in French. He asked me to help him write it. We worked on it together, until he was satisfied as to what he wanted to say. Then we rehearsed it privately, and I tried to coach Bill in the proper pronunciation.

At the end of the dinner, Bill got up with his typed French text in hand and began to speak. The audience stared at him in puzzlement. Is this a comedy act? they wondered. I shrivelled into my chair. Afterwards, a French Resistance veteran came up to me in obvious bewilderment, saying "You know, I understand English perfectly, but I couldn't understand a word Bill Casey said."

"That was not English," I told him, "Bill was speaking French." This became a standard oft-repeated joke for many years, and everyone loved Bill for it.

Friendship, when expressed in acts, can be more eloquent than when expressed in words. Such acts by Bill were manifested repeatedly. When my son Paul was held hostage in the Central African Empire by Bokassa, it was Bill who persuaded former Secretary of State Wiliam Rogers, his law partner at the time, to intervene personally with the Emperor. When DDI was meeting no success in its desperate effort to attract additional equity capital, Bill accompanied me on more than one visit to potential investors. These acts were spontaneous and freely given.

Finally, when my marriage broke up, the Casey women, Sophia and Bernadette sprang to Eva's side and cast me out of their lives. I became a pariah, no longer welcome at the Casey home. But Bill's friendship remained unshaken. We would meet on the outside, frequently for lunch, or at CIA headquarters in Langley, in the Director's office on the top floor.

When Bill lay mortally stricken at Georgetown University Hospital, in Washington, DC, Sophia and Bernadette relented, and allowed me to visit him towards the end. For this I was grateful.

My visit to Bill's bedside took place on February 6, 1987, one week after he resigned from the CIA. He could not speak, his whole right side was paralyzed and his face was twisted into an expression of terrible deformity. But he gripped me with his left hand. He could not raise himself from his bed. Then he mumbled incoherently. Bernadette crouched over him, trying to understand, saying "Say it again, Dad." This was within a few days of Bob Woodward's alleged conversation, which he describes in *Veil – The Secret Wars of the CIA 1981-1987*. (Simon & Shuster), Woodward purports to show that Casey, on his deathbed, made self-inculpatory admissions on the Iran-Contra affair. He has further stated that neither Sophia nor Bernadette were present on this occasion. Both women have confirmed that one of them was present at Bill's bedside at all times, and that Woodward could not have had such a conversation without one of them knowing about it. Sophia has flatly stated that Woodward's story is a lie.

In a review of *Veil* which I wrote for the **American Spectator,** I took issue with Woodward's claim to fair-minded objectivity regarding Bill Casey. I felt that by damning him with faint praise, Woodward was really out to "get" Bill. I concluded my review with these words:

"Finally, while far from suggesting that Bob Woodward is an instrument of Soviet active measures, I cannot resist quoting the admirable ditty of Humbert Wolfe, an Englishman, when describing British journalists:

> "You cannot hope to bribe or twist,
> Thank God! the British journalist.
> But seeing what the man will do
> Unbribed, there's no occasion to."

CHAPTER FIFTY FIVE

I MEET VLADIMIR BUKOVSKY

Finding myself in Europe one day in 1983, I fell upon an item in the *International Herald Tribune*. At a press conference in Brussels, three Red Army soldiers, deserters from Afghanistan, were presented to the public. The press conference was conducted by an Englishman, Lord Nicholas Bethell. Though we in the West had heard of such Soviet defections, this was the first time Red Army deserters had appeared in person. I was very excited. Knowing full well that such an event does not happen spontaneously, I was curious as to who was behind it. Friends in Paris told me: "Oh don't you know? This is the new organization called Resistance International."

"I've never heard of it," I answered. "Who is the moving spirit behind it?"

"It is Vladimir Bukovsky, the Soviet dissident," they told me. "Haven't you met him?"

"No," I said, "Tell me."

Vladimir Bukovsky had rebelled against the Soviet system since his days as a student. In June, 1963, as a young man, he was first arrested by the authorities for actions "inimical" to the regime. He was confined to a special psychiatric prison in Leningrad. Two years later, he was released in February 1965, only to be imprisoned again in December, and held for eight months in various psychiatric prisons. After six months of freedom, he was arrested once again and sentenced to a concentration camp for three years. After his release in January 1970, he spent a year extensively documenting the use of psychiatry and mind-bending drugs as a means of repressing political dissenters.

In March 1971, his famous "Appeal to Psychiatrists" was presented to the Western press. It attracted international attention. Nineteen days later, he was once again arrested and sentenced to two years in prison, five years in a concentration camp and five years of internal exile.

In December 1976, he was forcibly ejected from the Soviet Union in an exchange for the imprisoned leader of the Communist Party of Chile, Luis Corvalan. His autobiography, ***To Build a Castle,*** (Andre Deutsch, Ltd. – London, 1977) describes in grim detail his ordeal.

"Right now," I was told, "he is in Palo Alto, doing scientific research."

At the first opportunity, following my return to the U.S. I flew to the West Coast, and met with Vladimir Bukovsky, a pleasant stocky man with a broad slavic face, in his early forties as far as I could judge. He had an air of the street-smart intellectual about him and spoke perfect English. He told me how he and his friends brought the Russian deserters from Afghanistan to Europe, and how they were circulating clandestine newspapers among the Soviet troops still serving, and many other exciting things.

"I'd like to help," I said.

"There's only one thing we need," he told me, "Money!"

"I'm sorry," I answered, "I'm not rich enough for that. But maybe I can help you raise some. I'm not a professional fund-raiser, but one can always try."

"You think it will work?" he asked.

"I'm not sure," I answered, "but if your people need money to carry on their activities, its the only way to go about it that I can suggest. We should give it a try. Give me a little time to think this over, I'll get back to you as soon as I can."

CHAPTER FIFTY SIX

RESISTANCE INTERNATIONAL

" I went back to see Vladimir Bukovsky. "Give me the whole story," I asked him, "How did it all start?"

It started in Paris, in 1983, when Vladimir Bukovsky and a group of former political prisoners and exiled dissidents formed *"L'Internationale de la Resistance."* The organization had Bukovsky as President and Armando Valladares, the Cuban poet who spent twenty-two years as a political prisoner of Fidel Castro, as Vice-president. The latter's book, *Against All Hope,* (Alfred A. Knopf, 1986,) provides a hallucinating account of the ordeal of torture and brutality he and hundreds of others suffered in the Cuban Gulag.

Others in the group included Vladimir Maximov, editor of the exiled dissidents' magazine *Kontinent,* and Eduard Kusnetzov, both Soviet writers and victims of the Gulag and psychiatric prisons.

Resistance International was an umbrella organization embracing a broad spectrum of political, religious, and social movements from around the world, united by their common commitment to fighting Communist totalitarian oppression.

A list of those participating, and the message they broadcast to the world on the occasion of their highly publicized inauguration ceremony in Paris, in May, 1983, is reproduced in Appendix No.5.

The new group had already scored a number of successes in its short life. In addition to the presentation of Red Army deserters at the Brussels press conference, already mentioned, they included:

– The circulation among Soviet soldiers serving in Afghanistan of a dummy mock-up "Special" edition of the Red Army journal, Krasnaia Zvedzda (Red Star), urging them to "Stop the War and Go

Home!" This was also pasted on public walls in the streets of Kabul by the Mujahedeen. (See Appendix No.5.)

– An openly attended conference in Paris at which, for the first time in Europe, Soviet "Active Measures" and disinformation were publicly aired and discussed before the media.

– Street demonstrations in Milan, and other cities in Italy, urging freedom for the Soviet satellite countries of East Europe.

How does one grab a hold of such a complex proposition? Where to begin? "All it takes is money," said Bukovsky, sounding like the Beatles.

"In order to raise money to help your Paris friends," I said, "we need an American organization.

"We already have one," answered Bukovsky.

"Oh?"

"Yes, there's a man in Washington, DC, called Makarenko, who has formed a local branch of Resistance International."

"Fine," I said. "That will save us time. Please give him a call and say I'd like to come and talk to him."

That was the beginning of a false start that cost us several months of delay and much frustration.

*

In one of the seedier sections of Washington, DC, I found Mr. Makarenko, a huge bear-like man in his fifties with luxuriant bushy whiskers, almost filling with his sheer bulk the one-room cellar that served as home and office, one wall of which was completely covered with a large American flag. Mr. Makarenko did not speak a word of English.

A young man materialized – I could not see from where, – to serve as interpreter, and I explained my mission. Bukovsky had already alerted him, so he was full of excitement at the prospect of receiving unexpected support.

"Tell me about your organization," I asked him. "Who is on your Board of Directors? "Do you have a program? How much money have you raised?

As the answers came back, filtered in translation, I soon realized we had a fair-sized problem.

– There were three on his Board of Directors, himself as President, and his daughter and son-in-law, both of whom lived in Munich, Germany, who also spoke no English.

– No, they hadn't raised any money, and as for program, all that I gathered was, that Makarenko was in touch with a Congressman whose name I don't recall, and had once appeared before a Congresional Committee inquiring into slave-labor conditions in the USSR.

I told Bukovsky I did not think Makarenko was what we were looking for, and that we should form our own organization. Of course, that was the right way to go, except for an important difficulty, namely, Makarenko was using the name Resistance International with the approval of Vladimir Maximov, acting for the Paris group, and had registered the name with the U.S. authorities.

So, out of necessity, we decided to work with Makarenko. We explained to him that in order to attract support from private donors in the United States, it was most important to have an English-speaking Board of Directors, and at the very least he should add to his present Board some English-speaking members. Makarenko was not too happy at the idea, but in the face of it's obvious logic, he finally yielded. Then at a meeting we held in his lawyer's office in Washington, he agreed, subject to confirmation by his Board, to admit Bukovsky and myself as additional members. That meant getting agreement from his daughter and son-in-law in Munich!

We waited several weeks for an answer, and were finally informed one day, that those in Munich had declined to approve the measure. We were nowhere.

In exasperation, I told Bukovsky we had already wasted too much time, and should no longer delay forming our own organization.

Since we could not use the name Resistance International, I decided on the nearest thing to it, namely **The American Foundation for Resistance International.** Bukovsky, in his capacity of President of *L'Internationale de la Resistance,* wrote a letter to Makarenko

countermanding Maximov's previous authorization, to inform him
he no longer represented the Paris-based group.

*

The American Foundation for Resistance International (AFRI)
was incorporated in August 1984, with Vladimir Bukovsky, President,
Albert Jolis, Executive Director, and Charles Sutherland (a
Washington-based friend of Bukovsky,) director. Others who were
added later, included Armando Valladares, Vice-President,Jeane
Kirkpatrick, former U.S. Ambassador to the United Nations, and
Richard Perle, former Assistant Secretary of Defense, Midge Decter
and Yuri Yarim-Agaev.

One who proved of enormous help at the outset, was Midge
Decter, then Executive Director of the Committee For The Free
World. As a neophyte in such matters, I doubt whether I could have
gotten our project off the ground without the benefit of her experience,
her practical advice, and ever ready availability to answer my calls
for help.

Bukovsky did not remain in Palo Alto. He soon moved to
Cambridge, England, where he now permanently resides. His frequent
visits to the United States and mine to Europe, made it possible for
us to have a close and fruitful working relationship over the years.
Though we did not always agree on every day-to-day detail, we
agreed on most, and certainly on the broad objectives. Endowed with
a sharp perceptive intelligence and a burning commitment to his
beliefs, Bukovsky is the personification of the intellectual as man-
of-action.

One of our early actions, in 1985, made possible by a special
grant from the John M. Olin Foundation, was to bring to Washington
a delegation of European World War II Resistance leaders and
parliamentarians at the time when Ronald Reagan was trying to get a
balky Congress to approve his policy of resistance to Communist
subversion in Central America. Support for the anti-Communist
freedom fighters in Nicaragua, the Contras, was the big issue at the
time, and the Liberal-Left were opposing it furiously.

With Midge Decter's help, we were able to get a full-page ad in the *New York Times,* and as co-sponsors with the American Foreign Policy Council, we brought our delegation to Capitol Hill.

The group included, among others: Franz Ludwig Count von Stauffenberg, son of Hitler's failed assassin; Marie Madeleine Fourcade, French Resistance heroine; Edgardo Sogno del Valino, Italian Resistance leader; Malcolm Fraser, former Prime Minister of Australia; and three members of the British parliament, one of whom was Winston Churchill, (the grandson,) and Nikolaus Von Mach, German Anti-Nazi Resistance.

Through the good offices of my friend Michael Ledeen, I called on the Honorable Jeane J. Kirkpatrick, former United States Ambassador to the United Nations whom I had not met before, to inform her of the arrival of this group. I asked whether she would agree to chair a Capitol Hill seminar for them. Her unhesitating agreement encouraged me later to invite her to join our Board of Directors, which she accepted. From then on her participation in our activities was unstintingly given, often at considerable inconvenience to herself. At our Board meetings, her advice and counsel were invaluable. As keynote speaker at our public gatherings, her presence alone ensured their success. She remained throughout a precious source of strength and encouragement, and for me personally, an inspiration.

The Capitol Hill seminar, chaired by Jeane Kirkpatrick, was held in one of the Senate caucus rooms before an audience of Senators and staffers. The World War II Resistance leaders delivered a stirring appeal to the United States to exert leadership in stemming the spreading tide of Communist subversion which threatened to engulf the world. Should the United States fail in this, they argued, Western Europe would be gradually sucked into the Soviet orbit and end up as a Kremlin satellite.

Ronald Reagan subsequently received the group at the White House, and this was followed by a White House luncheon. Each member of the group was photographed individually, shaking hand with the President, which he subsequently dedicated personally. Mine hangs proudly in my office.

A memorable offshoot occurred on this occasion. One of the members of the delegation was a French Resistance leader, now member of the French Army General Staff, General Revault D'Allones. He had heard about the Strategic Defense Initiative (SDI), then in it's early development. He was very excited by the concept. "Just imagine!" he said, "A bullet firing at a bullet and hitting it – dans l'espace?" And he touched the tip of his left index finger to the tip of his right index finger. "C'est absolument fabuleux!" Could I arrange to have him briefed in more detail on this fantastic development?

I did better than that. I was lucky to be able to get an introduction to Lieutenant General James A. Abrahamson, Jr., the first Director of the Strategic Defense Initiative. He graciously invited me to bring General Revault D'Allones to lunch with him at the Pentagon. I pushed my luck a little further. Could I also bring Madame Marie-Madeleine Fourcade, the French Resistance heroine?

Marie-Madeleine, was something special. She had obviously been beautiful as a younger woman, and remained strikingly handsome now, well advanced into her seventies. Her visit to the White House had excited her beyond measure; she wanted to "be in on everything;" she was dying to hear about S.D.I.

"Of course!" answered the General. "Bring her along."

As the four of us sat down for lunch in the Senior Officer's dining room at the Pentagon, General Abrahamson began explaining the arcane mysteries of the Strategic Defense Initiative – Star Wars. General Revault D'Allones sat transfixed, and Marie-Madeleine Fourcade gazed at the General in rapt fascination, her eyes shining. But General Abrahamson did not only talk about SDI, he wanted to hear about World War II Resistance.

I could not help thinking what an extraordinary scene this was. Here were exponents of the two polar extremities in the art of warfare. At one pole, the farthest frontier of scientific and technological advance, and at the other, the lone resistance fighter whose armament is little more than quick wits and personal courage. And each was fascinated with other's story.

*

THE AMERICAN FOUNDATION FOR RESISTANCE IN-TERNATIONAL was originally intended as a support group for the Paris based organization, but this did not last. Soon, the Paris group fell apart due to personality differences. Vladimir Maximov was a difficult man to work with. He quarrelled with everyone, even with Armando Valladares, a man with whom, in my opinion, it is almost impossible to quarrel. He was jealous of Armando, whom he referred to as a "very small poet." He quarrelled with Bukovsky, of whom he was also jealous. I had my own problems with him, and used to refer to him as "homo sovieticus."

Resistance International's active life lasted eleven years. We will never know how much, if any, difference it made in the collapse of the Soviet Union. By the late 1980's, the collapse was probably irreversible anyway, though this was by no means the case when our organization was launched. Moreover, after the failed coup in 1991, nobody could rule out the possibility of a successful second try. The struggle went on till the end. In our own small way, we like to think we helped a little, and indeed in a few sharply focused instances, I think our actions did make a difference. Enough of a difference, at any rate, for Moscow to attack Resistance International as moral degenerates, which they did in 1987, in *Pravda*, *New Times* and *Moscow News*. This came in response to the publication by the *New York Times* on March 22, 1987, of a statement by Bukovsky and a group of other dissidents attacking Soviet policies, entitled "Is Glasnost a Game of Mirrors?"

The limiting factor of course, was always money. There were always more "great ideas" waiting to be implemented than money to pay for them. I had never been a fundraiser. I didn't like asking people for money, it went against the grain. But it is surprising what one can do if there is sufficient motive. Over the span, I was able to raise several million dollars, all private, not a cent from government. It sounds like a lot, but it was a pitiful drop in the ocean when measured against the magnitude of the task.

Our supporters included major foundations, corporations and private citizens. The most generous included, The Lynde & Harry Bradley Foundation, The John M. Olin Foundation, The Smith

Richardson Foundation, Sarah Scaife Foundation, The Milliken Foundation. In addition, we had over two thousand private individuals whose donations ranged from $25, $50, $100, into the tens and even hundreds of thousands. Among these, Mrs. Charlotte E. Cabot, deserves special mention for her extraordinary generosity.

Among the actions we were able to take, here are a few:

The Tribunal on Cuba

In April 1986, under the supervision of Armando Valladares, we organized a "Bertrand Russell-style" tribunal in Paris to expose to the world the killing, torture, mutilation, and degradation of political prisoners in Fidel Castro's tropical Gulag. Surviving witnesses testified before a prestigious international jury, (See Appendix No. 6)

The proceedings of the Tribunal were filmed, and later expanded into a two-hour documentary film by Nestor Almendros, the Oscar-winning cineast who made "Kramer versus Kramer;" "Sophie's Choice;" "Days of Heaven;" and "Places in the Heart." He was assisted by Cuban exile director Jorge Ulla. Entitled *Nobody Listened,* a riveting condemnation of Communist terror methods, it won numerous awards at international film festivals, and was smuggled into Cuba and the Soviet Union. It has been compared to the Holocaust documentary, Shoah, and also to the film *"Sorrow and Pity,"* the story of the German occupation of France.

Nobody Listened was shown widely in Europe and Latin America. But in the United States it was blocked by Liberal-Left opposition. Interminable efforts to get Public Broadcasting to show it on TV met with no success, until finally PBS agreed, only on condition that it be shown in conjunction with a left-wing pro Fidel Castro film. (See Appendix No. 6)

*

Helsinki "Parallel" Conferences

In April, 1986 In Bern, Switzerland, and again in November 1986, in Vienna, Austria,. Resistance International organized "parallel" conferences to coincide with the official Helsinki Review meetings of the thirty-five signatory nations to the Helsinki Accords, which were taking place in those same cities at the same time. Spokesmen for the pro-democracy and independence movements from the USSR participated, and included such well-known human rights activists as Anatoly Shcharansky, Yuri Orlov, and Eugene Ionesco among other intellectuals. Writing of the Vienna meeting, *U.S. News and World Report* described the event as "having stolen the political show from the C.S.C.E."

*

Martin Colman

Around this time, through the recommendation of Midge Decter, I acquired a close collaborator in the person of Martin Colman, a young man from California. With charm and intelligence he displayed public relations talents of a high order. His resourcefulness, ability to improvise in a pinch, and eager commitment, made him a real asset. Starting off as Director of Communications, he later became Executive Director of the National Council to Support the Democracy Movements, the special division of RI we had created to expand our fund-raising capacity, and which we later spun off as a separate entity. Never short of ideas; always ready with a "solution;" never daunted by setbacks, he was a perfect balance to my more cautious approach.

*

The First International Conference
on The Democratic Alternative
in The Soviet Union

Held in Paris, May 9 and 10, 1989, this meeting assembled for the first time, exiled representatives of the National Independence Movements of the Soviet Union, with the object of formulating a common program and a unified strategy.

Ambassador Jeane Kirkpatrick, in the midst of her crowded schedule, generously agreed to make a twenty-four round-trip trans-

Atlantic flight to deliver the keynote address. On this occasion, I endured some anxious nail-biting moments. Jeane's timing was calculated almost to the minute. It was the only way she could fit this into her other commitments. By the time the conference opened, her plane had not yet landed. Frantic calls to the airline company failed to elicit any hard information. I was about to make an announcement from the podium that Ambassador Kirkpatrick would regretfully be prevented from appearing, when I decided to make one final call to the airport. This time I got an answer. "Yes the plane would land in forty-five minutes." It was four hours late.

I left the conference and rushed out to Charles De Gaulle Airport, just in time to greet Jeane, fatigued, exasperated, but in good spirits. With remarkable good grace and cool aplomb, and as it were, without breaking her stride, she made a dramatic entry at the conference hall and delivered the keynote address. I considered it a most gallant performance.

In her address she pointed to the historical irony of the fact it was the Soviet Union that gave wars of liberation from colonial rule international legal underpinnings at the United Nations. "All peoples have the right to self-determination," says the resolution proposed by Nikita Krushchev, and adopted by the General Assembly in 1960. It is high time, said Jeane Kirkpatrick, that the West turn the argument against the Soviets and hoist them with their own petard.

*

The Prague Conference

During three days, July 4, 5 and 6, 1990, a historic meeting took place in Prague, Czechoslovakia, where, for the first time ever, democracy leaders from each of the Soviet republics, travelling from their homelands, met, at the invitation of President Vaclav Havel. How did such a noteworthy event come about?

The answer is, through Paruir Hayrikyan, an Armenian resistance fighter, who spent 17 of his 41 years of life in Soviet prisons and labor camps. He came to the United States after being forcibly expelled from the USSR, and now figured among the many former dissidents collaborating with our organization. The fame and reputation of Vaclav Havel had filtered through to Hayrikyan as he sat in his Soviet prison cell, and he now expressed a keen wish to meet his hero.

Martin Colman was quick to sense the political opportunity this presented, and cabled Havel directly. The latter responded, saying he would be pleased to meet with Hayrikyan. So Colman and Hayrikyan travelled to Prague, in February, 1990, and at their meeting, Havel extended his invitation that we hold our next conference in Prague.

Organizing such a conference in a country only recently emerged from behind the Iron Curtain, presented huge problems, both logistical and financial. We shared the task with a parallel group that Bukovsky had created in New York, called The Center for Democracy. Headed by Yuri Yarim-Agaev, this group was in closer day-to-day contact with certain dissidents inside the Soviet Union, thus facilitating the transmission of invitations and other organizational details.

Participants at the Prague meeting included delegates from the major constituent republics and pro-democracy movements in the Soviet Union. (See Appendix No7.)

These men and women knew of each others' existence, but had never met. Here, they had an opportunity to coordinate their strategy, exchange experiences, and meet with democracy leaders from the recently liberated countries of East and Central Europe.

I was not surprised to discover that there was opposition inside Czechoslovakia to this meeting. I expected it. During the weeks prior to the event, a whispering campaign spread through the coffee houses of Prague and was picked up by the local press. Backroom scuttlebutt in Czech circles had it that the conference was a dangerous provocation and a "snub to our neighbor to the East," that Havel had not really extended the invitation. Civic Forum, which Havel had originally designated to act as local co-hosts, quietly pulled out and was replaced by Charter 77. At one point, matters got so fouled up it looked as though the meeting might founder. Bukovsky jumped into the middle, and with lacerating invective, shamed the timid and silenced the naysayers. In the end the meeting got back on track,

Vaclav Havel delivered a warm address at the opening, and mingled with the delegates and guests.

The symbolism of the occasion was highlighted by the fact that during the same three days of its deliberations, the Communist Party of the Soviet Union was meeting in Moscow in a vain effort to shore up the crumbling edifice of its own power base.

Press coverage included *New York Times, Wall Street Journal, Washington Post, Boston Herald, Washington Times, Sunday Times (London), Le Monde, Figaro (Paris).* As for TV coverage, if Ted Koppel and Dan Rather did not feel the need to be there, Soviet TV on the other hand, certainly did. CNN was not yet around.

As chairman of the National Council to Support the Democracy Movements, it fell to me to open the conference and welcome the participants. As I mounted the podium, my mind flashed back forty-six years, to the time during World War II when I was smuggled into Switzerland in the trunk of Paul Mellon's car in order to meet with representatives of the same nationalities and ethnic groups as those now sitting before me. At that time they were convinced I was a special emissary of General Eisenhower who had come to help them in their quest for national independence. Alas, that was not the case, and I could not help them. This time, though, it is different, I can help them. What an extraordinary circumstance, I thought! "idée fixe," if there ever was one.

For the delegates who journeyed from the Soviet Union it was a milestone event. They returned home buoyed and encouraged beyond measure, armed with fax machines and word processors. They also took with them an invaluable store of information and contacts that were to prove crucial in the succeeding months as the Soviet System continued to disintegrate.

The gathering was not without drama closer to home. Personality clashes surfaced. Bukovsky took violent objection to Martin Colman, and demanded that I fire him. I refused. Colman had worked tirelessly in the preparatory stages of the conference. In fact it was Colman's initiative in bringing Paruir Hayrikian, the Armenian leader to meet with Vaclav Havel, that made the conference possible in the first place. Bukovsky felt Colman was attributing too large a role for himself, and was promoting Hayrikian without taking into account the feelings of the other delegates. There was evidently a good deal of jealousy and rivalry going on to which I had not been privy.

Though I refused to fire Colman, I realized it would be just as well to see that he and Bukovsky had as little contact with each other as possible, from then on. The best way to do this, I concluded, was to spin off as a separate entity, The National Council to Support the Democracy Movements. This we did in 1991, with Colman as Executive Director, and me as Chairman. Members of the Board included Richard Perle, Michael Novak, Charles Lichenstein, Paul Weyrich, Morton Blackwell, Midge Decter, Faith Whittlesey, and Robert Krieble.

*

Printing and Communications equipment for the democracy movements

Under the guidance of Robert Van Voren, of R.I's Amsterdam office, young Dutch students travelling to the USSR on Intourist visits, would pack short-wave radios, table-top copiers, and lap-top computers into their backpacks and duffel bags. These would be delivered to designated "safe" persons, once inside. Occasionally, a student was caught, arrested, held in prison for a few days, and then expelled. This student never got another visa to enter the USSR, but others carried on.

Offset printing equipment and computerized typesetting equipment, donated by private supporters, was airlifted to Armenia and Estonia respectively. It is better not to ask how the airlifting was arranged!

We were also able to send in equipment for a complete medium-wave radio station, from U.S. Army surplus; this too thanks to the generosity of a private donor. This station went on the air (pirate fashion) in support of Boris Yeltsin during his first presidential campaign.

*

Preparations for underground resistance

1991 was the year the Soviet Union died. But on January 1 of that year it did not look that way. At that time a repressive crackdown was clearly being mounted by the Kremlin. During January, the Red Army moved into the Caucasus, ostensibly to stop the fighting between Armenians and Azerbaijanis, but in fact to enforce control from the center. In the Baltics, Soviet Special Force troops, the "Black Berets" struck in Latvia and Soviet tanks crushed unarmed civilians in Lithuania.

Having anticipated this development toward the end of 1990, Vladimir Bukovsky had initiated a project aimed at creating a support base and training center for underground resistance. It was to be based in Poland.

After the failure of the August 1991 coup, there was clearly no further need for the project, and it was discontinued. But in the intervening seven months, with the assistance of friends in the "Fighting Solidarity" movement, a support infrastructure for eventual underground resistance in the Soviet Union had been established in Poland. Known as "Warsaw 90," it became fully operational on January 7 1991.

- A secret radio communications network was created, linking a number of locations inside the Soviet Union with the Polish base. These included Ternepol, Western Ukraine, Byelorussia and Lithuania. One station was located inside the Lithuanian Parliament building in Vilnius, and was operational when Red Army troops surrounded the Parliament.

- An underground broadcasting station was established in Tiblisi, Georgia. The station went on the air twice a week, Fridays and Sundays, for 15 minutes at a time, to avoid detection. *Moscow News* reported on April 29, 1991: "The Georgian opposition got help starting an illegal radio station from Polish members of Fighting Solidarity. They gave the Georgians the necessary American equipment."

– Some 76 underground activists received training at the Polish base between February 15 and May 15, 1991.

Fortunately all this was not needed, but it was a close call.

Democracy Bulletin

Every organization needs a newsletter, and ours was no exception. Who would do it? Who indeed? With no volunteers rushing forward, and the need obviously pressing, I stumbled into the job myself. With no experience in this field, it is amazing what one can do when there is no alternative. You learn as you go. Write the material; find contributors; meet the deadline. Learn how to operate computer equipment. Try to understand the incomprehensible "user handbooks". Stumble, fumble, start again. Try to catch the typos. It took time, but in the end I got it. *Democracy Bulletin* became our quarterly organ, 16 pages, with pictures and artwork. It went out to 5,000 readers, including members of Congress and college libraries across the country. A quarterly high-wire act – a tour de force.

Our Bulletin even had a Polish edition! A political science student at Jagiellonian University in Cracow named Grzegorz Hajdarowicz took it upon himself to translate every issue. He desk-top printed it and sold it on Cracow streets. He was a member of KPN The Confederacy of Independant Poland.

CHAPTER FIFTY SEVEN

TEN DAYS THAT SHOOK THE WORLD, AUGUST, 1991

The oceans of ink and hours of prime-time that TV devoted to "the coup-that-failed" are now but a memory, but oh, how I sat glued to my screen, and tore myself away only to rush to the newstand for the latest edition. In searching for answers, how frustrated I was. Was it a put-up job orchestrated by Gorbachev? Were the suicides really suicides? Who was really behind the plotters? What exactly went wrong? Why was it so badly bungled? Experts aplenty were giving instant answers. None were satisfactory, and I was not convinced. But how fascinating it was to speculate! All I knew for certain was that I was witnessing epoch-making events.

And I remember thinking, as I watched the unfolding action, how these events mirrored what took place 74 years ago in October, 1917, when Lenin's followers stormed the Winter Palace in Petrograd and ushered in the Bolshevik Revolution. John Reed, the American Communist newsman who witnessed these events wrote his classic *Ten Days That Shook The World* in 1919, for which Lenin made him a Hero Of The Soviet Union. He lies buried in the Kremlim today. With a preface by Lenin himself, his book became the preferred reading for generations of dedicated Communists the world over. For 74 years, left-wing intellectuals on four continents have praised its virtues as the seminal opus of the Workers' Revolution. In 1927, Sergei Eisenstein turned the book into a film classic. *Ten Days That Shook The World* still draws filmgoers at art theaters everywhere.

I saw it in London as a young man, and dreamed of becoming a cameraman like Eisenstein.

What I was seeing now, in August 1991, beamed through the TV screen into my New York City apartment was "ten days shaking the world again," except it was not ten this time, it was only four. Tanks rumbled through Moscow's streets and ringed the Parliament building, 200,000 people filled the Palace Square in Leningrad to protest the coup, the coal miners went on strike, confusion reigned, the coup leaders argued among themselves, rumors were flying. It was a 1917 replay in reverse.

Then Yeltsin climbed up on a tank to face down the coup plotters, a rare moment in history. And I thought how fitting it would be if at that very moment, somewhere in the crowd there might stand a young man as dedicated to human freedom as John Reed was to Socialism, recording in eloquent prose the death throes of the Workers' Revolution. I dared to hope he was there to write a book that would earn as much international acclaim as John Reed's, and would inspire the production of an epic film to rival Eisenstein's, so that my grandchildren can go to art theaters in the 21st century to learn of the monumental events of August, 1991, when one of the greatest tyrannies of all time was finally brought down.

*

CHAPTER FIFTY EIGHT

BY GEORGE – WE GOT AUSTRALIA!

When I was a youngster in the 1920s, Radio was in its infancy. Public broadcasting had just commenced. None of us had radio sets, and to buy one in a store was prohibitively expensive. So, a favorite schoolboy hobby was to "build your own." I don't remember all the details, but I do remember that part of the process consisted of mounting a small piece of quartz along with a copper-wire coil in a cigar box. The piece of quartz was known as "the crystal." Then a short length of curly-cue wire was fixed to a metal prong. This was known as the "cat's whisker." The whole contraption was linked to a battery and a pair of earphones, and now you were ready to go.

The trick was to poke the cat's whisker at the crystal until a sound came back to you in the earphones. It took a lot of poking and scratching, but with enough perseverance and luck you might finally be rewarded by a barely audible abrasive croak announcing: "Hello. Hello. This is London Calling." At that point you would leap up in triumph, and race a round the room shouting "I got it I got it."

In time, we got to be experts. We acquired bigger crystals, stronger batteries, and maybe, for all I remember, stronger cat's whiskers. Whatever it was, we started to receive broadcasts from abroad. We got Paris. "Allo! Allo! Ici Paris!" We got Brussels. We got Amsterdam. And we said to ourselves: "You know, if we go on like this, one day we'll get Australia." The idea was too preposterous to contemplate. "Good Lord, if we ever get Australia," we said, "there'll be nothing left. What on earth will we do then."

That's how I felt when the Soviet Union collapsed in 1991. **By George, we got Australia!**

It was intoxicating, while it lasted, but the "morning after" was inevitable.

Soviet power may have collapsed, but the Communist mindset has not. Old guard apparatchiks are still in charge under different labels. Fidel Castro still holds Cuba in thrall, and Communist dictatorships still rule in China and North Korea. And, irony of all ironies, what was originally foisted upon the Russian people by force, and maintained for seventy four years through blood and terror, now threatens to be legitimized by popular vote.

In an article he wrote for the Paris daily, *Le Monde,* on May 16, 1996, Vladimir Bukovsky deplored the passivity of today's Russian public in the face of the horrors being inflicted upon the people of Chechenya. They are free to demonstrate, he wrote. Why don't they? Why don't they pour into the streets of Moscow to demand and end to the barbarism? Yelstin would surely yield. When Russia was not free, we demonstrated; we protested; and we, all of us fellow dissidents, ended in the Gulag – the labor camps, the psychiatric prisons. "Was it all in vain?" he asks.

Elsewhere, new tyrannies loom, and human slaughter is sickeningly common across the globe. And with it all, there are still academics and pseudo-intellectuals in our midst obstinately clinging to the worn-out myths.

Of course, sometimes Good does triumph over Evil, but alas, never count on it. I was fortunate, I saw it triumph. To imagine that our lives can be so ordered that it would always be so, is a dream man has chased since the beginning of time. A return to Eden is impossible. Trying to force the Garden gates is how all the trouble started in the first place. Utopia will forever be just beyond our reach. That is its meaning. The dream has always carried us farther than the reality. More to the point – the dream is the reality – the quest is the reward.

Meanwhile, Chéri le Chasseur's Scottish professor struggles manfully to retain his balance on the high-wire.

ANNEXES

APPENDIX No. 1

Chapter 27 – ALLEN DULLES

A discussion was held at the American Embassy in Paris, in January, 1951, between David Bruce, Allen Dulles and Albert Jolis. Dulles was interested in developing ideas to support a "Defectors' Program" to encourage defections from Soviet Bloc countries. Following this meeting, Jolis sent a letter to Allen Dulles at his request, which is reproduced hereunder, in abridged form:

Paris
January 11, 1951

Dear Mr. Dulles:

I was glad to have the opportunity of talking to you just before my departure for Africa. Unfortunately, during that one talk it was not possible to cover all of the aspects and considerations implicit in a comprehensive "Defectors' Program." I would like to set down a few thoughts, however, which have occurred to me since, and I will ask David Bruce to be kind enough to forward this to you.

Many essential requirements of a "Defectors' Program" have, I believe, already been recognized. Such phases as Inducement, Reception, Interrogation, Screening, and, Rehabilitation, etc., are fairly well established as essential elements, each requiring fully elaborated supplementary programs. There is one overall consideration which in my view takes precedence over all these, however, and that is the question of our national policy.

I submit that our present policy of "Containment," that is to say the containment of Soviet aggression, is one upon which a successful "Defectors' Program" cannot be built.

Containment, by definition, implies resistance to further Soviet aggressions, but by the same token it implies acquiescence in past Soviet aggressions. A policy of Containment, if successful will ensure that no further aggressions take place, but it will also ensure the continuance of the status-quo behind the Iron Curtain. Now, a "Defectors' Program," if it is to be successful, must hold out to potential defectors the hope – at least the hope – that their homeland will one day be freed from the regime they detest, and that the United States, whose asylum they seek, will one day help them regain their freedom. A policy of Containment gives them no such hope.

What potential defectors have been vainly seeking from the United States these past years and have almost despaired of finding, is a bold clear lead in the realm of ideas; not ideas of sentimental and diffused "goodness" such as accompanied the Marshall Plan and Point Four debates; neither the defensive ideas which accompanied the North Atlantic Treaty build-up; but tough militant aggressive ideas born of our great traditions of Freedom and Liberty, and aimed directly at Police State Systems and Human Slavery.

The irony of the Containment principle is that we are it's prisoners, while the Russians are free. Once released, we can adopt the only possible state of mind that can give us victory, namely the Political, Psychological and Moral Offensive. The moral offensive demands that the area of freedom in the world be extended, and that the frontiers of slavery be rolled back. The alternative to Containment is not preventive war. It is a combination of great military strength in defensive posture with great moral and political strength in offensive posture.

Of direct concern to a possible Defectors' Program, Time magazine of January 8, 1951 quotes the United States Secretary of State as having said: "We do not propose to subvert the Soviet Union. We shall not attempt to undermine Soviet independence"

This illustrates exactly what I mean. Until there is a dramatic change in America's posture before the world, all efforts made to date will remain largely sterile. Then, and only then, will a "Defectors'" Program be more than a small-scale covert action in psychological warfare, and become a major weapon in our hands; perhaps the only one capable of offsetting our great inferiority in manpower.

With kindest regards, Sincerely
Bert Jolis.

As I re-read this letter today, forty-four years later, I am astonished at the depth of the romantic illusions I harbored at the time. Just five years after this letter was written, that is to say, in 1956, the United States failed to support the Hungarian Freedom Fighters in Budapest. And in 1968 we failed to support the Czechoslovak uprising. And so it went, on and on, downhill all the way, to the Bay of Pigs, and our cut-and-run-disaster in Vietnam.

It was forty years until America found a national leader in Ronald Reagan who had the courage and vision to awaken America's sense of destiny, which had for so long lain dormant. It is interesting to speculate how much sooner the Soviet Empire might have collapsed, had the United States never adopted the policy of Containment and followed instead the course outlined above.

APPENDIX No. 2

Chapter 44 – THE SEIZURE OF OUR MINES

Excerpt of message sent by Albert Jolis, on January 6, 1976, to Tom Buchanan, Director for Central African Affairs at the State Department, under the heading:

An Unprovoked and Unilateral Act of Discrimination Against an American Interest.

Bokassa's act in cancelling the tax agreement is totally fortuitous. It was preceded by no forewarning. There was no dispute involved, and no acts or omission of D.D.I. or it's C.A.R. affiliate, S.C.E.D., can be cited as a pretext. Personal relations between D.D.I. management and the government, from Bokassa on down, are good. The reasons for Bokassa's act therefore, cannot be sought in this area.

In attempting to understand the reasons, one can only suppose that the government, being chronically short of revenue, has suddenly discovered that this tax agreement with D.D.I. exists, and on the advice of some minister, has impulsively and inconsiderately cancelled it.

However, there are numerous other companies operating in C.A.R. enjoying the benefits of "Regime C" of the Investment Code, and these have not been touched. Only the D.D.I. affiliate, S.C.E.D. has been singled out. This is consequently a totally unwarranted act of discrimination.

D.D.I. cannot sustain it's planned investment program for 1976 in the face of this present decree. More seriously, no long range investment program can be contemplated when binding agreements, legally entered into, are capriciously broken.

Bokassa's present act, nullifying as it does an act of restitution for an earlier unwarranted expropriation, raises serious questions concerning the wisdom of further investment in the country. Should D.D.I. pull out the effect on other private sector investment will surely be felt.

NOTE: G.T.&E is currently installing a telephone and communications system with the aid of Import-Export Bank financing. CONOCO has a small petroleum search in progress as part of a larger program in the Chad. The U.S. Geological Survey is investigating an anomaly recently discovered by Earth Satellite which has received some publicity in the Press. A two-man mission is currently en route to Bangui. Bokassa is attempting to lure U.S. and other western private investment.

President Bokassa has announced that he wishes to travel to the United States this Spring, and hopes to be received by President Ford. It would be most unfortunate if this decree which he undoubtedly signed hastily and without due consideration were not withdrawn prior to his visit.

Albert Jolis

APPENDIX No. 3

Chapter 47 – MAX YERGAN SHOULD HAVE BEEN OUR MAN IN AFRICA

MEMORANDUM ON BLACK AFRICA,
submitted by Albert Jolis to Allen Dulles in November, 1951.

The struggle between Soviet power and the West extends throughout the continent of Africa, as it does to every other corner of the globe. The Soviet Union does not regard Africa as an area of immediate strategic benefit to itself – but it recognizes the enormous strategic and economic benefit it provides to the West. Soviet policy therefore, is directed towards the progressive destruction of these benefits and the eventual elimination of all Western influence from Africa. The total achievement of this objective may seem remote at first glance, and only possible after a Western defeat in Europe. But a partial achievement is not remote, and is perfectly possible without a Western defeat in Europe. Any measure of success towards this Soviet objective represents a set-back which the West can ill afford in this shrinking world.

In the global strategy of the Comintern and the Cominform, Africa has always occupied an important role. The program adopted by the 1928 World Congress of the Comintern included the following statement:

The revolutionary struggle in the Colonies, semi-colonies and dependent areas, constitutes from the standpoint of the world-wide struggle of the proletariat, one of the most important tasks of the Communist International.

Twenty-three years later, on March 2, 1951, "Humanite", French Communist Party daily, wrote:

At the present time, French Communists support all movements, all parties, all persons in the Overseas Territories who are effectively contributing to the weakening of the Imperialist Camp.

The Soviet Union has always made it a prime object of its policy in Colonial areas to infiltrate and capture the nationalist movements. Their dream for Africa has been of a Communist-led revolutionary uprising of the black masses against their white rulers. Moscow-trained Negro leaders have been working for years in obscurity. Some have risen high in nationalist movements. Today, while the eyes of the world are fixed on Korea, Indochina and the Middle east, these Soviet-trained agents in Darkest Africa continue to work devotedly, diligently and relatively undisturbed.

The quickening pace of world events has made their task easier. Black African nationalism, though less advanced than its Asian counterparts, has made tremendous strides in the last five years. The West is in danger of losing Africa as it has already lost a great part of Asia through failure to keep pace with its irresistible sweep.

There are two methods of dealing with nationalist movements in Colonial or semi-Colonial areas. One is repression by force. This is only effective when the Colonial power enjoys the necessary prestige, and when the prevailing moral and political climate supports it. The other method is to recognize nationalist aspirations as an inevitable and normal process. When this happens, enlightened self-interest produces a policy which will lead nationalist movements into progressive partnership with the Western colonial power concerned. This is indeed the policy which is generally followed by the Western world, with the notable and dangerous exception of South Africa. Progress towards implementation however, is irregular, and some-time contradictory. Furthermore, it's overall purpose is vitiated by Soviet policy which is bent on seeing it fail.

Though all the Colonial powers have moved slowly, and only when pressed by the force of events, it must be recognized that the boldest and most forthright approach has been made by the British Colonial Office. The granting of constitutions and large measures of self-government to the Gold Coast and Nigeria are important steps in the right direction.

In contrast, France's effort to achieve real colonial reform has been only partially successful. The existence of the French Communist Party is the main reason for this. The French Communist Party is the principle vehicle for the execution of Soviet policy in Black Central Africa. It's apparatus and influence extend beyond French Colonial frontiers into British, Belgian and Portuguese territory. The main instruments of French Communist action are the R.D.A. (Rassemblement Democratique Africain) and the C.G.T., the French Communist-dominated Labor movement. The areas of greatest Communist influence are, Togo, Dahomey, Ivory Coast, and Madagascar. Brazzaville and Dakar are also natural centers because of the concentration of educated and literate Africans.

In 1948, Communists succeeded in provoking a violent uprising in Madagascar, which was put down by French military force with considerable ferocity. This was a great success for the French Communist Party, who even today are able to exploit sympathy for the victims in France and throughout Africa.

Similar outbreaks of violence have occurred in Ivory Coast and Togo. At the time of writing, French officials are concerned about the possibility of further violence in Dahomey.

In the British Colonies, Communists are similarly active, though they do not enjoy the same powerful support from the British Communist Party that the French Party provides in French Africa. Nonetheless, there is evidence that Communists were active instigators in the riots which caused twenty deaths in Nigeria in 1949. Because of the weakness and relative impotence of the British Communist Party, the main task of furthering Soviet policy in British Africa has fallen to the Indian Communist Party.

The large Indian community in British East Africa and the smaller one in British West Africa, have provided Indian Communists with a good base of operations. At least one daily paper published in Nairobi and circulating among Africans is financed by the Indian Communist

Party. Indian Communists talk to Africans without having to surmount the barrier of color, an advantage they posses even over the French Communists. This is not to suggest that the Indian communities in Africa are communist-dominated. The contrary is true. But a small disciplined Communist minority is all that is needed to execute directives from the Cominform.

A vital area where Cominform strategy towards Africa is rendered most easy, is among Africans in Europe. There are over ten thousand Africans in Paris and London, students, writers, politicians and professionals. For the most part they are representative of the highest levels of African education and achievement. They come to Europe for varying lengths of time. The Communist Parties of France and Britain, but particularly France, engage in the most intensive political and propaganda activity among these Africans. These are the future leaders, and their visits to Europe should provide them with the groundwork on which they can build the future partnership of their countries with the West. But their experience in Europe usually has the opposite effect. Barriers of color, poverty and general social ostracism make them easy prey for Communist propagandists. The pseudo-intellectual circles of the Paris Left-Bank; the "existentialist" cafes; the jazz clubs; the student hostels, are all centers of the most intensive anti-American and anti-Western sentiment. It is here that Africans foregather, because it is here that the Communists make the greatest fetish of inter-racial social contact. And it is for the most part within the Communist orbit that Africans find social acceptance, where they are made to feel "at home." Communist possession of this citadel is of the utmost importance to the future of Africa. The West must recapture it decisively and urgently.

The Communist message to Africans is a straightforward and simple one. It is based on one, and only one concept, namely, "Africa for the Africans." This is the most powerful and emotionally intoxicating message that can be directed to a literate African. It even excercises a powerful draw upon semi-savage tribesmen, deep in the Equatorial jungles and forests. By proclaiming this slogan louder and longer than any other group, the Communists throughout Africa have succeeded in drawing within their organizational influence, large sections of nationalist sentiment, which otherwise would have no inclination or affinity towards Communism.

In the face of this, the West's only answer must be: "Africa's true liberation lies in the attainment of full partnership with the West. Africans, beware of the sweet sounds of nationalism in the mouths of Communists. They are the siren call to the New Slavery!"

How can the West deliver this message to Africans? How can it be given real content and real meaning? What should be the role of the United States in this effort?

This is the subject of the attached statement and recommendation prepared by Dr. Max Yergan.

APPENDIX No. 4

Chapter 47 – MAX YERGAN SHOULD BE OUR MAN IN AFRICA

Excerpt from letter published in *The New York Herald Tribune,* on April 23, 1949, from Max Yergan in which he publicly attacks Paul Robeson's pro-Soviet actions.

Yesterday's *New York Herald Tribune* reported statements made by Mr. Paul Robeson at the so-called World Peace Conference now in session in Paris. These statements assert that American Negroes would never fight Russia, and that President Truman's program for colonial development means new slavery for Africans... ...

It is reasonable to conclude that the Robeson statements had as their purpose the vicious and cynical effort which Communists in America have for a long time been putting forth, to drive a wedge between American Negroes and their fellow American citizens... ...

It has failed because Negro Americans know full well what their problems are, and know also how to deal with them. No thoughtful person in America, certainly no Negro, denies that most Negro Americans face limitations which, in the light of constitutional guarantees and citizenship rights, ought to be removed. Communists have not been needed, however, to point out that fact... ...

Few people know how Mr. Robeson has abused the confidence of American Negroes within the limited circles of the Council on African Affairs. It will be recalled that a little over a year ago, there was fundamental conflict within that organization when Mr. Robeson and the Communists who were associated with him sought to use that organization to attack American foreign policy and to support the foreign policy of Russia. Leading a majority of the members of that organization, I was in conflict with the Communist-led and Communist-inspired forces and with other council members, fought these forces. I count it as one of the most important actions of my entire life when, along with the majority of the individuals within that organization, I left it. Our leaving it established the fact that today it is what it is, an instrument of the Communist Party and Communist intrigue, not in the interest of the people of Africa, but in the interest of the Kremlin masters of Communists everywhere.

APPENDIX No. 5

Chapter 55 – RESISTANCE INTERNATIONAL

MEMBER ORGANIZATIONS:
The Bulgarian Liberation Movement
Comite Entr'aide et Action (Czechoslovakia)
Committee of Cuban Intellectuals in Exile
Independent and Democratic Cuba
Islamic Unity of Afghan Mujahedeen
Miskito, Fumo and Rama Indian Front (Nicaragua)
National Democratic Committee for a Free Albania
Nicaraguan Democratic Front
Resistance Front for the Liberation of Vietnam
Revolutionary Force of Young Vietnamese in Europe
The Khmer People's National Liberation Front (Cambodia)
United Front for the Liberation of Laos
UNITA (Angola)
Witness (Czechoslovakia)
Fighting Solidarity-Solidarnosc Walczaca (Poland)

*

Message broadcast to the world by Resistance International at it's inauguration ceremony in May, 1983:

Forty-four years ago Resistance fighters helped liberate Western Europe from Nazi totalitarianism, but Communist totalitarianism still holds East Europe in thrall and enslaves the Soviet People. It has spread its tentacles to helpless millions around the world and even now is reaching for the Philippines.

But the flame of Resistance was never extinguished. It burns brightly in Angola, in Cambodia, in Nicaragua, and yes, in the prison camps of the Soviet Union itself. Resistance takes many forms, ranging from wars of liberation on the outer rim of the empire to more subtle methods towards its center. The Polish shipyard workers of Gdansk, the dissidents in the Gulag and psychiatric prisons, the Cuban human rights activists in Castro's jails, Jonas Savimbi's jungle fighters, the Mujahedeen of Afghanistan, and Nicaragua's freedom fighters – are all comrades in arms resisting the same oppression, fighting the same war. Those engaged in such diverse theaters are well aware they are part of a global struggle, but they fight in lonely isolation. Coordination and a sense of unity must be supplied from the outside.

But from where? Who will provide this essential encouragement and support?

Governments of democratic nations, fearful of exceeding the limits of self-imposed diplomatic constraints and subject to Soviet blackmail, tread timidly and largely ineffectually in this area.

Only free men and women, acting individually and collectively, outside of government channels, can provide the popular support which alone will prove effective.

On the day of it's inauguration, Vladimir Bukovsky pronounced the following words:

"...the comfort of life in the West renders people insensible to the truth. It makes them deaf and blind, immutably ready to forget the crimes of yesterday... Look upon the map of the world, the so-called Free World is already no more than a tiny islet in a totalitarian ocean. But... enormous and frightening crowds gather in the capitals of Europe to demand a suicidal disarmament and capitulation. We must work indefatigably to remind them of the fate of the occupied countries. We must show that any kind of life is not better than death.

We must revive the spirit of resistance that once already has saved us from the darkness of Nazism."

And on the same occasion, Simon Wiesenthal, famous Nazi hunter, delivered the following message:

"The dictatorships of the Right and the Left are branches of the same tree, the tree of enslavement, of intolerance and of police states. We must remember the victims of yesterday, and fight for the liberty of today's victims."

These declarations of principles and aims received wide public support from a dazzling array of World War II Resistance leaders, writers, intellectuals and prominent public figures from around the world, including the U.S.A. (List attached.)

List of international personalities who sent personal messages of support on the occasion of the Founding meeting of l'Internationale de la Resistance – Resistance International, in Paris – May, 1993

AUSTRALIA
J. Malcolm Fraser	Former Prime Minister
Simon Leys	Sinologist

AUSTRIA
Simon Wiesenthal	Jewish Documentation Center

BELGIUM
Henri Bernard	Professor, World War II Resistance
Luc Beyer de Ryke	Member, European Parliament
General Robert Close	Member, Belgian Senate
Albert Guerisse	World War II Resistance
Nikolaus von Mach	German Anti-Nazi Resistance

FRANCE
Thierry Ardisson	Journalist
Raymond Aron	Philosopher (deceased 1983)
Fernando Arrabal	Playwright

Jean-Marie Benoist	Writer
Alain Besançon	Historian
Leon Boutbien	World War II Resistance
Père Bruckberger	Theologian
Bernard Chapuis	Writer
Joseph Czapski	Painter, Polish Resistance
Jean-Marie Daillet	Member of French National Assembly
Pierre Daix	Writer, Journalist
General Delaunay	Former Chief, French General Staff
Pierre Emmanuel	Poet, Member of French Academy
Marie-Madeleine Fourcade	World War II Resistance Leader
Marie-France Garaud	Director of the Geopolitical Institute
Monique Garnier-Lançon	V.P., European Institute for Security
Yves Gautier	Director, "Prospection Hebdo"
André Glucksman	Philosopher
Pierre Golendorf	Writer
Henri Hagdenberg	President, Jewish Renewal
Marek Halter	Writer, Painter
Eugène Ionesco	Playwright, Member of French Academy
Vladimir Jankelevitch	Philosopher, Musicologist
Christian Jelen	Writer, Journalist
Annie Kriegel	Journalist
Branko Lazitch	Journalist
Gerard Lenormand	Singer
Emmanuel Leroy-Ladurie	Historian, College de France
Bernard Henri-Lévy	Philosopher
Jacques Miquel	Lawyer
Jules Moch	Former French Minister
Yves Montand	Actor, Singer
Jean Pascalini	Writer, Journalist
Vladimir Radoman	Novelist, Physician
Jean-François Revel	Writer, Journalist
Claude Rey	Writer
Pierre Rigoulot	Professor
Père Riquet	World War II Resistance

George Sampson	Writer
Phillipe Sollers	Writer
Bernard Stasi	Member, French National Assembly
René Tavernier	President, P.E.N. Club of France
Olivier Todd	Journalist
Patrick Wajsman	Journalist
Simone Weil	Ex-President, European Parliament
Illios Yannakakis	Historian

GERMANY

Cornelia Gerstenmaier	Journalist, Writer
Kai-Uwe von Hassel	Member, Bundestag
Nicholas Lobkowicz	Dean, Eichstatt University
Renate-Charlotte Rabbetge	Member, European Parliament
Count Franz-Ludwig von Stauffenberg	Member, Bundestag
Gabrielle Taugner	Professor

GREAT BRITAIN

Nicholas Bethell	Writer, member of House of Lords
John Brown	Member of Parliament
Michael Brown	Member of Parliament
Alun Lord Chalfont	Former Minister, Foreign Office
Frank Lord Chapple	Former President, T.U.C.
Winston Churchill	Member of Parliament
Robert Conquest	Writer, Historian
Brian Crozier	Journalist
Leszek Kolakowski	Philosopher
Leo Labedz	Editor, *Survey*
Melvin Lasky	Editor, *Encounter*
Yehudi Menuhin	Violinist
Geoffrey Stewart-Smith	Foreign Affairs Research Institute
Hugh Lord Thomas	Chairman, Center for Policy Studies
Count Nicholas Tolstoy-Miloslavsky	Historian
George Urban	Journalist
Sir Huw Wheldon	Chairman, London School of Economics

ISRAEL
Dimitri Segal   Professor, University of Jerusalem
Avram Ben-Yakov   Professor, Martin Buber Institute

ITALY
Enzo Bettiza   Member, European Parliament
                                 and Executive Committee,
                                 Italian Liberal Party
Margharita Boniver   Member, Italian Senate
Roberto Formigoni   General Secretary,
                                 Movimento Popolare
Indro Montanelli   Historian, Editor *Il Giornale Nuevo*
Raymond Moretti   Painter
Massimo Pini   Publisher
Carlo Ripa de Maena   Senator, Member European
                                 Parliament
Roberto Mazotta   Secretary, Christian Democratic Party
Edgardo Sogno del Valino   World War II Resistance Leader

NETHERLANDS
Joseph Luns   Former Secretary General, NATO

NORWAY
Anton Frederic Andressen   Publisher
Leif Hovelsen   Writer, World War II Resistance
Aase Marie Nesse   President, P.E.N. Club of Norway
Gunnar Sonsteby   World War II Resistance Leader
Victor Sparre   Painter
Tore Stubberud   Journalist

SPAIN
Xavier Domingo   Journalist
Fernando Sanchez Drago   Journalist
Federico Jimenez Losanto   Journalist
Carlos Alberto Montaner   Journalist

Miguel Sales	Journalist

U.S.A.

Ronald Reagan	President, U.S.A.
Bruno Bettelheim	Psychologist
William F. Buckley, Jr.	Author, Founder *National Review*
Arnaud de Borchgrave	Author, Editor-in-chief *Washington Times*
Midge Decter	Executive Director, Committee for the Free World
Hon. Robert K. Dornan	Congressman
Sydney Hook	Writer, Philosopher
Hon. Jack Kemp	Congressman
Lane Kirkland	President, AFL/CIO
Hon. Jeane Kirkpatrick	Former Ambassador to the United Nations
Michael Ledeen	Writer, Senior Fellow Georgetown University
John McClaughry	Former White House Aide, Writer
Michael Novak	Religious and Political Writer
Hon. Richard N. Perle	Former Assistant Secretary of Defense
Norman Podhoretz	Writer, Editor *Commentary*
Mstislow Rostropovitch	Musician
Bayard Rustin	Civil Rights Leader
Albert Shanker	President, United Federation of Teachers
Jack Wheeler	Journalist
George Will	Writer, Journalist

VENEZUELA

Sofia Imber	Director of the Caracas Museum of Contemporary Arts
Carlos Rangel	Writer, journalist

YUGOSLAVIA

Milovan Djilas	Writer, political figure

Counterfiet edition of Red Army Journal, Krasnaia Zvedza (Red Star). The headline reads: "STOP THE WAR – GO HOME." Produced by Resistence International 1984 – Circulated among soviet troops in Afganistan, and posted on the walls of Kabul.

APPENDIX No. 6

Chapter 55 – RESISTANCE INTERNATIONAL

THE TRIBUNAL ON CUBA – APRIL 1986

Members of the Jury

René Tavernier,	President of the French PEN Club,
Fernando Sanchez-Drago,	Spanish Writer, Journalist,
Yves Montand,	French Actor-Singer,
Paul-Loup Sulitzer,	French Writer-Industrialist,
Osmund Faremo,	Member of the Norwegian Parliament, President of the Foreign Relations Committee
Jorge Semprun	Spanish Writer,
Jean-Francois Revel,	French Author of "How Democracies Perish",
Gunel Liljurgen,	Member of the Swedish Parliament,
Haing Ngor,	Cambodian Actor, Star in the film "The Killing Fields,"
Marie-Madeleine Fourcade,	French Resistance Heroine, World War II.

APPENDIX No. 7

Chapter 55 – RESISTANCE INTERNATIONAL

THE PRAGUE CONFERENCE
JULY 4–5 1990

LIST OF PARTICIPANTS

Yuri Afanasiev (Russia)	Congress of Peoples' Deputies U.S.S.R.
Karen Agulyan (France)	National Self-Determination of Armenia
Heiki Ahohen (Estonia)	Estonian Party for National Independence
Araz Ali-Zade (Azerbaijan)	Social Democratic Party of Azerbaijan
Sergei Broude (U.S.)	President, Action for Soviet Jewry
Vladimir Bukovsky (U.K.)	Honorary Chairman of the Conference
Gennadi Burbulis (Russia)	Congress of Peoples' Deputies U.S.S.R.
Georgi Chanturia (Georgia)	National Democratic Party of Georgia
Vyacheslav Chornovil (Ukraine)	Governor of Lvov Region, Ukraine
Martin Colman (U.S.)	Exec. Dir. Natl. Council to Support the Democracy Movements
Olgert Eglitis (Latvia)	Latvian Independence Movement
Tofik Gasymov (Azerbaijan)	Popular Front of Azerbaijan
Igor Geraschenko (Ukraine)	Ukrainian Democratic Movement
Cornelia Gerstenmaier (Germany)	Editor-in-Chief, *Kontinent Verlag*

Eduard Gudava (Georgia)	Exec. Dir. Center for Democracy in the U.S.S.R.
Tengiz Gudava (Georgia)	National Democratic Party of Georgia
Paruyr Hayrikyan (Armenia)	President, "Democracy & Independence"
Albert Jolis (U.S.)	Chairman Natl. Council to Support the Democracy Movements
Gary Kasparov (Russia)	Democratic Party of Russian Federation
Jeane Kirkpatrick (U.S.)	Georgetown University and American Enterprise Institute
Robert Kocharyan (Nagorno-Karabakh)	Supreme Soviet of Armenia
Anatoly Koryagin (Switzerland)	"Democracy & Independence"
Andrei Krastynsh (Latvia)	Supreme Soviet of Latvia
Charles Lichenstein (U.S.)	Heritage Foundation
Leonard Meri (Estonia)	Foreign Minister of Estonia
Ashot Nazaryan (Armenia)	Armenian Democratic Movement
Leonid Plioushtch (Ukraine)	Ukrainian Helsinki Union
Alexander Podrabinek (Russia)	Editor, *Express Chronicle*
Abdurakhim Pulatov (Uzbekistan)	Uzbek Democratic Movement
Irina Ratushinskaya (Russia)	Center for Democracy in the U.S.S.R.
Jean-François Revel (France)	Author, Political Philosopher
Yuri Rozhka (Moldavia)	Moldavian Popular Front
Yanis Rozkalns (Latvia)	Latvian Movement for Independence
Petro Rozumy (Ukraine)	Ukrainian Republican Party
Petro Ruban (Ukraine)	Ukrainian Cooperative Movement
Karen Simoyan (Armenia)	Supreme Soviet of the U.S.S.R.
Vasily Selyunin (Russia)	Economist
Ayshe Seytmuratova (Crimean Tatars)	National Independence Movement
Mikhtar Shakhanov (Kazakhstan)	Congress of Peoples' Deputies
Anatoly Shibyko (Ukraine)	"Rukh" Ukrainian Union
Sergei Skripnikov (Russia)	Democratic Union
Vitautas Skuodis (Lithuania)	Lithuanian Helsinki Group
Nadia Svitlichna (Ukraine)	Ukrainian Helsinki Union

Yakov Suslensky (Israel)   Society for
                                 Ukrainian-Jewish Relations
Vladimir Tikhonov (Russia)   Chairman, Union of Cooperatives
Nikolai Travkin (Russia)   Chairman, Democratic Party of Russia
Vitaly Urazhtsev (Russia)   Chairman, "Shield", Union
                                 of Servicemen
Kazimieras Uoka (Lithuania)   Chairman, Lithuanian
                                 Workers' Union
Armando Valladares (U.S.)   U.S. Rep. to United Nations
                                 for Human Rights
Arvo Vallikivi (Estonia)   Estonian Popular Front
Yusif Vekilov (Azerbaijan)   Popular Front of Azerbaijan
Alan Walters (U.K.)   John Hopkins University
Albert Wohlstetter (U.S.)   Pan Heuristics Services, Inc.
Yuri Yarim-Agaev (U.S.)   Pres. Center for Democracy
                                 in the U.S.S.R.
Ilya Zaslavsky (Russia)   Congress of Peoples' Deputies
Iosef Zisels (Ukraine)   Vaad-Federation of Jewish
                                 Organizations in U.S.S.R.

THE WHITE HOUSE

WASHINGTON

October 23, 1985

Dear Mr. Jolis:

Thank you and the members of the American Foundation for Resistance International for the brochure on your organization's activities.

For generations we Americans have enjoyed a common heritage of liberty that, we sometimes forget, was won for us by the blood and sacrifice of our Founding Fathers. It is necessary to remind ourselves that the battle they joined over 200 years ago against tyranny is still being waged today. The price paid for our freedom in America is now being paid by fighters in Cambodia, Angola, and Afghanistan, Nicaragua and in Poland and, yes, in the Soviet Union.

Your organization has set for itself the task of reminding free peoples everywhere of the bond they share with those who struggle to be free. That bond is our common purpose to resist oppression. Although resistance may take a variety of forms, it requires commitment and sacrifice by all of us to prevail. Beyond giving our support to those who are actively fighting totalitarianism, we Americans must do all we can to foster democracy and strengthen its institutions. Democracy offers the world an alternative to all tyrannical extremes. It is our best hope for peace, security, and freedom.

I want to take this opportunity to extend my own best wishes and appreciation to the American Foundation for Resistance International. Yours is a noble cause, and I hope your efforts will meet with continued success.

Sincerely,

Ronald Reagan

Mr. Albert E. Jolis
Secretary-Treasurer
The American Foundation for
    Resistance International
500 Fifth Avenue
New York, New York 10110

INDEX